LANGUAGE, IDENTITY, AND MARGINALITY IN INDONESIA

Indonesia's policy since independence has been to foster the national language. In some regions, local languages are still political rallying points, but in general their significance has diminished, and the rapid spread of Indonesian as the national language of political and religious authority has been described as the "miracle of the developing world." Among the Weyewa, an ethnic group living on the island of Sumba, this shift has displaced a once-vibrant tradition of ritual poetic speech used in prayers, songs, and myths, which until recently was an important source of authority, tradition, and identity. But it has also given rise to new and hybrid forms of poetic expression. In this first study to analyze language change in relation to political marginality, Joel Kuipers argues that political coercion or the cognitive process of "style reduction" may offer a partial explanation of what has happened, but equally important in language shift is the role of linguistic ideologies.

JOEL C. KUIPERS is Associate Professor of Anthropology at George Washington University. He is the author of *Power in Performance* (1990).

STUDIES IN THE SOCIAL AND CULTURAL FOUNDATIONS
OF LANGUAGE

The aim of this series is to develop theoretical perspectives on the essential social and cultural character of language by methodological and empirical emphasis on the occurrence of language in its communicative and interactional settings, on the socioculturally grounded "meanings" and "functions" of linguistic forms, and on the social scientific study of language use across cultures. It will thus explicate the essentially ethnographic nature of linguistic data, whether spontaneously occurring or experimentally induced, whether normative or variational, whether synchronic or disachronic. Works appearing in the series will make substantive and theoretical contributions to the debate over the sociocultural–functional and structural–formal nature of language, and will represent the concerns of scholars in the sociology and anthropology of language, anthropological linguistics, sociolinguistics, and socio-culturally informed psycholinguistics.

A list of books in the series can be found after the index.

LANGUAGE, IDENTITY, AND MARGINALITY IN INDONESIA

THE CHANGING NATURE OF RITUAL SPEECH ON THE ISLAND OF SUMBA

JOEL C. KUIPERS

CAMBRIDGE
UNIVERSITY PRESS

PUBLISHED BY THE PRESS SYNDICATE OF THE UNIVERSITY OF CAMBRIDGE
The Pitt Building, Trumpington Street, Cambridge CB 2 IRP, United Kingdom

CAMBRIDGE UNIVERSITY PRESS
The Edinburgh Building, Cambridge, CB2 2RU, United Kingdom
http://www.cup.cam.ac.uk
40 West 20th Street, New York, NY 10011-4211, USA   http://www.cup.org
10 Stamford Road, Oakleigh, Melbourne 3166, Australia

© Joel C. Kuipers 1998

First published 1998

Printed in the United Kingdom at the University Press, Cambridge

Typeset in 10/12pt Times   CE

A catalogue record for this book is available from the British Library

Library of Congress Cataloguing in Publication data
Kuipers, Joel Corneal
Language, identity, and marginality in Indonesia: the changing nature of ritual speech on the island of Sumba / Joel C. Kuipers.
p.   cm. – (Studies in the social and cultural foundations of language: no. 18)
Includes bibliographical references and index.
ISBN 0 521 62408 8 (hardback)
1. Weyewa (Indonesian people) – Rites and ceremonies.
2. Language and culture – Indonesia – Sumba Island.
3. Ethnology – Indonesia – Sumba Island.
4. Linguistic survey. 5. Ideology.
6. Weyewa dialect – Social aspects – Indonesia – Sumba Island.
I. Title   II. Series.
DS632.W48K84   1998   306.44'089'992205986–dc21   97–38770   CIP

ISBN 0 521 62408 8 hardback
ISBN 0 521 62495 9 paperback

CONTENTS

PLATES

FIGURES AND TABLES

PREFACE

On the island of Sumba, a poetic form of ritual speech once integral to the local system of religious and political authority has undergone a substantial shift in its meaning and use. This book is an examination of the history of that process of transformation and marginalization in its ethnographic and linguistic context. Transcriptions of recorded performances, Dutch and Indonesian archival materials, and first-hand interviews and observations over the course of 20 years of research on the island, form the core of the data on which much of this analysis is based.

This book differs in scope, method and approach from an earlier work (Kuipers 1990) in several important ways. That book focussed on the role of the ritual-speech tradition of verbal performance in the establishment of the "words of the ancestors" as textual authority. In that work, I emphasized the integral nature of the Weyewa system of ceremonial communication and its role in the enactment of what were regarded as the fixed and timeless ancestral words as guides to conduct and exchange.

I now see that in certain ways the authority system I described there was more circumscribed, fragile, and marginal than I had realized at the time. When I first carried out fieldwork on the island in 1978, only 20 percent of the population of the Weyewa were Christian, and the overwhelming majority were still practitioners of their indigenous ancestral religion, *marapu*, and this fact no doubt colored my perceptions of the importance of ritual speech in shaping their local system of authority. While what I said in that book is, I believe, still valid, it is valid for a system that was interacting with forces of history and ideological change that I describe more fully in the pages that follow.

What prompted a recasting of my views of ritual speech and authority was the growing realization on subsequent visits – especially in 1989, 1990, and 1994 – that the changes that were occurring were so substantial, so major, and so fundamental that they could not be explained by the immediate factors preceding them. While it is true that television was introduced, new varieties of rice were adopted, and new roads, schools and churches were built in the late 1980s and early 1990s, these factors alone did not seem to be responsible by themselves for the massive

Christian conversions, the large-scale rejection of feasting and ritual speech practices, and the widespread adoption of Indonesian in nearly all public gatherings.

To understand these changes in speaking practices and their relation to fundamental shifts in the structure of authority, this book argues that one cannot simply view the linguistic changes as passive reflections of external forces of material development and modernization, forces with which Sumbanese somehow calmly complied. One must look instead at the vibrant ways in which Weyewa attitudes, beliefs, and perception towards their own language have shifted. I argue that these changes did not begin in the late 1980s but had their roots much earlier, with the arrival of Dutch administrators and missionaries in the late nineteenth century. This provided the conditions for dynamic, ideological processes described in the chapters that follow: (1) dispersal from centers of ceremonial authority; (2) the marginalization of "anger"; (3) the expansion of the spectator/audience role; (4) the narrowing of practices of verbal reference; (5) the radical erasure of the diversity of ritual-speech fields of practices and modes of learning.

Following the fortunes of a special style of speech has broad benefits for the study of language change, especially in an archipelago so rich in liturgical languages (Adriani 1932; Fischer 1934; Grimes and Maryott 1994). By focussing on something self-consciously "special" and ideologically marked off from the ordinary ways of talking syntactically and pragmatically, ritual speech offers a privileged place from which to witness the operation of ideology as it organizes the language shifts associated with modernization and development; in the case of West Sumba, from center to margin, trunk to tip, whole to part, from speaker to spectator. These processes show how the very definition of what a language is, where and when it is spoken, how it functions, and how it is organized are all crucially mediated by language ideologies. If language ideologies mediate such important changes in exotic, special styles, might they also – as Molière's bourgeois gentleman reminds us – play a role in the redefinition, structure and use of "prose"?

While I suspect that many of the processes described here are applicable in a general way to all of Sumba, and indeed to much of Indonesia, the main focus of the research has been on West Sumba, and on the Weyewa highlands more specifically. Analytical slippage between "Sumba" and "Weyewa," however, occurs more often in this study than in the earlier, more ethnographic one, largely because of the ways in which Dutch sources tended to generalize from one ethnic group to the whole island, but also because of my own belief that in fact – in many cases – similar things were happening throughout much of the island. While it seems plausible that the east, with its more hierarchical and diarchic system of authority, has assigned a more "historical" role to ritual speech whereas speakers in the more egalitarian west view it as part of a lively, and dynamic "heritage" of ongoing relations to authority, this will have to await further study (see Hoskins 1996).

I am acutely aware that this book will be read by the descendants of some of the people described in these pages. I hope they will find much they can recognize, and much to admire in what was arguably one of the most vibrant and integral traditions of parallelistic speech anywhere in the world. By understanding how these changes came about, perhaps we can better grasp the historical implications of the present.

ACKNOWLEDGEMENTS

This book has been over ten years in the making, and inscribes bits and pieces of conversations, comments, critiques, and even elliptical asides and awkward silences in ways that surpass proper acknowledgement. To Ds. Enos Boeloe, a retired minister with the Sumbanese Christian Church and former assistant to Dr. Louis Onvlee, I offer my warmest thanks. He has offered me lodging, unfailing support, and wise advice, all the while maintaining such an open mind and lively curiosity throughout our twenty years of collaboration that he is a model for continuing intellectual growth. Petrus Malo Umbu Pati, who transcribed and helped me translate many of the texts in this study, has also been a reliable friend and energetic assistant, especially during my more recent short stays on the island. While Mbora Paila's responsibilities have made it difficult for him to participate in the past few years, I am grateful for the many years of effort he devoted to this research, particularly in its early stages. Neither Rato Kaduku nor Lende Mbatu lived to see this study completed, but their voices live on in these pages. Mbulu Renda, Mbora Kenda, and Dede Bobo all contributed time, effort, patience and much good humor to this project. The family Leng Kep of the Taguholo store in Waikabubak offered warm hospitality and assistance during my stays whenever I passed through that town. Drs. Darius Dairo Dady rented me his house and provided much useful advice. Mssr. Ney in the Elopada Catholic Church assisted with medical emergencies and good counsel.

In Indonesia, Drs. Munandjar Widiyatmika arranged for sponsorship of this project through UNDANA, a university in Kupang, Timor; while LIPI, the Indonesian Institute of Sciences, helped facilitate the visa-application process. Financial support came from the National Endowment for the Humanities, Fulbright CIES, Social Science Research Council, Wenner-Gren Foundation, Woodrow Wilson International Center for Scholars, George Washington University University Facilitating Fund, and the Southeast Asian Council of the Association for Asian Studies. This support I gratefully acknowledge.

Colleagues in the United States, Britain, Holland, and Australia have assisted with this project in important ways. Two anthropologists, Webb Keane and Janet Hoskins, have contributed the benefit of their long experience on the island of Sumba, and have each generously provided helpful comments on earlier versions of this manuscript. For comments and helpful criticisms I am grateful to John Bowen, Kenneth George, J. Joseph Errington, Charles Briggs, David Konstan, Ray MacDermott, Eugene Galbraith, Toby Volkman, Renato Rosaldo, Judith Irvine, Steven Caton, Patricia Spyer, Wim Stokhof, Frances Gouda, James Fox, James C. Scott, Paul Taylor, and Jean-Paul Dumont. At the George Washington University, my colleagues Catherine Allen, Alison Brooks, Peter Caws, Richard Grinker and Linda Salamon have all been helpful in creating a supportive environment for finishing this book. Institutional affiliations at various other times at Brown and Stanford Universities have provided library and other facilities at crucial stages. The Woodrow Wilson Center provided pleasant circumstances in which to write and discuss this work.

My wife and partner Teresa Anne Murphy has been my most constant source of encouragement and support. She has been, to paraphrase a Weyewa couplet, the audience who completes the event, whose attendance makes it whole. Without her, this book would not exist at all. To my children, Max, Nick, and Grace, who endured my absences while I was away in the field and my distractedness as I worked on the manuscript, I offer my thanks and apologies.

NOTES ON ORTHOGRAPHY

Bringing the Sumbanese languages to the printed page provides challenges to ethnographers and linguists (Onvlee 1973; Kuipers 1990; Hoskins 1993; Keane 1997b). Although I have described my rationale for the orthographic choices in greater detail elsewhere (Kuipers 1990: xvii-xxvi), it might be helpful to reprise here some of the main features of the system I use:

1. The semantic and formal couplet structure of ritual speech is depicted orthographically by attempting to make the lines visually parallel. Where the spoken line is too long for the page, the remaining portions of the poetic lines are further indented in a parallel fashion.
2. "The phonemes of the Weyewa language consist of five vowels i, e, u, o, a/, three nasal consonants /m, n, ng/, nine stops /mb, b, p, nd, d, t, ngg, k (glottal stop)/, one spirant /z/ two semi-consonants /w, y/, two lateral consonants /l, r/ one affricate /c/, and consonant length. There are four diphthongs /au, ai, ou, ei/" (Kuipers 1990: xix).

   While most of these sounds will be familiar to the readers of this book, there are a few sounds that readers from outside the island may find unusual, namely: /mb/ is a prenasalized, bilabial voiced stop; /b/ on the other hand, is a preglottalized, implosive bilabial stop. In a similar way, /nd/ is a prenasalized voiced, alveolar stop; /d/ is a preglottalized, implosive voiced alveolar stop.
3. Consonant length occurs intervocalically.
4. When consonant length occurs for sounds represented with a digraph (e.g. mb, nd, ng, or ngg), so as to avoid such unsightly words as *karambmbo*, I have used an accent on all vowels preceding doubled, digraphically represented consonants. Thus *karambmbo* becomes *karámbo*.

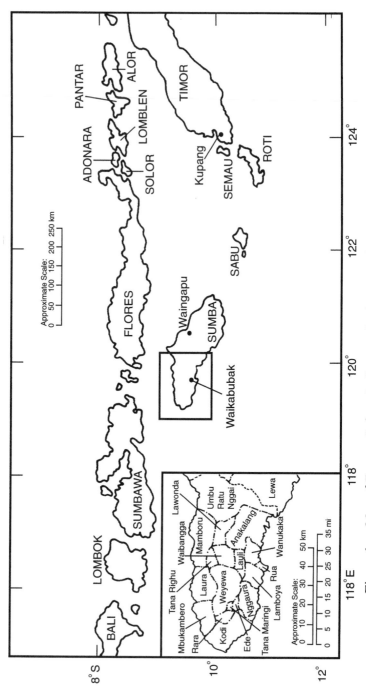

Figure 1: *Map of Eastern Indonesia (inset: ethnolinguistic divisions in Western Sumba)*

I

INTRODUCTION

When the third world . . . begins to modernize . . . a very old phenomenon, as old as the displacement of the American Indians, the Australian Aborigines, the Bushmen, the Bedouins, the Lapps, the Gypsies, gets a new lease on life. Those people who lack or who are denied the means of participating in such modernization, or who simply reject the terms on which it is offered, become marginal, and this leads to the creation of encapsulated societies, societies viewed by the majority population in the countries in which they live as "backward," "traditional," "archaic," "static," or "primitive." Go-ahead states, bent on "take-off," do not bring all their citizens with them when they join the contemporary world of capital flows, technology transfers, trade balances and growth rates.

(Geertz 1994: 3)

When I returned to the Weyewa highlands of the eastern Indonesian island of Sumba in 1994, I was surprised to learn that one of the most renowned and skilled practitioners of an elaborate and lively style of poetic ritual speech had converted to Christianity. With a wide, red, betel-stained grin, he held out his hand in the modern Indonesian style, and said, self-mockingly, "[allow me to] make your acquaintance, [I'm] David" ("kenalkan dulu: Daud"), then touched his hand to his breast after the Muslim practice. David! I was fascinated, because, when I first met him in 1978, he had been one of the most defiant towards the government's intense programs of educational, religious and political modernization and development. He had loudly dismissed the idea that native religious feasting practices were "wasteful and backward." It seemed to me that if anybody had the personal savvy to turn what used to be regarded as a key, if not the key political and economic resource – namely, one's ability to fashion eloquent and persuasive discourse from poetic couplets – into a modern asset in the courtrooms, marketplace, and political forums of the modern Indonesian state, – it was he, Mbora Kenda, now named David. He had in many ways, beaten the system, by Sumbanese standards: although functionally illiterate, he had won title to his lands through successful litigation in modern courts, he had negotiated several favorable deals for the sale of his coffee and rice crops, and he was able to create and maintain politically important alliances with several powerful people

1

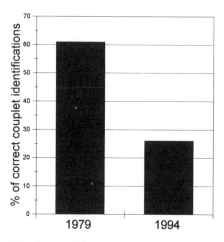

Figure 2   *Ritual speech knowledge among Weyewa sixth graders*

through strategic marriages of his own and his children. He had done all of this while proudly maintaining his identity as a leader of the indigenous religion based on ancestor worship and resisting government pressure to convert to one of the "modern" religions: Protestantism, Catholicism, or Islam.

When I asked him, "Why did you do it?" he responded with a phrase that I heard many times in 1994, but which defies simple political or psychological interpretations: roughly glossed, it goes, "In the past, I was angry all the time, and hot inside; now I feel cool, but cunning." What fascinated me was his rhetorical positioning of the emotions as a way of talking about transformations in the local system of authority, and the implications of this shift for the use of language in public and private settings. Ritual speech used by men in their native religion had to be "angry" to be authoritative, perhaps not unlike rap music in the US; but in Sumba, it was not confined in the relatively safe and neatly defined aesthetic frame of song – in Sumba, this form of ritual speech was a required part of the most important economic and political transactions of their lives.

 During the past decade, after nearly a century of linguistic resistance, accommodation then marginalization, a dramatic shift has occurred in language use on the island of Sumba. Use of ritual speech for religious and political purposes has plummeted, apparently pushed aside by the national language, Indonesian. Figure 2 shows (see p. 12), the number of Weyewa sixth graders (i.e. children of 12 years of age) in the same school who could discern the meaning of couplets was significantly fewer in 1994 than in 1979.[1] It is a shift which reflects the growing presence of the

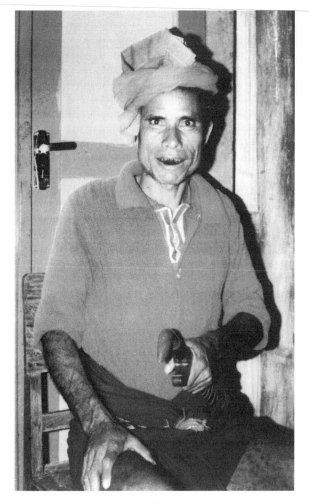

Plate 1 *Mbora Kenda*

state in the everyday lives of the Sumbanese, particularly through government-sponsored programs of economic development and expanded access to the educational system. However, even as some traditional forms of Weyewa speech atrophy, others have blossomed, and been transformed into a new kind of discourse, an ambiguous realm of "custom," "tradition," and "art."

Mbora Kenda is often now a silent spectator in an ever-expanding number of Indonesian-language events in the Weyewa highlands, such as state-sponsored rallies, local government meetings, and church services.

When he does speak, he sometimes orates Weyewa ritual speech, or offers ritual applause (*yawao*), but it is usually brief, and often framed as the voice of a newly narrowed and secularized domain of "native custom" (*adat*), a relatively novel category used by government officials to refer to the ways in which local culture legitimates state practices. There, his passion and "anger" have a special place. Since his Indonesian language skills often do not permit him to take a public role in negotiations, he can nonetheless participate in a way that is both authoritative and yet contained.

Yet life as a Christian holds profound paradoxes for him. He has two wives, a fact of which many in his Calvinist congregation disapprove. While he feels he has forsworn the "angry" life, with many of its economic risks and liabilities, he faces a loss of status. Economic moderation and steady accumulation of wealth may have its satisfactions but the lavish feasting – as was customary in his past – is not one of them. As a Christian, he now feels himself to be more fully a citizen of Indonesia – since the government did not recognize ancestor worship as legitimate – and he feels his children now stand a better chance at getting a full education, but he also sees the Chinese and government elites driving about in cars, trucks, and motorcycles which he cannot afford and which seem beyond his reach. Unable to perform in rituals, and incapable of full participation in Indonesian bureaucracy, he expresses his growing sense of irony in ritual-speech "laments."

This book is about new and emerging features of ritual speaking in modern Indonesia – laments, applause, prestige naming, and contest songs – and it seeks to understand them in their cultural, linguistic, and historical context. I argue that these new ways of speaking, singing, naming, and cheering cannot be explained only by external forces such as political or religious coercion – the barrel of a gun or threats of hellfire – nor can they be accounted for as the logical outcome of an autonomous linguistic system requiring "stylistic reductions" and cognitive "simplifications." A less obvious explanation, but one of crucial importance in the developing societies of Southeast Asia, is that these new features make sense in relation to an historical and ideological shift that I call "marginalization," in which highly valued verbal resources are reinterpreted, drawing on a spatial idiom, from whole to partial, from trunk to tip, from "total" to "local": i.e. from center to margin. In a country like Indonesia, an aspiring Asian "tiger" where "modernization" of language, culture, and economy is central to political legitimacy, space (e.g. centers and margins) is a modality through which the contradictions and disruptions of change are normalized, naturalized, and neutralized: ideologized.

Language ideology and social change in Sumba

The case of the transformation of this special poetic style of ritual speaking over the past hundred years provides an extraordinary sociolinguistic lens with which to examine more general problems concerning the relationship between linguistic and social change. As "modernization" and "development" transforms the societies of the "third world" such as Indonesia, it is also having a profound impact on their language. However, if I had limited my attention in this analysis to a study of "dialect shift" – on the level of sound or morpho-syntactic change – it might have been possible to conclude that relatively little change was occurring. Yet by turning the focus of the study to what the Sumbanese people have long considered the most valued words in their culture – their ritual-speech register – then it becomes clear that major changes are afoot. On the other hand, if I had concentrated entirely on the sociocultural aspects of the changes – conversion to Christianity, agricultural production, and political reorganization – I would be at a loss to explain why, in this apparently standard narrative of modernization, detribalization, and development, some ritual-speech genres have not only survived but thrived, and others have withered.

As the example of Mbora Kenda suggests, an important clue to the shifting fortunes of this prestigious and ideologically prominent speech code are the local beliefs and attitudes about the structure and function of language, and how these play a role in the transformation and reallocation of political, economic, and social resources. Sumbanese speakers care deeply about their verbal culture, and are not passive bystanders to the changes that are occurring. They actively represent aspects of their culture to themselves in ways that provide valuable clues about how they perceive its changes. Keyed by locally significant terms such as "speech," "anger," "humility," "name," and "cunning," Sumbanese *linguistic ideologies* (Woolard and Schieffelin 1994) about expressive performance, audience structure, naming and reference, and grammar organize verbal shifts interpretively in a manner that reveals the powerful role that language has played (and still plays) in the shaping of their history.

In the Weyewa highlands, the local "science" of language – a systematic language ideology, in this sense – begins with a classification of language varieties. Most prominent among these types is ritual speech. Consisting of couplets in which the first line parallels the second line in rhythm and meaning, this ritual-speech form is known as *tenda* or *panewe tenda*. As the "words of the ancestors," it has been an intense focus of ideological interest, and has long been regarded as a privileged medium of ritual wisdom and ancient truth. Weyewa ritual speakers draw on a stock of about 3,500 traditional couplets and link them together as they perform any of about nineteen different genres – narratives, chants, oratory, divination, songs and laments. These discourses must be fluent, eloquent, and frequently last all night. Thus a man singing in a placation rite refers to his audience as

a mattu-ba-na mata	The complete sets of eyes
a tanga-ba-na wiwi	the paired sets of lips

i.e. they are an attentive and complete audience. He may continue by saying

nyakka ku nonga powi	because of them, I blow my flute
nyakka ku bale dungga	because of them, I pluck my guitar.

i.e. because the audience is complete, the singer modestly attempts to perform in front of them. By linking such couplets together, one after another – hundreds in the course of an evening – performers of ritual-speech acquire reputations as skilled orators, singers, and mediators among living descendants and deceased ancestors.

To understand the relationship between linguistic and social change, I find it useful to first to adopt locally defined concepts of *genre* as the starting point for analysis, rather than beginning with sentence structure, phonemes, or morphemes. In Bakhtin's evocative image, genres are the "drivebelts" between the history of language and history of society (1986; see Hanks 1987). In standard linguistic approaches to change and shift, the "uncontroversial point" that "dying languages exhibit 'stylistic shrinkage'" in fact assumes that "style" is a formal set of options that "shrinks" in a neutral fashion when such affixes, certain syntactic constructions, and phonological resources are no longer used (Campbell and Muntzel 1989: 195; see also Mougeon and Beniak 1989: 299-302). In the Weyewa case, such "style reductions" are not impartial. They are inseparable from the ideologically charged genres in which those styles are embedded. Which genres survive and are reinterpreted, which remain as "folklore," and which ones are erased altogether, is a matter crucially mediated by language ideologies, and has fundamental implications, in turn, for understanding which syntactic, phonological, and morphological resources actually "shrink" and are "reduced."

As Jane Hill observes, strictly linguistic approaches to "endangered languages" tend to assume a relatively homogeneous stylistic repertoire (1993: 69). When discussing "abrupt transmission failure" or "tip" (e.g. Dorian 1989: 9), the assumption is that this refers to an "entire" language, not a specific style, or context of use, or genre. If declining styles are mentioned, they are discussed as one symptom of an overall decline in shared property belonging to all members equally. It is assumed that speakers wish to use it in appropriate, orderly, and traditional ways. In fact, such stylistic registers – as Mary Louise Pratt points out – can also be seen as internal fault lines that, particularly in situations of rapid social change, can be and are used as tools of exclusion and critique that fracture, divide, and rearrange groups and sub-groups in new ways (Pratt 1987; Hill 1993: 69).

It is only by understanding the language ideology as interpreted by local actors that we can explain why personal songs such as *lawiti* have been elaborated not only in villages but in settings such as schools. The more formal, religious, and political genres – despite interventions and support from church and state – have not received much local interest. Only when we appreciate how laments (*lawiti*), for example, were constructed as the voice of marginality, subordination, dependency, and "humility" can we understand why Weyewa did not simply change the addressees of the more authoritative political and religious genres from the ancestors to God and government. They could have, but did not.

Linguistic totality

A key feature of many linguistic ideologies is a belief about the nature of linguistic totality – a conception of a complete, pure, or coherent verbal whole against which improper usages, partial performances, and less valued features can be constructed. A good example of such beliefs emerged in the recent, passionate debate about Ebonics in the United States in the late 1990s. This debate revealed starkly the importance of "completeness" and "wholeness" in American linguistic ideologies. African-American vernacular English, it was alleged by its critics, is "broken" English, and not a "full"-fledged language deserving an institutional place along with other varieties of English.[2]

Assumptions about linguistic wholeness have long been important to the field of linguistics and linguistic anthropology. While in the past, this preoccupation arose out a concern with the linguistic fragmentation of society in Europe (Eco 1997), in the United States in the early 20th century, it was associated with a broadly liberal, democratic spirit of defending the integrity of non-Western cultures (e.g. Hall 1955). Sapir, for example, describes the wholeness of language from a structural standpoint in terms of its "formal completeness": "no matter what any speaker . . . desires to communicate . . . he will never need to create new forms or force upon his language a new formal orientation" (Sapir 1949: 153). The affective correlate of this formal completeness is the "whole feeling": the "feeling of inability or unwillingness to break up an object into smaller objects" (Sapir 1930: 7).[3] Note how "formal completeness" is thus linked with autonomy, i.e. the lack of a "need" for new forms, or external "force" imposing such forms. Sapir notes elsewhere, however, that no language is a completely integrated system, for "all grammars leak" (1921: 31).

Other scholars have extended such ideas about totality and completeness at different levels of linguistic structure. Anttila (1980), for instance, argues that the "totality" of the phoneme is a *Gestalt* enabling its contextual invariance and relative autonomy. Leont'eva (1974) observes that, while structural and semantic completeness requires formal repetition, most text-building traditions offer structural devices for reducing redundancy by creating logical ellipses. On the level of style, Paul Kay (1977) argues, drawing on Basil Bernstein's (1974) notion of "elaborated and restricted codes," that elaborated languages are more advanced because they are more "complete" and whole unto themselves, since no knowledge is needed to interpret them other than the language itself.

It is useful, however, to recall the cautions expressed in other areas of anthropology about formal completeness. There is, after all, no inherent reason why one language *must* express everything that a speaker wishes to say, if another language is available – other things being equal – to do the job. Most of the debate, unfortunately, has focussed on either attacking or defending the speaking varieties accused of being marginal and partial, with little questioning of the cultural representations of "completeness" and "wholeness" that such evaluations ultimately rest on. In the realm of sociocultural anthropology, critics have for over a decade now been criticizing the tendency in ethnographic writing to represent societies as complete totalities, and have pointed out that many of these societies were in fact marginal, partial, even dependent. Is it possible, then, that many of the languages represented by linguists as having a full "grammar" might, from a different perspective, be regarded as themselves marginal and partial? If so, what difference would it make? While much effort has already gone into a critique of the anthropological construction of "tribes" and "peoples" into ethnographic "wholes" (Clifford and Marcus 1986), little comparable critical scrutiny has been devoted to the common assumption that "language" is a neatly integrated totality.

Ideologies of linguistic totality in Indonesia

Indonesia, formerly the Dutch East Indies, with over 680 distinct ethnolinguistic entities (Wurm and Hattori 1983), is a particularly fascinating place to study the historical and ideological construction of totalities and their margins. The archipelago has a long history of deploying spatially defined imagery of identity for the legitimacy of systems of political and spiritual authority. Exemplary centers (Heine-Geldern 1942; Geertz 1968; Tambiah [1977] 1985), *adat* "circles" (Van Vollenhoven 1934), and localized "self-rule" were all part of a spatialized idiom for understanding indigenous processes by which subjects make moral, political, and economic choices about highly valued verbal, political, and social alternatives over time. Specifically, in eastern Indonesia, concepts of margin and center, "tip" and "trunk', part and whole, have been crucial to understanding the local Weyewa ideologies through which social and linguistic changes have been interpreted (Fox 1980; Fox and Sather 1996).

The history of ritual speech on a colonial periphery like Sumba challenges some central ideas about Dutch imperial history, as it reveals the ambivalence of the Dutch towards their own language and its cultural authority. As their polyglot island empire grew and developed, Dutch struggled to define what was whole, complete, and correct speech, and often could not agree among themselves. Groeneboer (1992) chronicles the fascinating, centuries-long doubts of the Dutch about the adequacy and appropriateness of their language as an instrument of empire, an ambivalence not found among any other European colonial power. Partly as a result of this ambivalence, and because it was the only major European colony administered through a non-European language, Dutch scholars and administrators were more concerned about the completeness, adequacy, and wholeness of local languages as a policy issue (particularly after the British reforms in the early nineteenth century) than were other colonial regimes. As Siegel points out, many of the Indies-born Dutch and Eurasians spoke Malay, not Dutch, as their first language, and "were told by colonial authorities and sometimes by their fathers, that their first language was not a language" (Siegel 1997: 15; see Maier 1993).

As a particularly self-conscious example of "language," ritual poetic speech and its changing fortunes in the history of this island empire reveals the strong ideologies of language operating among the Dutch at the time, and the crucial role that these ideologies played in the organization of their empire. Van Vollenhoven, one of the intellectual architects of a legal framework for the administrative organization of the Dutch East Indies, claimed that native languages were wholes that were "likely to correspond to a law group" (1934: 58). Thus the classification of native languages could provide valuable clues about the legal organization of the archipelago. Just as the surface differences among European languages justify national boundaries, differences among Indonesian languages can legitimate the boundaries and extent of legal claims.

But what is "language"? For Van Vollenhoven, the language of Indonesian law is not "utilitarian, expedient, and practical, like a telephone book or almanac, but originates out of something higher . . . that affects the mood and evokes feelings of devotion, respect and dedication" (1934: 119). In an essay entitled "Poetry in Indonesian Law" ["De Poëzie in het Indische Recht"], he suggests that, for example, the reason why local Minahassan (Northern Sulawesi) rules for dividing family land among in-laws are so inflexible has to do with certain local poetic sayings that have religious and moral force to them (1934: 120–121). Poetic speech, for Van Vollenhoven, deserved closer scrutiny as an important contributing factor in the more emotional, and thus non-rational, organization of Indonesian law and social structure.

Their approach to language defined the Dutch as a Southeast Asian empire (see Anderson 1996). As the field of linguistic study itself became increasingly professionalized and intellectually legitimate in the Dutch East Indies, the establishment of the Batavian Society of Arts and Sciences in 1778 and the Royal Institute of Linguistics and Ethnology (KITLV) in 1851 in Delft significantly enhanced the professional authority of scholars promoting the use of Javanese and Malay. As linguists gained in stature, the extractive, production-oriented character of Dutch political and social colonial policy was in constant tension with its linguistic policy (Groeneboer 1992). From the colonial government's perspective, the goal of language study was to develop a way for administrators effectively to communicate with their people so that they could effectively keep order; and, secondarily, to use the local languages as a means of identifying "rational" units for administrative structure, e.g. *desa*, "village." Relatively few resources were devoted to promote language study among the natives themselves. The goal of language study was thus the smooth functioning of the social order itself, and not to define, create, or meet local "needs" *per se*. For the British, by contrast, one important goal of language study in colonial India was a kind of "market research" to better understand, create and shape consumer needs and thus enlarge their markets.

As for the scholarship on Sumba itself, the impact of Van Vollenhoven was indirect, since the man who did the most important linguistic research on the island, the missionary linguist Louis Onvlee (1973), was most influenced in his early training by two legal philologists – Johan Jonker and Samuel Philippus van Ronkel. Both of these men, however, were scholars who had distinguished themselves through study of Indonesian languages in order to discern native laws: Jonker on old Javanese laws (1885), and van Ronkel on old Malay laws (1929), and thus were very much aware of Van Vollenhoven's writings. Both of these men taught Onvlee.

Onvlee himself investigated the Sumbanese languages not only to provide practical assistance to those wishing to learn it, and to develop a

Bible in the local Sumbanese languages, but also to discern the laws of the local culture. In an article on the building of a dam in Mangili (1977), Onvlee shows how an investigation of language, particularly ritual speech, provides new insights into Sumbanese legal understandings of land use. Central to his argument was his idea that "culture is a response" *"cultuur als antwoord"* a total world view in which meaning is organized, including language, culture, and society (1973).

The emphasis on meaningful coherence of totalities in Onvlee's insightful cultural analyses worked in some unusual ways in his linguistic researches. In his dictionary (Onvlee et al. 1984), he emphasized the coherence of Sumbanese languages as a unit in his dictionary by including under a single entry all the known cognate forms among other Sumbanese languages, as if these words were somehow dialectal variants of one another. Indeed, although he was well aware of the lack of mutual intelligibility of the Sumbanese languages, he often refers to them as "dialects" (e.g. Onvlee 1930). Such an approach also elides all evidence of borrowing, and implies that they have grown from a common source. Teeuw (1994) and Kridalaksana (1979) have both discussed the unique characteristics of the Dutch lexicographic tradition. As Ellen points out (1976), such emphasis on the coherence of totalities cannot be simply assimilated to British functionalism: Dutch anthropology and linguistics have their own unique intellectual traditions, which need to be explained in relation to debates about the autonomy of *adat* law (see Van Vollenhoven 1934) and orientalist views of language.

Linguistic completeness as a language ideology in eastern Indonesia

Beliefs about the wholeness of languages (or conversely, the relative "broken"-ness, "partial"-ness and marginality of language) are not simply a western, colonial invention imposed on the passive "natives" of Indonesia. Research carried out in the past twenty years has revealed the central importance of ideologies about linguistic completeness and wholeness in eastern Indonesia, although these studies – with some exceptions – have not usually examined the role of these ideologies in the process of linguistic and ceremonial shifts taking place in the region (see Fox 1980; Barraud and Platenkamp 1992). Among the Rindi of East Sumba, Forth notes that ritual speech is described as *peka pamangihingu*, "speech which is full." In contrast to ordinary speech, ritual speech is whole, full and dense with meanings (1988: 134). Among Rindi, as among many other folk in eastern Indonesia, the fullness and richness is used as a "veil" and "ruse" to exclude others.

In Traube's research among the Mambai of East Timor, however, she explores the ways in which local symbolic constructions of completeness have assimilated historical processes. She begins with the observation that "indigenous conceptions of the whole are symbolically constituted" (1986: 4). Ritual speech is "the primary means of [ceremonial] formalization" (1986: 22). Among these talkative ritualists, the "whole" of their cosmos is expressed in terms of "rhythmic alternations of white and black, of life and death, of receiving and giving" which are the basis of a ritual system's "total" character. As they put it,

Buti ba rat	When white is not enough
Nor meta fe tlut	Increase it with black;
Meta ba natou	When black is not sufficient
Nor buti fe naur	Augment it with white. (1986: 11)

Traube, however, notes the ways in which Mambai incorporated the Portuguese into their cosmology by viewing them as late-arriving "little brothers" whose recent arrival on (and conquest of) the island of Timor nonetheless left them deficient in ritual knowledge of the "wholeness of Mambai life" embodied in ritual-speech (Traube 1986: 60).

In my research among the Weyewa of Sumba, ideologies of linguistic completeness and change cannot be separated from the problems of performance (see Kuipers 1990). Indeed, completeness arises as an issue in relation to the ceremonial performance. In ceremonial procedure, for instance, a common question is: did the speaker "follow the [proper] steps?" ("*deku nauta*"). One of the most important of these steps – as we shall see in chapter 3 – is convening a complete audience, as expressed in the common couplet:

mattu mata	the faces are complete
tanga wiwi	the lips are paired.

Failure to complete a ritual in its proper way is often attributed to "forgetting" the "true ways" of the ancestors, and the widespread influences of the modern world.

On a more general level, the "wholeness" of ritual-speech is described as "the ultimate speech" (*ndukka li'i*): full, whole, and complete discourse of the ancestors. The sense of wholeness evoked by this phrase is intimately bound up with the idea of margin, since *ndukka* means "limit, edge." One can say, "*Na kako ndukka Amerika*" ("he went [all the way to] America"). Margins are linked to wholes in intimate and interesting ways in the Weyewa language. *Uppu*, for example, means "margin" as in *uppu-na lara*, "edge of the road," but it also means "limit," or "climax," and "fulfillment" (of a prior effort) as in *uppu-na li'i*, "fulfillment of one's word, promise." "Complete speech" in this sense does not carry the same prescriptive force as it might in English, where it has an almost allegorical sense of model behavior quite apart from any particular enactment of it. In Weyewa, speech is only "ultimate," "complete," and "whole" when it is appropriately performed as such (Kuipers 1990; cf. also Bauman and Briggs 1990). As ritual spokesmen often told me: "everything has its pair." Failure to pair something appropriately in its ritual context could result in a fine or supernatural sanctions.

Linguistic ideologies of marginalization cannot be studied only by what people say *about* their language: it also emerges in *performance of* the language. Both Tsitsipis (1988, 1989) and Dorian (1982) have noted the role of performance in the process of linguistic marginality and decline. In a study of the decline of the Arvanitika language in Greece, Tsitsipis (1989) argued that speakers with partial competence are nonetheless capable of using the language in meta-linguistic contexts, to "clarify things for some older folks," to impress a foreigner, or "consciously [to] turn the language into an object of play and inquiry" (1989: 120; cf. Keane 1997b). In the context of traditional storytelling, however, often such partially competent speakers *do not* respond appropriately (Tsitsipis 1988). Dorian (1982), in her study of Scottish fisherfolk, reports that many speakers who did not have productive syntactic fluency in the language nonetheless possessed many of the conversational inferencing skills required for fluency. They were able to participate in conversations, understand the jokes, make requests, take leave, and other speech routines without offending anyone.

Like Dorian's Gaelic speakers, who are not syntactically fluent but are pragmatically competent, many of the remaining ritual speakers on Sumba increasingly specialize in responsive forms, but are wary of placing themselves in a performative context in which their own communicative competence as producers can be evaluated. By focussing on genres such *lawiti* "laments" that are seen as responses to other genres, they are able to deflect some of the responsibility for communicative competence. Laments and other such dialogic genres of communication also allow for frequent use of "performance disclaimers" – such as hedges, asides, and codeswitches – to suggest that they are not actually performing. Because Weyewa possess a "strict compartmentalization ideology" similar to that described by Kroskrity (1992) for Tewa speakers, authoritative ritual genres cannot be diluted, they must be performed in their entirety, and lapses in performances can be punished by supernatural retribution. Thus it is safer to rely on genres such as "laments" in which performance is not so strictly compartmentalized, and in which performers are not so responsible for full performance.

Marginality

Wholes, "sources," and totalities require parts, "tips," and margins. The metaphor of marginality is interwoven through much of this analysis.

Arising from the textual realm – the edge of the page – the term "marginality" suggests a spatialized, perspectival, and hence (at least potentially) experiential idiom for understanding a condition of being at the border, a transitional zone of a defined totality. In colonial and neo-colonial Indonesia, in which redefinitions of place and identity have been crucial to the legitimacy of systems of political and spiritual authority, marginality can offer a usefully spatialized idiom for understanding cultural processes by which individuals and groups select among verbal options over the course of their histories. As I point out below, concepts of the "margin" and center, "tip" and "trunk," part and whole have been critical for understanding the local Weyewa linguistic ideologies through which linguistic changes have been interpreted.

Linguistic ideologies can provide an interpretive link connecting more radically subjective, experiential perspectives and more "objective," system-based approaches to understanding marginalization. On the one hand, for example, bell hooks (1990), eloquently describes the liberating radical subjectivity of postcolonial actors as *choosing marginality* as a site of resistance; in my reading, her account is not so very different from the experience of people like Mbora Kenda, and some of the "angry men" and "humble" women described in this book. However, to explain how such "choices" play out over time, it is useful to examine the ways in which such interpretive strategies have themselves affected, and been affected by, the dynamic socioeconomic and political structures in which those choices take place. Thus "anger" as a feature of expressive performance, for example, was once regarded as a noble and righteous rage, a central feature of linguistic, political, even economic ideology in Sumba; with the arrival of the Dutch, new bureaucratic and institutional meanings were attached to displays of anger, thus engendering a reinter-pretation of "anger" as a subjective experience. Rather than focussing only on marginality as an *experience* of exclusion, or, on the other hand, entirely on the systemic implications of marginality as "deviance" or "liminality" (e.g. Turner 1974), the approach I have adopted examines how aspects of this process (which I explain below) – hierarchic inclusion, essentialization, spectatorship, indexicalization and erasure – mediate between locally constructed meanings and experiences of change, and the institutional system of practices undergoing transformation.

With a hitherto robust economy, and the home of a national language regarded by some as the "miracle of the developing world" (Fishman 1978), Indonesia is a critical site for studying the process of margin-alization and displacement, and the role of speech within that process (see Errington 1992). Within Southeast Asia, few countries have been more unabashedly pro-growth than the Suharto regime of Indonesia, which bases much of its political legitimacy on the promise of economic "development" (*pembangunan*) (Schwartz 1994). Across this large island nation – now the fourth largest country in the world – the social experience of this astonishing growth – to use the current vernacular of Indonesia's five-year plans – has been "uneven" (*tidak merata*), and most officials describe some groups, indeed some whole peoples, as having been "left behind." As Indonesia's economy began to lurch toward the "take-off stage," a "by-product" of this dynamic development was the creation of categories of marginal peoples: people like Mbora Kenda, who refused or were refused the experience of modernity. An entire bureaucracy was formed to control this category of "marginal peoples" (*suku terasing*), to analyze who they were, and how to "lead" them into the modern world. However, as Koentjaraningrat has observed (1993), the peoples living on the edges of Indonesia's economy interpret and express their condition in a variety of ways – with resentment, pride, envy, resignation, perhaps sharing only the experience of exclusion and difference.[4]

Most studies approach marginality from a broadly sociocultural standpoint (e.g. Turner 1974; Germani 1980), and do not specifically focus on language. In Anna Lowenhaupt Tsing's (1993) detailed, insightful, and theoretically self-conscious study, *In the realm of the diamond queen*, however, she relates the institutional marginality of the peoples of the Meratus area in Kalimantan to the ways in which the people themselves creatively interpret their marginality, often through ironic, fanciful, and irreverent verbal arts. While their tendency to "move" is enough to get them labeled *terasing* ("marginal, estranged"), key evidence of their marginality for Tsing is a subjective, inner state expressed through subtle verbal arts, poetic means that may be concealed from powerful visitors from the outside. When a Javanese engineer visited the village of Kalawan in the Meratus area, for instance, Tsing speculates: "I doubt if he saw anything other than a typical rural settlement . . . I believe the engineer got no hint of the anger and fear that had seized the community with the news of the transmigration agency's plans" (1993: 290). While the appearance of the village indicated suggested normal participation in society, the ironic uses of language, the double meanings of fanciful stories, the ambiguous meanings of assent are only available upon a closer inspection of the society and the subject positions of its members.

Approaches to the role of language among socially marginal groups

Speech use – specifically, verbal art – plays an important role in the production and reproduction of marginality. But while there have been a number of books that have made this point vividly and persuasively – e.g. Scott (1990), Stallybrass and White (1986), Abu-Lughod (1986) – as

Gal (1995) points out, there are many important questions that remain about how pragmatic and grammatical features of language use relate to marginality and how these features change over time. Furthermore, she argues, one cannot always assume that the ironic stance often attributed to the underclass is in fact intrinsically subversive or expressive of subordination. Interacting subjects do not necessarily see their social world in polarized categories such as dominant–subordinate, public–private, "acting" versus "real": indeed, sometimes they hold and express simultaneously contradictory opinions. Furthermore, the data used in analyzing the expressive forms of subordinate groups and marginal peoples have overwhelmingly been focussed on the referential and representational forms of language, leaving out the pragmatic and grammatical complexity of the data.

Careful attention to the linguistic processes by which marginality is constructed can provide new insights into the ways in which this condition develops, is experienced, and is reproduced. Many of the ethnographies most well known for depicting marginality are of peoples who frame and indeed construct their marginality through the control and manipulation of linguistic resources. Tsing makes the intriguing observation that

> Banjar [a dominant ethnic group who live near the Meratus people] claim that the Meratus language is unintelligible to them; Meratus are more likely to argue that they speak exactly the same language.   (1993: 53)[5]

The ways in which such ideological constructions of bilingualism and monolingualism get played out in actual settings of use can have important implications for explaining how marginality develops and is reproduced on a day to day basis. Kulick, for instance, in his study of a largely bilingual New Guinea village of Gapun (1992b) shows that the pragmatic structure of language socialization practices has contributed to the failure of children to learn their native language, Taiap, and instead prefer Tok Pisin – despite their parents' wishes. He observed that when the youngsters fail to respond to parental directives in Taiap, the same directive is then rephrased in Tok Pisin to get results. Without Kulick's careful attention to the interactive structure of how the language actually gets used and how that interactive pattern is part and parcel of a larger ideological process of marginalization, it is difficult to understand how the Gapun people – relatively isolated, subsistence farmers with limited exposure to neighboring groups – could find themselves in their present predicament.

Grammatical structures also play a role in the organization of marginality and language shift. Gal and Irvine (1995), for example, show how French scholarly interpretations of the relative grammatical "complexity" of west African languages – Wolof and Sereer – played an important role in the ways in which linguistic and cultural boundaries in those societies were constructed (Gal and Irvine 1995). They describe how nineteenth century French linguists, by labelling Sereer as grammatically "simple" set in motion a series of choices about its uses. In a similar fashion, Dutch linguists" attitudes towards the structure of Malay languages had implications for its suitability in schools, textbook development, and use in administration (e.g. Wilken 1892: 141;[6] see Maier 1993). However, without an analysis of how these grammatical features were understood and analyzed, the kinds of evaluations and subsequent boundary determinations and relative allocations of resources would be hard to comprehend.

But if cultural anthropologists can learn valuable lessons by paying attention to linguistic structures, linguists, too, can benefit from the *actor-oriented*, experiential perspective employed by many of the cultural anthropologists whose work I have mentioned above. Many linguists have tended to look on marginal languages as "dying languages" as though this were somehow a natural process in a "life cycle." Buoyed by arguments for structural patterning in "language birth" processes such as creolization (e.g. Bickerton 1983), many linguists have devoted their attention to searching for predictable patterns of structural attrition, simplification and rule loss (Schmidt 1985). Others, more sociolinguistically inclined, have concentrated on searching for universal patterns of bilingualism and borrowing in language shift and decline (e.g. Myers-Scotton 1992).

All, however, have tended to borrow from models in the natural sciences in ways that do not capture the experience of the people using those languages. Marginal languages are often described as "endangered languages," a phrase which calls to mind the botanical and zoological analogy of "endangered species." While the implicit stance of political advocacy may be laudable (if occasionally condescending) such a model often fails to appreciate the way in which the actual speakers themselves (as "actors," "agents," "subjects") make *use* of their languages in creative ways that affect their social situation. The term *obsolescence* (deriving from a term "to grow old') also bears connotations of naturalness and inevitability. Yet other scholars – more neutrally – call this process language "shift," which, in some hands at least, suggests a rather impersonal framework of change, unassignable to specific agents or experiencers.

Marginality as an ideological and semiotic process

Languages, dialects, and speech varieties, and the boundaries between them, are not "things," unaffected by human will, somehow waiting to be discovered by scholars, cartographers, politicians, and national-development experts. As a growing number of scholars have observed and documented, language ideologies have played a crucial role in the construction of the boundaries between languages, and varieties of languages (Kroskrity, 1992). Drawing broadly on Silverstein (1979), Woolard and Schieffelin (1994) and Gal and Irvine (1995: 970–971), I view language ideologies as ideas with which "participants frame their understandings of linguistic varieties and the differences among them, and map those understandings onto people, events, and activities" (1995: 970). These ideas are ideological in the sense that they are deeply interwoven with the political, moral, and economic interests of the bearers, who may be the actual speakers themselves, or the various observers, scholars, philologists, and linguists who describe and map the boundaries of those languages and language varieties.

Thus language ideologies held by many Americans have played a role in the definition of African-American vernacular English, for example, as a substandard variety whose use defines one as uneducated and unsophisticated. Language ideologies have played an important role in the construction of national and tribal boundaries in places like Macedonia and west Africa (Gal and Irvine 1995). The definition of what constitutes a separate language is often a highly ideological one, but has been crucial to the legitimation of tribal identities, cultural "character," and national frontiers.

The semiotic processes by which linguistic ideologies contributed to language change have been described as iconicity, recursiveness, and erasure (Gal and Irvine 1995). Iconicity

involves a transformation of the sign relationship between linguistic practices, features or varieties and the social images with which they are linked. Linguistic practices that *index* social groups or activities appear to be *iconic* representations of them – as if a linguistic feature somehow depicted or displayed a social groups" inherent nature or essence (cf. Irvine 1989).   (1995: 973)

In the United States, the southern accent is often taken as an icon of a certain laziness. The pattern of pronouncing vowels is sometimes regarded as a transparent reflection of a lazy unwillingness to muster the energy to pronounce one's vowels "correctly." Among Weyewa, the "angry" character of ritual speech came to be seen by the Dutch as a "natural" and inherent feature of Sumbanese discourse, an icon of the savage condition of Sumbanese leadership, from which the "people" must be delivered.

Recursiveness "involves the projection of an opposition, salient at some level of relationship, on to some other level. For example, intra-group oppositions might be projected outward onto inter-group relations or vice versa" (1995: 974). Thus when Nguni speakers incorporated clicks in order to express social distance and deference, they were projecting the perceived contrast between their own Bantu language and the very different Khoi languages *on to* the realm of speech registers *within* their own language – i.e. socially intimate speech versus socially distant and deferential speech (Irvine and Gal 1998).

Erasure "is the process in which ideology, in simplifying the field of linguistic practices, renders some persons or activities or sociolinguistic phenomena invisible" (Gal and Irvine 1995: 974). In nineteenth-century descriptions of African languages by Western scholars, the complexity of the linguistic practices that involved borrowing, code-switching, and other evidence of "mixing" were often stripped away from grammatical descriptions in order to effectively to support claims to the distinctiveness of the groups (1995: 980). Among Weyewa, the variety of ritual speech genres were reduced in efforts by the local school system to present it as an aspect of local "culture." Only when the more authoritative genres are erased from the curriculum can these local poetic languages be taught as an object of contemplation.

Plan of the book: theoretical perspectives

In the spirit of Gal and Irvine's (1995) efforts to identify processes by which linguistic ideologies mediate sociocultural and linguistic change, I propose – using a more spatially oriented idiom of centers and peripheries, wholes and margins – five related processes of a general nature that I believe have occurred and are occurring in the Weyewa highlands: *hierarchic inclusion*, *essentialization*, *spectatorship*, *indexicalization*, and *erasure*. These rather abstract labels correspond, in turn, to a cluster of more "experience-near" and ideologically salient local terms for describing sociolinguistic relationships of which speakers age more or less aware (see Geertz 1983: 56–57; see also Silverstein 1981). Each of these processes is a theme in the roughly chronological arrangement of chapters explained below.

In chapter 1, I argue that one of the first and most fundamental processes in the marginalization of ritual speech was one carried out in a spatial idiom, in which Sumbanese languages were put in their place in relation to other languages on the territory of the island. I call this process hierarchic inclusion, which refers to the transformation of ideas about speech in which a language, or language variety, once seen as complete and integral by virtue of its relation to a locale comes to be viewed as included in a larger grouping. I describe how Weyewa ritual speech came increasingly to be seen as a part of the everyday, colloquial Weyewa language, which was in turn a part of the larger set of languages included in the relatively novel category of the Dutch East Indies. This process, although set in motion by the Dutch invasion, *pax neerlandica*, and the subsequent dispersal of the ancestral villages, cannot be explained in purely political terms, since the Dutch actively sought to shore up symbols that bore connotations of the autonomy of local, "self-ruling" (*zelf-bestuur*) authority, including ritual-speech.

In chapter 2, I argue that as the Dutch mapped out the island, they sought to characterize Sumbanese leadership in terms of its emotional and political alignment to the *bestuur*, "administration." The primary evidence for these alignments were the communicative and expressive styles used in the (rather limited) encounters between nobility and Dutch authorities. A key process at work in these encounters was essentialization (cf. "iconicity" above), whereby a linguistic feature that indexes a social status, group, or category comes to be seen as essentially or naturally linked to it. Among Weyewa, the "angry" character of ritual-speech, which was a feature that indexed the social category of "angry man," came to be seen by the Dutch (and by the Sumbanese themselves) as a "natural," core, and essential feature of Sumbanese leadership, an inner emotional state, and characteristic of the savage condition of Sumbanese authority, from which the "people" must be delivered. As angry speech came to be associated with "traditional leadership," new forms of "cunning" and "humble" emotional expression began to occupy the peripheries of passion in ambiguous and uncertain ways. This chapter thus argues for the importance of emotion as a cultural factor in linguistic and social change.

By the late 1920s and 1930s in Sumba, political participation – viewed as a communicative relation between the leaders and followers, performers and audience, production and reception of meanings, had become verbally unstable, and morally problematic. In chapter 3, I describe how spectatorship emerged as not only as a status but as a process in which the pragmatic opposition between performer and audience is projected onto a more generalized relation between the authoritative discourse of the state and the citizens of the state. Thus in Weyewa, the audience, embodied in the image of the "orphan" in sung laments, was increasingly cast in the role of responder to the voice of Indonesian authority. As an account of linguistic change, the chapter describes a process guided by norms of verbal interaction; as an account of sociopolitical change, the chapter explains a process that is locally understood and represented in communicative terms.

After the Second World War, the declaration of Indonesia's independence, and the folding of the Dutch administration, ironically, conversion to Christianity finally began to occur at a more rapid pace. Converts began to adopt Christian names at a rapid pace, and discarded their ritual-speech prestige names, along with the elaborate feasting practices in which those names were bestowed. In chapter 4 I describe a process of indexicalization in which the function of Sumbanese linguistic signs (e.g.

a "name"), once viewed as designating a more general cultural category (i.e. a "semantic" category), came to be viewed primarily as an act of pointing to something more specific (i.e. as an ostensive and "pragmatic" act). Thus Weyewa names, which once served to classify people in terms of address and reference, soft and hard, and as high status, are increasingly giving way in both address and reference to Christian names used to refer to and identify specific individuals on tax forms and in all state and personal functions. Government-led campaigns against ritual "name-seeking" feasts suggest an implicit ideological preference for more practical, indexical functions of naming rather than more classificatory functions. Modern Christian names have little in the way of semantic functions – other than to indicate one's religion and gender. This chapter examines the role of such ideologies in mediating the shift by which the most prestigious forms of ritual-speech names are now applied only to pick-up trucks, businesses, and race horses.

By the mid-1980s, nearly all school-age children were attending school. In chapter 5, I examine how changing learning practices affected ritual-speech. The process I propose, erasure, among the Weyewa is similar to the concept of erasure proposed by Gal and Irvine (1995), except that in simplifying the field of linguistic practices, the processual character of diverse forms of discourse is systematically ignored. I describe how in teaching and learning ritual speech, the process whereby novices make mistakes and are sociolinguistically supported by their elders is system-atically denied any communicative or interactional reality. By only teaching "laments," Indonesian schools render the more authoritative and potentially challenging "source" and originary forms of ritual speech invisible. Increasingly, laments are coming to stand for ritual speaking as a whole.

By placing verbal practices at the center of this study, this book is part of a growing genre of anthropological writing known as the ethnography of speaking or ethnography of communication (Hymes 1974; Duranti 1984). It departs from most such ethnographies in that its primary goal is explanation and interpretation of change, not a more synchronic analy-sis. By chronicling the demise of a cherished cultural form, I risk incurring the dismay of some of my more modernist friends on Sumba, who might favor a more triumphal narrative of progress and moderniza-tion. On the other hand, by adopting a non-nostalgic view of new, emergent and hybrid forms of speech, I may be offending some of my more traditional friends, who would prefer to focus on true and more "authentic" versions of past practices. Despite these limitations, I hope it does provide a reasonable account of the operation of linguistic ideolo-gies in the shift of a once-valued style of communication from trunk to tip, from whole to part, from center to margin.

2

PLACE, IDENTITY, AND THE SHIFTING FORMS OF CULTIVATED SPEECH: A GEOGRAPHY OF MARGINALITY

What is the role of place in linguistic change? Is there a link between the changing locale of a community of speakers and its social position as marginal or central to the society? If a language is positioned – or conceived to be positioned – on the edge of an island, a nation, a continent, or a trade route, how does that affect its evolution and development? Is it a symptom of decline? In European linguistics, there are certainly some suggestive cases: Gaelic, for instance, is spoken now only in the western and northern tips of Ireland and Scotland (Watson 1989: 43). Breton is a language spoken in tiny enclaves of northern France, pushed up against the sea (Kuter 1989: 83). Both of these are widely regarded as languages in decline. Is there some special linkage between the whereabouts of speakers and the status of a language as marginal?

To understand the significance of place for linguistic change, I argue in this chapter that we need to investigate its meaning for the speakers themselves. Location in and of itself does not in any simple way determine the nature of linguistic change, or result in linguistic expansion or decline. Instead, place affects linguistic shifts via linguistic ideologies – local beliefs about language and its characteristics – which mediate the relation between locale and linguistic features. For example, some speakers maintain a strong belief in a linguistic homeland; sometimes this source is viewed as an especially "pure" form of speech; other times it is seen as simply antiquated and marginal. Some people think their language "belongs" in a particular location and sounds strange and out-of-place in new and unfamiliar locations; others think their language can be used comfortably anywhere. In situations of rapid social change, in- or out-migration, such ideas about place and its relation to language use can be crucial to the survival or decline of a language (see also Tuan 1991).

In linguistics and anthropology, there is a long and venerable history of studies that investigate the relation between place and language. Carried out variously under the banner of dialect geography (Chambers and Trudgill 1980), areal linguistics (Goossens 1977; Emeneau 1980), or contact linguistics (Weinreich 1966), all have been concerned with variations and their distributions in three categories: (1) subsystemic (or intra-

22

linguistic studies) in which variation is examined internal to a language system; (2) diasystemic (or distributions between different dialects); and (3) intersystemic relations (or contact linguistics). Features of "place" in these formulations generally plays one of the following interpretive roles: (1) A local feature of the place is noted as coinciding with linguistic distributions, as when different dialects are found on different sides of a mountain range. (2) It may be regarded as an external explanatory factor, as when a mountain range is seen as a cause of the linguistic boundaries. Overall, however, these approaches have tended not to focus on the experience of the speakers, but rather tend to treat the language as an independent autonomous structure quite separate from human will, intentions, and agency. I wish to emphasize that language ideologies – beliefs about language that arise out of the socioeconomic interests and positions of cultural actors – selectively emphasize certain features of place as being important while disregarding others (see also Haugen 1972; Mannheim 1991).

More specifically, the language ideologies about place in Sumba have changed via a semiotic process I call hierarchic inclusion. By this, I refer to a transformation of ideas about speech in which a language, or language variety, once seen as complete and integral by virtue of its relation to a locale comes to be viewed as included in a larger grouping. Thus Weyewa ritual speech came increasingly to be seen as a part of the Weyewa language, which was in turn a part of the larger set of languages in Indonesia.

Before intensive contact with the Dutch began in the early twentieth century, an important concept of place that organized ritual-speech use was a notion that Geertz described as the "doctrine of the exemplary center" (1968). On resource-poor but verbally rich Sumba it was less of a visual, architectural, or sumptuary concept than a linguistic one. As the Dutch gradually guaranteed the security of the island by controlling inter-island trading and raiding, the population began to rise, and, in the Weyewa highlands at least, a population dispersal was set in motion. This diaspora saw the creation of new, smaller pioneering settlements of hamlets that were marginal to the ritual centers, but agriculturally more autonomous. For Weyewa, this kind of distance from ceremonial centers meant that only seldom were the most authoritative genres of ritual speech performed. More often, the less authoritative and more marginal genres were performed instead.

The varieties of ritual speech performed were increasingly not the encompassing, authoritative varieties, but more simple, derivative forms that were closer to, and included in, the everyday Weyewa language: "garden talk." At the same time, Dutch missionaries and scholars, rather than communicating in Malay or Dutch, began studying Weyewa intensively as an example of a "local language" (*landstaal*). In order to be viewed as local, it had to be part of a locative hierarchy, in which the "local" was successively grouped into ever-larger entities (see Keane 1997a).

The ancestral village, the exemplary center, and linguistic ideology

The concept of marginality requires a center. For the past three decades, both Tambiah (1977, 1985) and Geertz (1968: 35–43; 1980, 1983), drawing on earlier work by Heine-Geldern (1942), have devoted much effort to explicating the politically, spiritually, and architecturally ornate cosmographies of the meaning of centers in classical Southeast Asian states. In Geertz's formulation, such states exhibited three implicit principles: (1) the doctrine of the exemplary center; (2) graded spirituality; (3) theatre state.

By "exemplary center," Geertz means the notion that "the king's court and capital, and at their axis the king himself, form at once an image of divine order and a paradigm for social order" (1968: 36). The doctrine of graded spirituality holds that spirituality is not equally distributed among people, and that the king has the most, by virtue of his office, and those who are further from the palace have less by virtue of their spatial and social remove from him. The principle of the theatre state is the idea that the ritual practices of the court are not just the trappings of rule but its *raison d'être*; the purpose of the state is not so much to govern as to make "inequality enchant."

As Tambiah points out in his essay on "The galactic polity in Southeast Asia" such concepts are "not a distinctive feature of complex kingdoms and polities only. The evidence is quite clear that [these ideas] appear in tribal, lineage-based segmentary societies practicing slash and burn agriculture" (Tambiah [1977]1985: 253). He cites as an example the case of the Atoni of Timor, in eastern Indonesia, where house and village design are organized on a center and periphery model (Cunningham 1964). While these societies do not possess elaborate courts and kingdoms in the usual sense, the imagery of the exemplary center is nonetheless pervasive and profound.

When one first enters a Sumbanese village, one's eyes are immediately drawn to the center. One of my first experiences in Sumba was a visit to a *wanno kalada*. From a distance, one can often miss them entirely, as they are often on hilltops, and shrouded from view by the fronds of coconut and areca palms, thick plumes of bamboo, and broad-leafed banana palms. At the base of the hill, one must dismount one's horse, or park one's motorcycle or jeep, because the broken and jagged pieces of chalky limestone that pave the trail are treacherously slippery and uneven.

Plate 2   *A Weyewa ancestral village*

After what is sometimes a climb of several minutes, past thorny hedges of cacti meant to keep people out, suddenly a view opens up of somber intensity: two rows of solemn, high-peaked houses facing each other across a courtyard filled with massive, moldy, megalithic ancestral sarcophagi (see Plate 2). As the scrawny dogs erupt into a frenzy of barking, residents of the houses silently stare from their dark verandas as one passes by.

In the very center of the village, there is an altar, sometimes consisting of a stripped and bare tree placed upright in a pile of rocks. This is the *marapu wanno*, "village spirit," sometimes also called the *katoda*. The relative proximity of a house to this village center may be taken as a broad reflection of status and genealogical history. As a rule of thumb, those closer to the center, with taller roof peaks, are regarded as being of higher relative status. Those with smaller houses, farther from the center are relatively marginal, relatively late in settling in the village, and hence of lower status, at least initially. Particularly in older, ancestral villages, however, these initial settlement histories may no longer be a reflection of current status conditions, since the first settlers of a village may now be poor and marginal while the latter-day immigrants may have stronger economic and ritual positions. These

Plate 3   *The steep, rocky path leading to an ancestral village*

relative status issues are matters of debate and contest at times of the ritual renewal and rebuilding of the houses. Where family members cannot agree on these matters of relative status, the houses are simply allowed to become dilapidated.

Weyewa use couplet speech such as the following to describe the relation between the ancestral villages as magnificent ("amidst tributes/gifts") and central ("source/base") and the descendant villages, which are dependent and marginal ("bound by rhizomes/attached by tendrils").

Wa'i ma-ngge newe-ngge	We are all here amidst
wolo pondi	the tributes of the princes
rawi rato	the gifts of the priests
pu'u-na wazu	at the base of the tree
mata-na we'e	at the source of the water
ka ta kako ne'e-ngge	so let us go
pandou ndari tana	where farm land is bound
mangu baba	by rhizomes
pandou mbatu rutta	where the grass land is attached
mangu lolo	with tendrils

Thus ancestral villages – ideally – are not only a nucleated center of population, but are likened to a parental "source" (*bei wanno*) from which other villages spring, which are then attached to the center by symbolic "rhizomes" and "tendrils" of filiation. I describe this in an earlier work:

> There were [and are now] three main ranks of Weyewa "villages" (*wanno*), in descending order of status and genealogical proximity to the origin village: 'ancestral villages" (*wanno kalada*), "corral villages" (*wanno nggollu*), and "garden villages" (*wanno oma dana*). When asked to name his or her village, a Weyewa might reply with any one of these three, depending on the context. Ancestral villages [Plate 1] represent the apical nodes in a kin-based and, derivatively, botanical discourse about the classification of collective life. They are spoken of as the "source" and "trunk."   (Kuipers 1990: 18–19)

Lesser, offshoot villages are spoken of as "tendrils," "gardens," as "field huts," and as temporary settlements, even if people have lived there for decades. Their spiritual potency is correspondingly diminished. Promises made, rituals performed in "garden villages" are less authoritative than those in the ancestral villages. I was often told that conversations about ritual and religious lore could only go so far with particular individuals because we were not in the sacred village. Unless we were sitting in the sacred village, discussion about ceremonial matters could not concern matters of great genealogical depth.

Evidence of similar stratification of villages according to their relationship to the center is found elsewhere on Sumba (Forth 1981; Hoskins 1993; Keane 1997b) and in many other islands in eastern Indonesia (Fox 1980; Traube 1986).

THE VILLAGE OF BEINDELLO

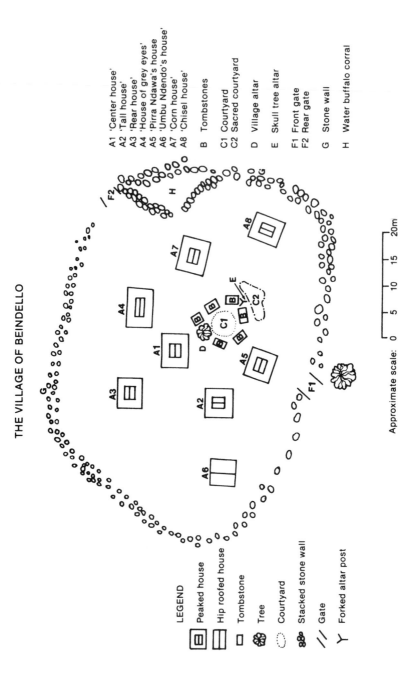

A1 'Center house'
A2 'Tall house'
A3 'Rear house'
A4 'House of grey eyes'
A5 'Pirra Ndawa's house'
A6 'Umbu Ndendo's house'
A7 'Corn house'
A8 'Chisel house'

B Tombstones

C1 Courtyard
C2 Sacred courtyard

D Village altar

E Skull tree altar

F1 Front gate
F2 Rear gate

G Stone wall

H Water buffalo corral

LEGEND

▣ Peaked house

▥ Hip roofed house

□ Tombstone

❀ Tree

⋯ Courtyard

∘∘∘ Stacked stone wall

// Gate

Y Forked altar post

Approximate scale: 0 5 10 15 20m

Figure 3 Plan of an ancestral village

Verbal performance and the establishment of the exemplary center

In the verbally rich but resource-poor islands of eastern Indonesia such as Sumba, verbal performance played an important role in the establishment of the authority of the center as spiritually and politically exemplary (cf. Errington 1992). In many places, such as Sumba, there is a special style of speech that is held to hark back to an earlier period of revelation, and these words are seen as sacred, morally foundational, and unchanging, immune to "shift" (Fox 1988c). Angry displays of verbal virtuosity using this elaborate form of couplet speech played a key role in the establishment of oneself, one's village, and one's clan as the bearer of the word of the ancestors and thus the "center" and "source" of authority. Powerful charismatic men – called *kabani-mbani*, "angry men" – used ritual speech to legitimate economic exchanges and feasting displays, create political obligations and alliances and fulfill old obligations to dead ancestors. I discuss the ideological significance of "angry men" more fully in the next chapter.

Ritual speech among the Weyewa is regarded as the "words of the ancestors" (*li'i inna li'i ama*, literally "words of the Mother, words of the Father"). As I explained elsewhere:

The paired structure of the couplets is mirrored in a fundamental and productive aesthetic principle of Weyewa ritual ideology by which social arrangements, objects, and events of all kinds are symbolically represented as pairs (e.g., "inside/ outside," "mother/father," "left/right," "elder/younger," "trunk/tip") constituting a pervasive scheme of dual classification. When the "word" is neglected and misfortune ensues, specialist performers of ritual speech recover it through a culturally recognized "path" of atonement and feasting. They begin with divination, then re-state the neglected promises or "words" in placation rites, and finally fulfill these promises in celebration and housebuilding feasts. As both the special medium for describing the *li'i marapu* "words of the ancestors" and the vocal instantiation of it, ritual speech represents a "performative" evocation of what is held to be an enduring, ancestrally established order.

(Kuipers 1990: 2–3)

These verbal performances are not the trappings of authority, they are the very stuff of which it is made.

For example, when a ritual speaker stands on top of an ancestral sarcophagus in the middle of the village, and proclaims that

All the ears are paired, and the faces are complete, the tip is matched and the trunk is parallel the land is flattened smooth, and stones are cut evenly here in this gathering of the children of princes, the heirs of nobility

(cf. Kuipers 1990: 145ff.)

he is not simply dressing up the authority of the village; this verbal performance is an enactment of the "words" and "promises" handed down from the ancestors. By performing these words, accompanied by

lavish feasting, beautiful costumes, and elaborate exchange, he is fulfilling his obligations to his forebears and establishing himself and his
village as an "axis" of spirituality.

Village size

From a reading of the earliest colonial sources, it appears that the
Sumbanese villages before intensive Dutch contact tended to be larger
than they are now. In 1872, Roos says that there are some villages with
"40, 70, 110 and more houses. In Laura the writer personally counted
more than 300 houses [in a village], who all lived there with the raja"
(1872: 18). In the village of Laura, "one finds between two rows of
houses hundreds of graves, some of which are covered with colossal
stones" (1872: 19). Roos says he was told that the villages in the Weyewa
highlands were "ten times as dense." Ten Kate, on a visit to West
Sumba, observes that the "villages are densely populated, and in general
West Sumba is more densely populated than [elsewhere in Sumba]"
(1894: 630–631). In Wielenga's visit, he finds that in Lauli and Wadjewa,
there were about forty to fifty houses in a village ("Reisen op Soemba
III"; p. 332). During a visit in the 1840s, Gronovius mentions *negeri*
villages ranging in size from 200 (Laura) to "Wai Jewang" (=Weyewa)
possessing fifty houses (1855: 285). Even allowing for the inevitable
inaccuracies of such unsystematic estimates, since there are currently no
traditional villages in the Weyewa area with even twenty houses, it seems
to reasonable to infer that villages were larger in the past.

According to Hangelbroek (1910: 14), one important reason for these
large villages was security.

In the interior [of Sumba], nearly all of the villages or *negorij* are located on
stony, high and difficult to reach hilltops. As we unwillingly climbed these, we
asked ourselves, why do these people, in a region so rich with unused farmland,
put their villages in a difficult and inaccessible place, where women and girls day
after day must descend and climb for at least a half an hour to fetch water from
the streams and rivers? We find this stupid and impractical. But the Sumbanese
consider it safer. Out of fear of surprise attack, they build their villages up high,
and they hike back and forth to their walled villages.

Kapita concurs:

During this period, all of Sumba was unsafe; villages that were formerly dispersed
had to be brought together into a *"paraingu"* located on top of a hill, fortified by
stones and sharp and thick [cactus] thorns. If a person went out of the village, he
had to go with a group equipped with weapons, to the point that even to go and
fetch water one had to be accompanied by an armed group.

(1976: 28; see also de Roo Van Alderwerelt 1903: 231)

Most elderly Weyewa would agree with this interpretation; an important reason for living within the walled confines of these "great villages" and submitting oneself to the authorities within them was security.

Among the security concerns were slave raiders, headhunters, and even theft from neighboring villages. According to Needham, slave raiding by Endenese traders was common in the nineteenth century, particularly along the north coast of Sumba (1983). When the Dutch gradually took control of the waterways around the coastlines, things only got worse inland, as Endenese searched deeper and deeper into the interior of the island for captives.

Pax neerlandica

The first step in changing the meaning of the ancestral villages as sources of security and ritual authority began with the Dutch effort to begin to establish what they regarded as an "orderly administration" on the island in 1866. According to the missionary Douwe Klaas Wielenga, an historical turning point for Sumbanese (at least on the eastern part of the island), was the arrival of Samuel Roos, the first official government officer whose goal was to win the trust of the Sumbanese, to learn their language, customs, and behavior.

"[Roos] not only forms a beginning for our administrative time reckoning [on Sumba], but also for the Sumbanese he has become a point of time reckoning. When one replies to a question about how long ago something occurred, it is before or after Ama Rohi.   (Wielenga 1916)

In 1906, with the appointment of the militarily inclined Van Heutz as Governor General in the Dutch East Indies, the pacification of Sumba began in earnest.

In the rhetoric of the day, missionaries and administrators described the Sumbanese political system as "primitive," "backward," "chaotic," and "anarchic," recognizing only the "law of the jungle," and "law of the strongest," thus justifying their invasion of an island with little or no economic significance to the Dutch East Indies. As we shall show in the next chapter, the primary symbols of this despotism were the "angry men" who controlled the village. To rescue the population from these people, they sought to bring an "administration" (*bestuur*) to the island.

By 1914, Couvreur proclaimed that "East and Central Sumba are entirely pacified, and West Sumba is mostly pacified" (1914: 65). The actual techniques of "pacification" were so violent and brutal that they left little doubt among the Sumbanese as to who was actually in charge of this "self-ruling" island (see Zentgraaff 1912). A typical scenario was as follows: a group of mounted officers and about forty foot soldiers would approach a village and demand to see the village's leader about some theft. If the leader did not surrender, or worse, attempted to fight, immediate battle would ensue, usually resulting in heavy casualties among the Sumbanese (Zentgraaff 1912). If the leader surrendered himself, the troops would demand payment of a fine and possibly tribute in acknowledgement of the government's authority. Resistant Sumbanese leaders were then placed under detention and often exiled.

For Wielenga, the military occupation was a good thing. He did not emphasize the excesses of the military. Although he admits that the practice of forcing the people to work on road-building was not popular, nonetheless "the word 'imperialism' has little application in this case" ([1908] 1987: 144).

Population growth

Once the fines were paid by the leadership, yearly "head taxes" paid by local people, and the "new hierarchy" was acknowledged, the Dutch administrators seem to have left most of the Sumbanese people alone, largely because of a lack of staff. From a Sumbanese standpoint, the ensuing period was one of stability and relative calm in Sumbanese lives, ideal conditions for rapid population growth.

As one can see from Figure 4, the Weyewa highlands experienced a rather robust growth rate. This is in marked contrast to the relatively slow growth rates of some other areas, such as Rindi and Wanukaka, and Laboya, which experienced endemic gonorrhea (see Mitchell 1982; see also Rodenwalt 1923; Kloosterhuis 1936).

Why did the population grow in the highlands? There seem to have been at least three factors at work: (1) access to basic medical services such as vaccinations; (2) lowered mortality owing to decline of warfare; (3) greater fertility linked to gradual increases in food production. It should be noted also that the Weyewa were relatively insulated from endemic gonorrhea that affected the coastal populations (Mitchell 1982).

European medical services to the island came from missionaries and government officials. De Roo Van Alderwerelt (1903: 568) notes that Sumbanese appeared to have had little hesitation about use of medicines: "They place much trust in European medicines; vaccinations also meet with their approval." Van Alphen, one of the earliest Dutch missionaries to the island, brought with him some basic medical training as part of his preparation for the mission. Wielenga had training from Livingstone College in London and in his first seven months on the island, saw 2,000 patients. In 1898, the missionary W. Pos opened the first hospital on Sumba in the eastern Sumbanese village of Melolo in 1898. Wielenga followed suit in 1904 in the village of Payeti, not far from Waingapu. In 1912, the government of the Dutch East Indies placed a health officer on Sumba, who was responsible for the supervision of the mission hospital.

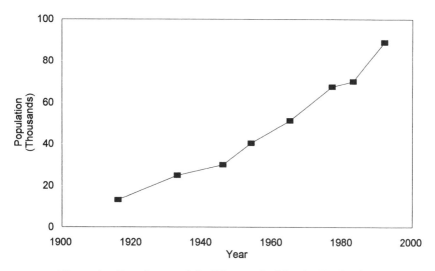

Figure 4   *Population of the Weyewa highlands, 1916–1992*

Couvreur reports that in the year 1914, 18,962 people were vaccinated, or 15 percent of the population of the island. From the early 1920s onward, regularly maintained clinics were held in Waikabubak, and in many of the subdistricts of West Sumba (Van Den End 1987: 22).

The overall production of food per capita has also increased in West Sumba. According to estimates by one agricultural officer who had served in that capacity since 1948, most West Sumbanese traditionally expected between 0.3 and 0.5 tons of rice per hectare each year; and, indeed, many years were considerably worse than that due to drought, mice, and other pests (Sastrodihardjo 1958: 77–82; Van Den End 1987: 579n1). By the 1970s, however, farm yields were improving, partly due to agricultural training programs (Van Den End 1987: 673ff.) and irrigation programs (Onvlee 1977).

Dispersal (*uitzwerming*, literally, "swarming forth")

The administration-guaranteed security . . . resulted in more and more people abandoning their old walled and fortified villages and spreading out and settling in the farmlands . . . . this results necessarily in the building of new villages because the location of the old villages was as a rule chosen with an eye to security.   (van Cambier 1928: 8).

By the 1930s the size of villages had begun to decline. Groeneveld (1931: 3) observes that "villages with not even 100 souls are not a rarity" (1931: 3).

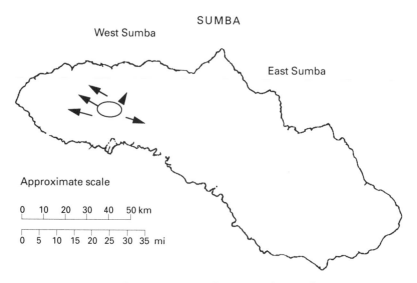

Figure 5   *Map of Weyewa dispersal*

The Dutch administrators viewed this movement out to the gardens with some dismay. Referring to it as *uitzwerming* (literally, "swarming forth'), this dispersal was seen as one of the main obstacles to setting up a rational administration. The Resident of Timor, Dr. Hoven, visited West Sumba in October and November of 1930 and found village administration in disarray: "The Government is attempting to establish an effective village administration, aimed at concentrating the settlements, but this has met with little success" (Hoven, 1930: 22). From his report, it is clear that one of his main difficulties in West Sumba was that

in addition to the actual village, one finds all sorts of garden villages (*wano goloe* [corral village], *kalimboe, galoe,* [*sic*] etc). Mostly these are under the authority of the mother village, from which they have spread out, unless they have have been elevated by our administration into a true village *wano kalada* (kalada = great). In the garden villages one finds that the inhabitants belong to a variety of clans.

(p. 23)

For Hoven, establishing a local, village-based bureaucratic structure when lines of authority were so dispersed into garden and corral settlements was an administrative problem. Moreover, even in the villages that existed, often there was more than one clan represented, thus requiring that one family group claim authority over another, thus causing further confusion.

The dispersal of the population seems to have been agriculturally motivated. Groenevelt writes that "the village resettlement program [i.e. an effort to centralize residences near the road] which the Administration earlier had launched had to be abandoned perhaps because of the fear of starvation" (1931: 9). He notes the somewhat caustic remarks of a civil administrator who wrote in 1917 about the efforts to get Sumbanese to live in nucleated villages: "it's all well and good, if the landscape lends itself to the stated goals. [However,] the people do not make their swiddens far from their houses purely for pleasure" (1931: 10).

Although Sastrodihardjo (1958: 77ff.) complained that in many parts of Sumba, people remained in their mountain villages because of a lack of land reform; in Weyewa it appears that there were never such large landholdings as were found in the eastern parts of the island, and thus many pioneer settlements were established by the 1950s. Furthermore, the extent of available arable land was greater than in the coastal areas. Many mountain settlers were actually pioneer settlers who were taking advantage of the weakened authority of the *rajas* and big men to set up their own settlements on open land.

As one can see from the illustration in Figure 5, the western Weyewa region has been growing rapidly. This area of growth is occurring in an area marginal to the main ritual and wet-rice complex for the Weyewa region.

Ritual marginality

The significance of these changes in village size, population growth, and dispersal for ritual-speech use is that it resulted in ritual marginality. By this I mean that the genres of ritual speech regarded as most authoritative by Weyewa were performed with less and less frequency as they moved further away from the ceremonial centers.

To understand how this could be so, it is necessary to give a brief overview of the varieties of ritual speech and their relative centrality and marginality from a Weyewa point of view. Weyewa label ritual speech as *tenda* and consider it to be a form of *panewe* or "speech"; it is considered a special variety of speech, however, since, unlike ordinary speech, it consists of conventional couplets in which the first line parallels the second line in rhythm and meaning. One speaks of *panewe Weyewa*, "the Weyewa language," *panewe Kodi*, "the Kodi language," and also of *panewe tenda*, "ritual speech." While the actual words of *tenda* draw mostly on the Weyewa everyday language in the construction of its couplets, it would sound strange to say that "ritual speech is [a variety of] the Weyewa language" although increasingly this is what is taught in schools. Traditionally, *tenda* is not included in any higher category except "words" or "speech." If *tenda* contrasts with anything, it is with *panewe bora* ,"plain language."

As the category *tenda*, "ritual speech," is further subdivided, not all subvarieties are equally "central" in a ritual sense. Some are more authoritative, central and directly reflective of the words of the ancestors, while others are more marginal, "noisy," and peripheral to the original ancestral voices and more concerned with the latter-day preoccupations of contemporary descendants. Since all genres of ritual speech are seen as exemplifying the "words of the ancestors," when one of these "words" of obligation is broken, then it sets in motion a ranked process of atoning for the transgression through performance of genres devoted to identifying the transgression (*urrata*, "divination"), those concerned with placating the angry spirits by reaffirming the "word" of obligation, and the most prestigious forms of speech devoted to re-enacting the "words of the ancestors" and thereby fulfilling them through acts of spectacular sacrifice, stone dragging or village building (Kuipers 1990).

In Table 1, the genres of ritual speech are divided into two main categories: political and religious genres, and personal genres. The political and religious genres are systematically planned performances carried out by males for an audience of ancestral spirits, and are obligatorily accompanied by some sort of animal sacrifice, minimally chicken, but more often pig, goat, or water buffalo. The more "personal genres" are more spontaneous, performed primarily for a human audience, and may be led by women as well as men.

Within the category of religious and political genres of ritual speech, the majority of these items are most appropriately performed in a *wanno kalada* "ancestral village." Indeed, two of these genres – the "lightning song" and the "headhunting song" – are regarded as so sacred, so ancient, and so closely associated with the sacredness of the most senior of the "ancestral villages" that no longer exist, that they are not now performed anywhere in the Weyewa region as far as I know. I have only heard these songs by specifically requesting that they be performed for me out of context.

As I argued earlier in this chapter, when Weyewa moved out of their hilltop ancestral villages, they were also moving away from their ceremonial centers. Once out in their garden villages, when ritualists performed the asterisked varieties of ritual speech – if they performed them at all – they performed relatively stripped down versions of the more sacred genres performed in the *wanno kalada*. Several men told me that in a garden village "ancestral narratives" could only include genealogies three generations deep, while in corral villages narratives could reach as far back as seven generations; in ancestral village centers, however, there were no restrictions on the genealogical depth of the narration, and the names of the most ancient ancestral figures could be mentioned.

Table 1. *Genres of Weyewa ritual speech*

I. Political and religious genres	
pazimbala	"ceremonial greeting"
bara	"offertory prayer"
urrata	"divination"
tauna li'i	"oration"
zaizo	"placation song"
ndondo	"celebration song"
we'e maringi	"blessing song"
pawowe	"headhunting song"
payoyela	"lightning song"
oka	"chant"
kanungga	"migration narrative"
newe marapu	"ancestral narrative"
ngi'o newe	"narrative lament"
II. Personal Genres	
nggeile	"wet-rice planting song"
padéngara	"worksong"
pawaiyonggo	"dragging chanty"
nggeloka	"wailing"
matekula	"eulogy"
lawiti	"personal song"

Such constraints on the genealogical depth of the ritual-speech performance in the increasingly populated gardens and garden settlement had implications for the authority of the speech performed in those settings and the relatively peripheral status of the ancestral villages. Increasingly, most people were living in a relatively shallow ritual universe, at least in a genealogical sense.

One effect of this rule has been that the ideological role of ritual speech as an encompassing form of language was diminished. In conversations with several elder men who lived through this period of decline, I often heard nostalgic expressions of loss of plenitude, wholeness, and completeness. While these of course are commonplace in ethnography around the world, what is novel is the specifically linguistic idiom with which these ideas were understood and its close linkage to the dispersal from the ritual centers. Often I would hear expressions such as "now that we all live in the gardens," "since everyone has now left the ritual centers," or "now that we've come down from the hilltops," – as a way of explaining why ritual discourse is more colloquial, ordinary, and less encompassing and authoritative than it once was. As many ritual speakers have put it, ritual speech is now "garden talk" (i.e. not true ritual speech).

Hierarchic inclusion

As Weyewa moved out of the ritual centers, they increasingly slipped beyond the jurisdiction of their ritual leaders in the ancestral villages. Although these migrants worked to set up their own autonomous ritual centers, from the standpoint of the Dutch, they were increasingly subject to colonial rule, at least insofar as this movement loosened the grip of the "despotic" rajas.

As for the "rajas" (*toko*) and once powerful men of Sumba who controlled the central villages, they had to learn, as Prins put it in 1916, a "new hierarchy":

An altogether new hierarchical relation must be continually worked towards, particularly among the headmen, who were accustomed to having unlimited authority in their own domains and only in name dependent on the [central authority] . . . .Thanks to our own influence the power of the head of the region has become greater.   (Prins 1916: 106)

Another administrator, 16 years later, also remarked, "the Soembanese [leaders] must learn to follow the appropriate hierarchy" and limit their "independent activities" (Groeneveld 1931: 14).

What this hierarchy entailed was a system of nested spatial groupings in which the ones below were totally included in the ones above. Thus in the *afdeeling Soemba*, "regency of Sumba," there were four *onderafdeeling* or districts: east, northwest, southwest, and west. Within each of these *onderafdeeling*, there were then "subdistricts" or *landschaap*s (see Figure 6). What took some getting used to – for rajas and performers accustomed to enacting their own authority as an exemplary center – was the idea that each of these discourses was hierarchically included in the one above it. Thus whereas ritual performers were once accustomed to enacting the history of their domain as the center of the world, they now needed to see their discourses as a sub-species of a larger more authoritative discourse that issued from a colonial metropolis.

Another implication of this ideology of hierarchic inclusion concerned translation patterns. While residents of border zones between linguistic domains frequently were (and are) bilingual in both of the regional languages, with the establishment of this new administrative structure, such skills have little official significance, except in the occasional marriage negotiation. As Keane observes, "Rarely is anyone called upon to translate from one local language to another. Translation is largely "vertical" from the local language to the language of administration – Malay and, later, Indonesian" (Keane 1997a: 43).

The Dutch *controleurs* attached spatial and administrative meanings to the use of colloquial language use in ways that must have struck Sumbanese as odd. Fortunately for the Dutch, in many cases, the border

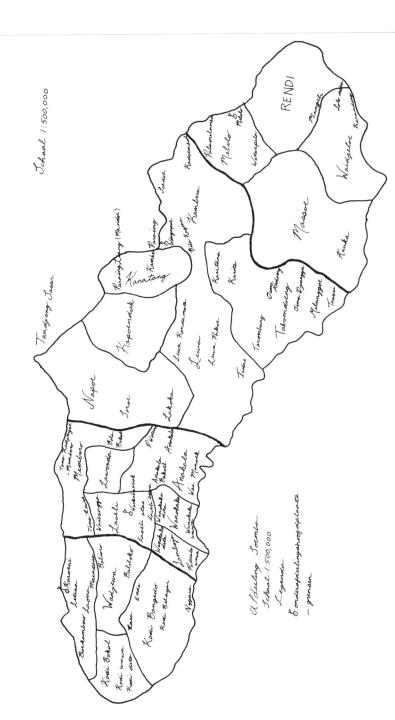

Figure 6   Couvreur's sketch map of ethnolinguistic divisions in Sumba, 1914

zones of the territories they sought to establish were inhabited by relatively recent pioneer settlers taking advantage of the *pax neerlandica* to locate in a former no-man's land. Unlike the Thai–Burman border, where modern cartography and linguistic geography imposed a foreign, "either–or" spatial reasoning on a local population long accustomed to accommodating the demands of dual (or more) sovereigns (Tongchai 1994: 62ff.), in Weyewa garden settlements, Dutch geographical models (e.g. Couvreur 1914) inscribed a dispersal relatively fresh in the historical consciousness of local people. This proposed Dutch inscription of territorial sovereignty came at a time when local models were vulnerable to a more secular, colloquial language-based reinterpretation, a time when ritual obligations to former ancestral centers were loosening anyway. I asked one rather humorously laconic old man, a pioneer settler to a remote region in the 1920s, whether he considered his land *tana Weyewa* ("Weyewa land") when he moved there. He thought for a bit and replied:

"We didn't talk about it that way: "Kodi, Weyewa, Laura" like that. No. There were only "earth spirits" [*marapu tana*] out there then. When the foreigners came and said [is this] Weyewa land? [*tana Weyewa?*] I just said "fine [It's] Weyewa land" [*ya, tana Weyewa awa*] [Laughter].

Not only did Dutch officials privilege cartographically and administratively the significance of colloquial, non-ritual speech, Dutch missionaries privileged it as a way of gaining access to the souls of their flock. At a time when many Dutch regarded Malay as a code which was "not a language of the people and [which] would never become one" (Emeis 1917), the local languages (*landstaal*), spoken in local genres, were seen as offering direct evidence of personal agency and emotional involvement. In a letter to his supporters in Holland about his research into the local language, the missionary linguist Onvlee describes how West Sumbanese women use the local language to bring the catechism closer to their hearts:

[In Loli] it appears that song is one of the most powerful media for evangelizing. What was remarkable about this case was that among the baptismal candidates, there were a few women who were renowned as good singers. Whenever a certain section of the cathechism was discussed (in the pre-Baptism class), they sang it to the village that evening . . . in this way they held fast to what they had learned and pushed it further . . . And every time my words were joined with song, a word of mine would be picked up by the women and they would break out into song, with Sumbanese words, and Sumbanese melodies. I began to believe they were getting the picture.   (1951: 540)

At a time when the Dutch in Holland were very concerned about the sincerity of public communication (Wouters 1987), missionaries implied that even though *landstaal* were provincial, isolated, and politically subordinate to national languages, they were nonetheless epistemologically privileged: they were vehicles of honesty, sincerity, and truthfulness. As we shall see in the next chapter, however, for Sumbanese, this sincerity often translated as "humility."

Conclusions

Place cannot be viewed as an objective "thing" that influences the direction of linguistic shift in any particular way. Rather, its influence on linguistic change is mediated through local ideologies about the meaning of such features on linguistic structure and practice. In Weyewa, the marginalization of ritual speech occurred in relation to a local concept of a ritual, exemplary center. The meaning of these centers, especially the walled, fortified "ancestral villages," changed as the Dutch altered security and health conditions, the population grew, and agricultural opportunities shifted. Encouraged by colonial guarantees of security, Weyewa farmers increasingly settled in the relatively unprotected farmlands farther and farther from their ritual centers. In these garden settlements, Weyewa only seldom performed the higher-ranking and more authoritative and encompassing genres of ritual speech. The varieties that appear more frequently in such contexts are more colloquial, more everyday and less markedly different – either in structural form or in performance style (see Kuipers 1990) – from ordinary speech.

Meanwhile, the growth of Dutch education, government, and religion via the Malay language increased the contexts in which bilingualism, code-switching, and translation between the Sumbanese languages and the national language were required. In such juxtapositions, the relations between the languages were unequal: Sumbanese languages belonged to the category of *landstaal*, "local language," while Malay was the *voertaal*, a "language of wider communication." The semiotic relation between the two was one of hierarchic inclusion: everything that one could say in Sumbanese could be included in, appropriated by and translated into Malay. The government and missionary officials had categories, labels and descriptions for all of Sumbanese social experience. The reverse did not hold, because the Sumbanese were so *primitief* and *onbeschaafd*, "uncivilized" – they could not be expected to have an appropriate way of talking about the modern world.

Demographic shift (move away from ritual centers) →
change in ritual speech use

3

TOWERING IN RAGE AND COWERING IN FEAR: EMOTION, SELF, AND VERBAL EXPRESSION IN SUMBA

Scholarly literature on language "shift" and language "death" often makes these changes appear to be impersonal, structural processes. Of course, speakers are occasionally depicted as sad and angry or dismayed – retrospectively – *about* the loss of their language; but discussions about the role of emotion *in* the creation of the conditions of shift themselves are not so easily found. Language shift is not only a structural and pragmatic process, but it is one that is mediated by emotional attitudes and assumptions about the structure and use of language in a particular context. Emotions do not only enter in after the fact, but are part and parcel of the process of shift itself. As Kulick observed in Gapun, New Guinea, women's angry speeches (*kroses*) in the native language and men's more polite speeches in Tok Pisin were in effect competing ways of representing relations to the outside world: they are choosing the less "angry" and (for them) feminine way (1992a: 294). Similarly, for Mbora Kenda, converting to Christianity – and thus abandoning most forms of ritual speech – was a way of choosing "cunning" over "anger."

But if emotions have played little role in the study of linguistic change, linguistics has also had a relatively small part in the study of emotional change. When the verbal aspects of emotion are given scholarly recognition, the focus is usually on explicit emotion terms and "hypercognized" (i.e. self-conscious and culturally elaborated) categories of emotional experience such as "shame" and "honor" (Abu-Lughod 1986), or "anger" (Rosaldo 1980; Levy 1984). In a recent comment on an article on emotional change, Donald Brenneis notes that "emotion discourse is more than a matter of labels and their personal referents" (1997: 340). Affect is conveyed on many different levels of linguistic structure (Irvine 1982; Ochs 1986: 256), including structures of interaction. In Sumba, "anger" – and all the intonational, structural, and generic features that accompanied it – was once a central aspect of authoritative communicative interactions.

In Sumba, the Dutch played an important role in these changes. Like Europeans in many parts of Southeast Asia in the late nineteenth and early twentieth century, Dutch administrators, soldiers, and missionaries

42

were greeted on Sumba with a variety of verbal expressive forms,
including "anger" (*mbani*). Because ritualized displays of "anger" were
important indigenous symbols of masculinity, potency, and spiritual
authority in Sumba, the strong negative reaction by the Dutch played an
important role in the marginalization of ritual speech. For Weyewa,
angry displays of ritual speech legitimated the spiritual and political
exemplariness of the "big men," while for the Dutch these were seen as
acts of defiance that legitimated intervention by the Dutch East Indies,
the administrative containment of the role of these men, and the moral
peripheralizing of such performative display as mere bluster, swagger,
and braggadocio. As such anger was gradually contained militarily, the
Dutch sought to cultivate "respect" among the Sumbanese, but what
they got instead was "humility" (*milla ate*) and "cunning" (*pánde*).

   These emotional categories – anger, humility, and cunning – not only
provided local models through which agency of individual speakers was
interpreted, but were also ideological icons that were seen as displaying a
group's inherent nature or essence, an ideological construction which
had an effect on the process of linguistic marginalization and change (see
Gal and Irvine 1995). Both Dutch and Weyewa constructed "anger" – as
enacted in verbal displays and ritual-speech performances – as a naturalized icon of the essential characteristics of Sumbanese leadership:
characteristics that the Weyewa regarded as exemplary of natural
authority, and from which the Dutch sought to deliver the Sumbanese.

Anger in Sumbanese life

"Anger" was a high-status emotion in West Sumba in the nineteenth
century, and into much of the twentieth century. The most renowned
ritual speakers, the most powerful and persuasive leaders, the most
charismatic individuals – people such as Mbora Kenda – were all "men
of anger" (*kabani-mbani*). Through ritualized expressions of anger, men
defined their position in the group; reciprocally, others defined their
position in relation to these powerful individuals through ceremonialized
expressions of "humility" and self-pity (*milla ate*). By the 1930s,
however, at the height of colonial rule, "angry men" were already seen as
limited and circumscribed in their powers, and the growing number of
Sumbanese Christians contrasted themselves with their non-Christian
neighbors in terms of their control of "anger."

   More Christian and modern forms of emotional expression featured
"humility." But while this emotional posture was one of subordination
and marginality, it also permitted a kind of clever, cunning autonomy
outside the watchful eye of authority. Drawing on the image of the
orphan, Weyewa depicted themselves as at once humble, but cunning.

The hybrid genres through which these emotions were expressed – *lawiti* – were neither official nor private forms of discourse. While these songs belong to the category of "ritual-speech" (*panewe tenda*), they are also personal; while they are conventional, they are also biographical and historical. These hybrid forms were the ones through which the Dutch evangelists sought to influence and transform the local culture (Onvlee 1951: 540), and they exist today as a major site of intersection between nation, self, and verbal expression.

Popular poetic songs about the self and emotions have a history of unstable autonomy from, and in some cases opposition to, the forces of authority in Indonesia. As Reid observes (1988), in many parts of Southeast Asia in the "Age of Commerce," a prevalent form of oral literature was the love song, or in some places, poetic repartee and duels between lovers. These songs were rarely public challenges to authority, but since marriage is widely viewed as an alliance of social groups (cf. Fox 1980), the rhetoric of emotions and personal experience associated with marital and sexual relations can be a potent idiom for talking about the self in the context of social groups, categories, and relations (see also Yampolsky 1989; Lockard 1996).

Mbora Kenda's use of the rhetoric of emotional experience to explain his own language shift – from being a potent and "angry" ritual-speech performer to being a spectator-citizen in Indonesian-language events – is revealing on several levels. It not only helps us understand why he made the choice he did, but underscores the importance of emotions as a factor in the language ideologies that mediate language differentiation and change.

The colonial discovery of the "angry man" in the nineteenth century

For the Dutch, the "angry man" as a social category on Sumba first appears in the writings of Samuel Roos, the first Dutch government officer assigned to the island for a lengthy stay. Roos was an energetic man who rose from being a lowly cavalry trumpeter to become the Resident of Timor. He was sent to East Sumba in 1860 to learn the language and customs. He was quick to note the link between nobility and anger. In an early report, he describes the Radja of Bata-Kapedoe as

Oemboe Daij and is considered a *meramba bokoel* (great person). He was formerly an angry man (*meramba bani*) and a dangerous enemy. For very small mistakes he would kill his subordinates, and especially those whose wealth he desired, so that he has committed many murders.   (1872: 101)

After several months on the island in 1860, Roos decided to carry out a sort of tour throughout the island, visiting each of the "rajas" in the eastern half of Sumba. He records his encounter with a category of person called an "angry man." His effort to display paternal affection to this Sumbanese "angry man" nearly resulted in bloodshed:

The man on the horse was . . . an orang brani . . . [angry man]. I walked up to [him], laid my hand on his shoulder and spoke to him calmly and affably to let him know that he had no reason to fear or be restless, for I had come to him like a father to a child.

As Heryanto (1986: 21) has observed, such father–child imagery is now widespread in Indonesia, for it is used to suggest the "natural authority" of leadership. Roos describes being taken aback when the man's response was simply: *"I am not afraid of you."* The response suggests the man interpreted the gesture of "affection" for what it in fact was: a threat to Sumbanese autonomy. Roos continues by describing his fear of being attacked and his response of swashbuckling bravado:

It did not escape my notice that he had observed the line of my beard, and had his hand on the handle of his sword. Judging from the anxious look on the face of my interpreter, my all-too-friendly greeting had done no good; I sensed that the man had misconstrued my intent, and so I decided that I would have to cut my way out of this impasse as soon as possible:
"You are the Raja of Kalala, no?"
"Yes!"
"Well, I am the 'Raja of All of Sumba,' and I am not used to such treatment, and for that I am angry."
Then I let him see I also had a *kabela* [a knife] in the form of a revolver.
"Show me quickly, where the Raja of Karita lives, I must go there."
The way in which I said that to him, combined with the look I gave him, made the man back up and release the rope to my horse. (Roos 1872: 107)

By 1906, while the paternal imagery ("like a father to a child") continued on the part of the administrators, the military forces conducted their military operations on Sumba on explicitly gendered terms (Gouda 1995). Before conducting any raids on Sumbanese villages, for instance, the attacking force made it clear their battle was not with women. In one description of a battle in 1906, the military historian says that after an attack was decided upon,

word was given to the defenders that *women and children should be brought to safety*. Later it appeared that indeed this was carried out, although our messenger received the arrogant message that they did not harbor any feelings of fear towards us. (Oort 1906: 750; my emphasis)

What the Dutch saw as arrogance – and the Sumbanese describe as *mbani* ("anger") – was interpreted by both sides as masculinity and defiance.

Using imagery of the jungle, "law of the strongest," and of an arbitrary leadership exerting control through random, primitive war-like rages, the Dutch pointed to such displays of ritual-speech "anger" as a clear justification for their intervention on the island. According to

Wielenga ([1908] 1987: 144), the "administration" offered "protection from the arbitrariness of the princes and freemen." As the campaign proceeded, settlements were no longer referred to by the more exalted *nagari* ("state") but as the more rustic *kampong* ("village"), thus making them somewhat less legitimate.

From the standpoint of the Sumbanese, there was plenty to be angry about. According to Zentgraaff, a Dutch reporter who accompanied the "pacification campaign," the gendered imagery had a violent sexual basis to it. In 1911, while on a patrol in the middle of Sumba, a Sergeant Diesenroth and a soldier named Iding

> in midday . . . came from their border patrol to the residence of the women. Deisenroth grabbed Banja Oeroe [a Sumbanese woman], and Iding seized Dahi Waha [the raja's third wife]. Both women struggled and screamed, but were dragged off to their barracks, where the women were stripped completely naked and then raped.   (1912: 15)

Sexual connotations are clear in the Sumbanese interpretations of the systematic Dutch invasion of the island that began in 1906. As the Weyewa put it, the Dutch "mounted" the island (*na penne dawa*).

Is the "angry man" a local category or a colonial stereotype? Probably both. The *kabani-mbani* no doubt fed into colonial stereotypes about primitive despotism and thus provided justification for further acts of repression. On the other hand, the use of local lexemes, and its clear referent and contrastive significance in the present suggest that it was a category not wholly dependent on colonial discourse, especially since it does not appear to have been a part of the colonial discourse in other regions of Indonesia, such as Sumatra (Bowen 1991; Steedly 1993), Kalimantan (Tsing 1993), or Central Java (Pemberton 1994).

From my interviews with people who lived through this period, it appears that if the *kabani-mbani* ("angry man") was a colonial stereotype, it was one that many Sumbanese, especially Weyewa elites, bought into and supported. When I discussed the issue with Dede Bobo, a prominent man who served as *raja kecil* ("little raja") under the Dutch and as a clerk under the Japanese, he strongly supported the idea that leaders should be angry. With nostalgia mixed with indignation, he lamented the current lack of truly fierce men in positions of leadership. As he made his point, he rose into something of a rage of his own against the general lack of current moral leadership. Starting slowly but gradually rising in volume, he began gesticulating and posing ever more rapid rhetorical questions, spittle flying from his lips as his expressions and vehemence came ever more rapidly.

> There are no "angry men" any more. They are all "yes master" type of people. That's how they got to be where they are. Do you think any of our ancestors

would sit at a desk, take their paychecks and say "yes sir" the way our leaders do now? Do you? Do you? Huh? Well then. Impossible.

The cultural organization of anger: status, verbal style, and performance

The fierce persona that Mbora Kenda once proudly projected clearly emerges in many other parts of Sumba over many historical periods. Many Dutch colonial reports indicate the cultural salience of the "angry man" (*kabani-mbani*) in the early colonial period. Dutch colonial officers, soldiers, and missionaries all mention this category (usually in a negative light), and discuss their attempts to understand and control him. Three features stand out: he is high–ranking, he is verbally expressive, and he is central to their society.

Couvreur, another early Dutch officer, describes many of the Sumbanese leaders as being "angry men." Lara Loengi, the "crown prince" of Rendi, Couvreur describes as a "wild character" whose anger towards the Government was "well known"; as evidence of his character, Couvreur tells of how Lara Loengi "was once out traveling and came upon a man who did not answer an ordinary question fast enough and therefore with his knife he slashed the man's face" (1914: 29). In another incident, Couvreur describes an uprising (*opstanden*) in Laboya. "The village head, known as an *ata mbani* – a angry man, a willing fighter and terrorist among his circles – procured weapons and came after us in battle."

Not only are these men considered high rank, they are highly verbal as well. The missionary Wielenga devoted an entire book to portray the downfall of such a man, *Oemboe Dongga*:

He was a man of strength and brute force . . . he had a booming voice that could command. The sound of his voice, the sparkling of his eyes, and the gesture with which his right hand would reach for his long knife, was more than enough to make one take him seriously. (1928: 7)

Verbal fluency was essential to creating an impression of competence, ferocity, and ability to protect, if not from slave raiders, then from malign spirits. Wielenga described his encounter with Oemboe Pati, the Weyewa raja in 1909:

Then Oemboe Pati stood up and laid open the floodgates of his eloquence. He has no equal in all of Sumba. With unbelievable speed his words came out of his mouth, tumbling and splashing, one following the sound of the other. His countenance was taut and his carriage erect. Now and then making a single broad gesture with his right hand, he stood there talking, getting all excited, so that one thinks: with lashing words he flogs his enemies. In fact, it was a "word of welcome." To the ear of the uncomprehending, he spoke friendly words like a rabble-rousing braggart. Oemboe Pati cultivates his renown and makes an impression . . . as one who is "powerful" [*geweldigen*]. (Wielenga 1912: 330)

Roos (1872: 104) also notes the "gruff and passionate words" of an "angry man's" oration: "*Why did you come here? What do you want?*"[1]

In the nineteenth and early twentieth centuries powerful men were symbols of the village and lineage. Spoken of as the "leafy white banyan tree, the shady yellow banyan" that protects the village, these men used personal charisma, coercion, and family connections to gain control over the symbols of clan identity as well: gongs, cloth, and temple head-quarters, even cattle and rice fields. The familiar botanical symbolism of "trunk and tip" as an expression of hierarchy fit these men well; they were often referred to by themselves and others as "the trunk of the tree, the source of the water." Ritually and politically, they were associated with the inside, the source and the center of Weyewa social life (Kuipers 1990: 16ff).

Their central authority was legitimated partly by a charismatic per-sonal style of fierceness and competitiveness used as a means to attract cattle, pigs and other goods for large-scale feasting and displays of wealth. Particlarly in the late nineteenth and early twentieth century, when most ordinary Sumbanese were in great danger from the depreda-tions of slave raiders (Needham 1983), these men forged powerful alliances with other "angry men" who headed other lineages in order to trade women, cattle, and other goods and thus reproduce their position in society.

The word *mbani* can be glossed as "anger, daring, threatening, rage." Unlike the English usage, it is not primarily associated with a "feeling, [emotional] experience" (*podda*), but is more closely linked to forms of expression and interactional strategy. For instance, it refers also to threatening activities in which an animal moves dangerously in one's direction, for example, "that horse is threatening!" ("*na mbani-wa ndara!*"). It also has distinctively masculine connotations: when Weyewa speak nostalgically of "real men," the expression they use translates literally as "angry men" (*kabani-mbani*). In a recent biographical account of Yusup Malo, he was described as "a real man" (a daring young man (*kabani-mbani*)). Only men have this institutionalized, public anger. Women's anger occurs in the home, often at children, relatives, or their husbands. There is no women's equivalent of the *kabani-mbani* – the angry woman.[2]

Mbani also commonly designates a social category. One can speak of "an angry person" in Weyewa (*ata mbani*), or a *kabani-mbani* "an angry man," something culturally recognized as a sort of status. Although it has some similarities to the "angry young men" (not women!) in the West in the 1950s (see Osborne's *Look back in anger*, 1957), it has more positive, and indeed, socially central connotations than the Western usage. Rosaldo has written about the "anger" of headhunters among the

Ilongot, where the experience of this emotion makes one liminal, in transition, heavily burdened and in need of resolution (Rosaldo 1980, 1983). For Weyewa, an "angry man" is not liminal or marginal (cf. Rosaldo 1980), or "feminine" (Kulick 1992a: 287–288, 294), he is *central*, masculine, defining, indeed *exemplary* of the social order. While the expression of "anger" for Gapuners in New Guinea something concealed by men (Kulick 1992a), in Weyewa ceremonial ideology, ritualized anger, and passionate performances are ideally an enactment of the congruence of charismatic individual will and the harmonious structures of the ancestral order. "Anger" in this sense for Weyewa is defined through verbal attributes, while, for Ilongot, "angry men" are defined by their silence, their quiet moodiness. Although many Western representations of "anger" depict it as an uncomfortable emotion for the experiencer, there is no evidence that the Sumbanese ever viewed it as such: indeed, many Sumbanese represent it as something that is desirable for the potency it can provide.

There are expressive conventions by which one displays oneself in one's capacity as an "angry man."[3] First, the speech of angry men is louder than normal. Loudness is, of course, a relative matter, depending on the situation; *panewe mbani* ("angry speech") is louder than is usual for a given situation. I once was surprised when an elder, ritual spokesman, during what I regarded as a casual interview, seemed to be shouting at me throughout the entire encounter. I found this to be an aggressive act, but my assistants who accompanied me assured me it was not. "Old men of his generation often speak that way – they are *kabani-mbani* 'angry men.'" Second, such speech is fluent. Angry men do not start, stop, compose their thoughts and speak again. There is no hesitation. They must keep up a constant stream of verbal activity. Third, it is orderly. When someone exhibits anger, but makes little sense, and has no pattern to the speech, the audience may laugh and ridicule the speaker as having lost control. One way in which coherence can be displayed is through the use of ritual speech. Finally, the angry person's face is said to "go dark" (flushed) when speaking.

There are certain structural features associated with angry speech. It makes sparing use of locutives (Kuipers 1993) – phrases like "I say," "you said," "he said," etc. – in which the discourse of others is received, framed, circulated, and delivered in a dialogic sort of way. To avoid any appearance of asking for ratification or approval, falling intonation is preferred over rising intonation, unless the questions are rhetorical or bitingly ironic. Modal particles such as -ki-, -po-, -do- that indicate subtleties, hedges, or uncertainties in the speaker's attitude toward the veracity of what he is saying are minimized. The most culturally salient feature of the discourse of an "angry man" is his capacity to silence his

Plate 4   *An "Angry Man" (Kabani-mbani)* [Photo: H. J. May]

critics through forceful monologues. One of the renowned ritual speakers, Lende Mbatu, gleefully described a particularly triumphant rhetorical moment in one of his performances by saying, "and no one could answer me! They all sat in silence! No one could say a thing!"

The exemplary expressions of the *kabani-mbani* are forceful, monologic ritual-speech genres in which a man may present his reasons for doing something in a forceful and compelling manner. One such genre is *pazimbala* ("ceremonial greeting") in which two orators face one another in a competitive debate. Yet another is *oka,* an emphatic chant, that may be used to announce, proclaim, or herald some important news or sacred knowledge. While these genres are often an opportunity for the display of *mbani* characteristics, more spontaneous and less generically constrained performances are also common. In general, speech is preferred over song, ritual speech over prose, and monologic genres over more dialogic, interactive ones.

Humility, marginality, and the meaning of *milla*

The Sumbanese do not understand the meaning of *hormat* [Indonesian, "respect"].
(Roos 1872: 121)

In the Weyewa expressive economy, if "anger" has an opposite, it is not "love," but rather "humility" (*milla ate*). Anger connotes strength, potency, domination; "humility" suggests weakness, impotence, subordination, and dependency. As those who spoke with anger came to be increasingly subordinated to the Dutch, their anger lost some of its meaning. The ideological construction of "humility" (*milla ate*), and particularly "cunning" (*pánde*), came to represent the expressive experience of many Sumbanese under Dutch colonialism; if *milla ate* once referred only to the comportment of low-status orphans and slaves, it soon came to refer to the expressive experience of high-status, but subordinate, Sumbanese as well. The generic vehicle through which these emotional positions were enacted was the expanded and hybridized forms of ritual speech known as *lawiti,* "laments." While laments are old, their use to express discontent with contemporary political regimes is relatively recent and is increasing in its variety and elaborateness.

What the Dutch sought were expressions of "respect" (*hormat*), along with its associated economic and political benefits; what they got instead, from the Weyewa anyway, appears to have been expressions of *milla ate* – a sort of self-pitying humility. From examining oral history, ritual-speech genres, and written accounts, I have not found any native genres devoted entirely to expressions of *paaka* ("respect"). Nor does one find comic expressions of subordination and resistance, such as emerged in Western literature. There is no institutionalization of laughter, comedy, and ridicule, no rites of reversal, no "inversion of reality" such as that described by Bakhtin (1979; Babcock 1977). While there is public laughter and buffoonery, as Anthony Reid notes, "the public festivals of Southeast Asia appear to have reinforced rather than challenged hierarchy" (1988: 174).

Rather, when emotional expression took an organized, institutional

Plate 5   *A "humble" man* (milla ate)

form, Weyewa expressed a complex mix of self-pity and humility about the changes the Dutch brought about, and their new relation to the powerful masters. While *milla* literally means "poor, impoverished, miserable" (Onvlee et al. 1984: 288), it also refers to (self-)pity and compassion.

Milla "humility" is sometimes expressed as part of the affected modesty of orators (cf. Curtius 1953: 83; Sweeney 1987: 149ff.), in which Weyewa speakers typically denigrate themselves in front of their audience. In such cases, statements of the speaker's incapacity ("I have the tiny mouth of a bottle, tiny lips of a basket") are closely associated with expressions of submission and subordination ("I am like a liverless water spider, a locust without a heart"). These acts of modesty seek to glorify the audience and ancestral interlocutors.

The quintessential embodiment of *milla* is an "orphan" (*ana lalo*), and the orphan's "laments." This image crystallizes powerful tensions between *pánde* "cunning, cleverness" and *milla* "humility, sadness", the personal and the social, between autonomy and dependence, and individual desires versus obligation to tradition. While universally pitied, orphans in songs and spoken narratives nonetheless often exhibit admirable personal traits such as magical talents and ingenuity. In the dozens of narratives and songs I have collected concerning orphans, there is a pervasive sense that extraordinary individual attributes and spiritual strength can help one to overcome adversity and establish one's identity. But on the other hand, one still needs family recognition to legitimate one's position in society.

A cultural icon of humility: the orphan Mada Luwu

This double-edged meaning of orphans in Weyewa society clearly emerges in the story of Mada Luwu, which I summarize:

Mada Luwu and his older sister Kyazi were orphans who lived alone in the jungle. One day a handsome young man named Ndelo was out hunting on his tall horse and saw Kyazi and fell in love. He asked her to come home with him, but she refused, for she had to care for Mada Luwu. He persisted, however, saying that they could leave him plenty of food, a magic top and a magic dog to look after him. So Kyazi left her baby brother alone in the jungle. Before departing for her new village, she charged Mada Luwu with the "word" (*li'i*) that when he grew up, he must seek her by following the trail of yarn which she unraveled behind her on her way.

With the help of the magical dog and an enchanted toy top, he managed to survive to adulthood. One day, he resolved to search for her following the trail of yarn. Along the way, he met a group of children playing with their tops. Mada Luwu set his top spinning, and the other children could not knock it out of the ring. When it was his turn to try to knock theirs out, he spun his top and smashed all of theirs to pieces in one blow. They were very angry, so they grabbed him and tied him up and beat him. He sings a lament, to which his dog responds by releasing his bonds, and he continued on his way.

When finally he discovered his sister's village, he was prevented from entering it by children playing a game of tops. When he set his top to spinning, it destroyed their tops and his sister's garden as well. They became very angry and beat him till he died. They threw him down underneath the house where the livestock live. That night, his magic dog came to lick him till he came to life again. He sat on the tombstones in the middle of the courtyard and sang a sad tale of his life and broken promises. Kyazi, after listening for several nights to this beautiful song, finally recognized his "voice," at the same time she also remembered her "word" to him. With grand feasting and lavish gifts, Mada Luwu's identity is re-established as her true brother and the rightful recipient to her marriage payments. His wealth soon "filled the valley, and covered a mountain."

When it came time for him to marry, he overcame the challenges of his father-in-law with the help of his dog and top, and he soon became very wealthy.

This tale can be mined for meaning at several levels (see C. Forth 1982 for a fuller discussion of such tales), only a few of which can be explored here. One of the more striking features of such stories in general is that the heroes (who may be male or female) tend to be young people who achieve wealth or status from a state of poverty through individual talents, cleverness (*pánde*) and personal magic, without the help of agnates or ancestral spirits (*marapu*). Although the hero is frequently and brutally maltreated because of his *ana lalo* "orphan" status and is therefore *milla* ("poor, humble"), with individual initiative, verbal prowess, and cleverness, he or she is able to rise above the impotence, impoverishment, and subordination with which many Weyewa identify. In most cases, however, the mythical hero does not attempt to use his or her powers to move outside of or to threaten the existing social hierarchy.

The exemplary genres of verbal expression associated with such *milla* figures are not monologic ritual-speech oratory, but songs: laments (*lawiti*), eulogies (*matekula*), and tuneful weeping, or "keening" (*nggeloka*). Such songs are performed by both men and women upon request on relatively informal occasions: harvest work, fireside gossip, funeral wakes. No animal sacrifice accompanies them, no ancestors are addressed: the audience is a distinctly human one. When they have thematic development, the songs tend to be narrative biographies or autobiographies of a particularly sad or pitiful person. They tell various tales, most often of children rejected, abandoned, or left behind by their angry, deceased, or cruel elders. The tales do not often directly criticize the figures of authority, although their expressions of misery are taken as a sign of discontent with the circumstances for which the elder bears some responsibility.

The structural features of such songs are different from those of more angry speech. They are not loudly projected, fast, or staccato in tone but tuneful, slow, and relatively soft. The singer is not expected to be perfectly fluent; indeed, occasional pauses can be interpreted as signs of deep emotional involvement (Kuipers 1986). Careful coherence does not matter as much as in angry oratory; if the rhetorical organization of a lament does not completely make sense the audience is not likely to condemn the performer for a lapse in memory but rather to interpret such ellipses in the context of the situation. Unlike the genres associated with the performance of "anger," in lament performances couplet structure is often violated, sentences are not finished, words are mispronounced. Such songs are likely to have modal particles indicating the qualms of the singer about what she is saying. They are likely to include other voices, sometimes without quotation or attribution. They may also include stylistic inconsistencies such as foreign words and phrases.

Dada Nggole: weeping at the margins

The case of Dada Nggole illustrates well the relation between *milla ate* ("humility") and the lament genre. When Dada Nggole was about sixteen years old, her father died from cerebral malaria. About twenty-two years old in 1984, she was pretty, pensive, and unmarried. She was relatively well educated, since was among the first graduating classes in what was then a new middle school close to her father's home. She had badly wanted to go on to high school, but when her father died, she and her mother and her two brothers went to live with her uncle, her father's brother. He "embraced" (*wapu*) Dada Nggole's widowed mother. In this levirate arrangement, he took her as his second wife, working her fields, repairing her house, and helping tend her cattle. While her mother seemed contented with this arrangement, Dada Nggole had many conflicts with her uncle, a man noted as an *ata mbani* ("angry man"). Perhaps partly due to this ill-will, she was to be sent back to her mother's village to help out with a sick aunt. Whatever the reason, she was about to be, in Sumbanese terms, "orphaned."

One morning in 1984, I heard her perform an orphan lament that exemplified many features of the *milla ate* affect. As I sat on the veranda of a house in which a performance had taken place the previous night, I chatted with Dada Nggole before she was to be sent off to her mother's natal village as a result of the previous night's deliberations. As we chatted about her upcoming move, she paused, and nodded towards a tape recorder I had in my bag. I turned it on and she began to sing.

wu inna lango leiro	You, my mother with the gentle embrace
la tandyaza elu tana	who is now in the eternal earth
ndau pandunnimongga mata	your eyes don't follow me any more
Wu ama lango baba	You, my father with the open lap
léngana takoro rindi watu	who is now in a room of stone walls
nda pa-mbali-mo-ngga limma	whose hands no longer reach for me

Since one parent was dead, and the other was sending her off to a strange village, Dada Nggole depicted herself as an orphan both of whose parents are dead, buried in the "eternal" earth, and entombed in "stone walls."

Kundende la katota, yauwa	As for me, I stand all alone
innangge ya katota ate	my mother, with a lonely heart
kuwaina weiya mata	I use the tears in my eyes
taniri wai kawendo	at the eaves of the house
kuzallungo kanuwa, yauwa	As for me, I try to amuse myself
amangge yakanuwa wiwi	I speak with my own lips
kuwaina weiya wirro	as snot flows from my nose
taniri wai kawendo	at the eaves of the house.

Since her parents abandoned her, she was no longer a part of any household, so she stands in between houses, under the eaves, and cries all alone. Among Weyewa, if one is alone it is usually only to get from one place to the next, so as to be with other people. To represent oneself as motionless and alone, is an image of utter desolation. In short, she is at the margins of society, a spectator condemned to watch, hear, and not participate.

Dada Nggole depicted her life among her new caretakers as cruel and harsh, full of hard labor and arbitrary orders.

kulipali kalerre	I run around getting ropes
kalerre dekke wazu	ropes for gathering wood
kuli padede wazu	I run about gathering wood
kawulla yoddo nale	I run about like a sea worm hunter,
pamalenggani loddo	I turn day into night
kunggattana padede	I quickly go and get
palele oke weiya	a headpad for carrying water
kuli paoke weiyo	and I go and fetch the water
kawulla timbu teri	I run about like a sardine gatherer
panggiringgawe tana	I work until sunset.

Like a person frantically scrambling for sea worms washed up with high tide, she runs about following orders, gathering firewood, until day turns into night.

While she accepts her fate, she laments that her parents did not tell her it was going to be like this: it does not, she weeps, "follow your words":

ndewa memangguni inna-o	this is indeed my fate, O mother
nda leduna	which did not follow
kadia tupalangimu	the basis of your words
urra memangguni ama-o	this is indeed my destiny, O father
nda manena	which did not follow
kalerre tu patekkimu	the strand of your words.

What she is stressing here is the lack of continuity, the lack of any meaningful sense of connectedness, indeed involvement with, the words and obligations that make up the authoritative structures of Weyewa life.

Thus having no defenders, she is forced to listen passively to those who gossip about her, even though she tries to shut her eyes and ears to the painful words.

lángo ka nda peikodangga ole	Even if they act so badly to me
ba panewe dukki waikingga	and I come upon their gossip about me
ka melle mata nda ku eta	as long as my eyes don't have to see it
langngo kanda peikodangga ole	Even if they act cruelly to me
ba panewe dukki waikingga	and I come upon their gossip about me
melle katillu nda ku rénge	as long as my ears don't hear it.

She goes on: even if her tormenters blame her for their misfortunes, and force her to undergo an ordeal of proof by grasping a burning log or grasping a thorny branch, she will do it; but she does not want to.

lángngo kau padeitonggandi	even if you make me carry
inna – o	O mother
pa-tunne mángu apingge	a flaming log
ka deito ka ndaku deitowi	I'll carry it, but I don't want to
langngo kau patoddunggandi	even if you make me carry on my head
ama – o	O father
hidda ponda mangngu tara	a thorny pandanus leaf
ka toddu ndaku toddundi	I'll carry it, but I don't want to
ndukka-ba-na.	that's it.

When she stopped singing, she appeared to me to be momentarily overcome by her own feelings of sadness and embarrassment, for she turned away from me and the small group of listeners, drew part of her sarong over her head, and turned away to face the wall. While others commented quietly to me that "her words are from the heart" (*"wale ate pongu"*) "she is very sad" (*"na milla takka ate-na"*).

Dada Nggole's antagonist in the song is never clearly represented. She sings of people gossiping, "acting cruel," and making her "fetch water," but they are not named, nor are they engaged directly in dialogue. Instead, she addresses her complaint to her deceased parent, and her antagonists are supposed simply to overhear her lament. She is a spectator who is performing her act of reception, as it were.

Dada Nggole speaks Indonesian, which she learned in her nearly nine years of school. She has lately taken to speaking only Weyewa, and wearing a traditional woven sarong pulled up over her breasts, which she wears over a store-bought dress with sleeves covering her shoulders. When asked, she sometimes sings in a clear soprano as the lead singer in planting and harvest-time worksongs. For this, she has achieved some renown in her neighborhood of hamlets, and she is often asked to perform when such occasions arise. She does not consider herself a performer or an artist; she would be surprised if she were offered money for her services. While she is proud of her ability to sing in ways that increase her renown, she remains frustrated and confused by her inability to affect her own social circumstances.

Humble marginality in a colonial context: Ninda Dappa sings Wini Mbolu's lament

If Dada Nggole's lament fits well with Weyewa images of "self-pitying humility," Ninda Dappa has elaborated on that emotion in more modern terms. The laments through which this emotion is expressed are among the ritual-speech genres to adapt to colonial experience. One such song, for example, records the lament of Wini Mbolu, the lover of First Lieutenant (*Letinani*) Barendsen. Barendsen, described by one of the "in-laws" as having been "young, tall, handsome and bald," was civil

Plate 6   *Woman singing an ironic lament*

administrator in West Sumba for a number of years following the pacification in 1912 (Van Den End 1987: 685–686). As the story goes, he shot Wini Mbolu in the shoulder during a Dutch raid on a village in Kodi where she was married to Wona Kaka, a local hero in the struggle against the Dutch. After Wona Kaka's defeat, she returned to Waimangura, her home, where her father gave her in "marriage" to Letnan Barendsen (Dapawole 1965). According to her surviving kinfolk, Barendsen was impressed with her spirit, her beauty, and the fact that her father was a raja. While he never paid brideprice, they lived together as man and wife until he had to return to Holland. According to people who remember her, she went everywhere with him, wearing Dutch-style jodhpurs, riding in a masculine style with a hat and using a riding crop. She never married again after he left and remained childless all her life, which ended in the 1940s.

I often heard about her lament even before I heard someone sing it. Whenever I had questions about the colonial period, Barendsen's name would inevitably arise. People would say, "Oh yeah, there's a song about him. Have you heard it?" To which I would reply hopefully, "no, can you sing it for me?" A reflective pause and then an excuse would always ensue. I experienced this same frustration at least a half-dozen times with various people until finally one day Enos Boeloe, my friend and assistant, suggested that we go visit a village not far from Karuni where Barendsen was stationed more than half a century ago. There was an elderly woman named Ninda Dappa who was the niece of Wini Mbolu, who was said to be able to remember it.

We found her lying alone in a dark back room of their traditional bamboo platform house, half-blind, and frighteningly frail and thin. When her cloudy eyes focussed on me, her stick-thin body twitched violently, and she clutched me to her chest: "it's you! It's you!" she shrieked, and began gasping frantically for breath. Fearing for her health and sanity, my friend and I gently tried to explain that I was not Barendsen, but that we sought the song about him. After she calmed down, and stared at me a long time, she began to sing her aunt's song:

oo mori aroo	ah my lord alas
ba-ku mburru-wangga cana	as I go down the steps
wu Marommba leti-nani	Master Lieutenant
Ooo mori maingge nemme oo	Ah my lord come hither
kau kondo kiku kakongga	and let me follow your horse's tail
kata pala-ngge	and we'll cross the
mbonnu a matimba	deep oceans together
Na yullu moto pakandiwu	he played me like a child's game
na marommba leti-nani	that Master Lieutenant
na yullu kurra pa-kazele	he eluded me like a tricky shrimp
na marommba dawa kaka	that White Foreign Master.

When he left Winni Mbolu behind after his tour of duty on Sumba, she expresses her regret and loneliness. Using the melody and many of the phrases from mythical orphan laments, she implicitly compares herself to someone abandoned by family and close kin.

As Ninda Dappa finished performing the song, her son arrived on the veranda and sat reflectively for a while. He explained that his mother was once in love with a Dutch-speaking Ambonese teacher who later left her. The case of Wini Mbolu is very near to her heart.

By adopting a posture of lament, she evokes the the sentiment *milla*, a kind of self-pitying humility, the sentiment here also clearly tinged with "anger." While certainly the Dutch East Indies (*kompeni*) is never mentioned explicitly in the song, it is not too much to suggest that for her and for many Sumbanese, legendary figures like Barendsen embodied the Dutch East Indies. These songs suggest that the framework of the dialogue was not that of confrontation, anger, or negotiation. Wini Mbolu does not say, "All right, to make amends, you owe me ten head of cattle" – rather it is a tone of lament, sadness and humility, framed as inner experience, something that occurs in the "heart" (literally, for Weyewa, the "liver").

Many ritual-speech representations of Dutch presence on the island that have been preserved have a gendered character to them in which a Sumbanese is depicted in a female role. The voice of the Dutchman typically does not appear anywhere in the song; the verbal genre represents emotional experience, not dialogue. Although this song contains expressions of indignation and dismay over perceived injustice, the interactional conventions of the genre chosen for this expression do not require any response on the part of the accused or even members of the audience. Indeed, the tone is one of resignation.

Dada Nggole and Ninda Dappa were both expressing *milla ate* ("humility") in their own way. Dada Nggole's humility comes from her loss of autonomy, and her experience of domination and oppression; the entire system of domination was not questioned. Ninda Dappa's lament was born out of her experience of abandonment, but was juxtaposed with the new context of Dutch colonialism. The Ambonese were widely regarded as surrogate Dutchmen ("dark Dutchmen"), and Ninda projects anger at her rejection on to the entire Dutch government; using the voice of Wini Mbolu, Ninda Dappa directly addresses her Dutch lover – *qua* Letnan Barendsen – and expresses her pain to the one who caused it, implying a critique.

The orphan metaphor is one that has deep roots both in Sumbanese oral literature and also in many other societies, but has been a surprisingly powerful and widespread image around the world for organizing feelings about the emergence of the nation state (see, e.g., Hunt 1992).

For Ninda Dappa, it is cast in both a national and a gendered framework. As a woman she is thus doubly orphaned: cut off by custom from her rights in her natal family after marriage, she is especially vulnerable when the nation state fails to take care of its citizens. Like many Sumbanese, citizens such as Ninda are caught between two worlds: she is "wedded" to the more contractual kinds of authority in the emerging world, yet she is orphaned from the more involuntary, familial authority in the old, original world.

As is the case in many literary traditions, the "orphan" is a liminal figure in a situation where natural (parental or kingly) authority is no longer present. As someone denied natural community, the orphan is required to conjure an "imagined community" in ways that pose questions about the very authority of social life itself.

The evolution of "cunning" (*pánde*): from "deviousness" to "development"

Evaluations of emotional attitudes and orientations played an important role in Dutch administration on Sumba. Some of the ambivalence can be seen in these two remarks by colonial administrators:

The current police inspector who had also served in Sumatra, said euphemistically he'd rather deal with 5 Bataks than 1 Soembanese. His predecessor was of this conviction. He was convinced without doubt of the cunning and cleverness of the Soembanese. He is *"pinter"* [clever] alas, *pinter* in the wrong way: *pinter boesoek* "clever rotten" = stinker.   (Riekerk 1936: 47)

Riekerk draws on an ambiguity in the Malay term *pinter*, an ambiguity also present in its Weyewa counterpart *pánde*. On the one hand, it refers to cleverness and skill, but, on the other, it also refers to cunning and deviousness. Their emotional and personality characteristics are crucial features that mediate between their material circumstances and their capacity for change. On a more positive, but similar note, Couvreur observes: *"[The Sumbanese] have gained the sympathy of all the previous administrators. The [Sumbanese] are absolutely vigorous, eager, courageous, and cheerful: therein lies their capacity for development (*ontwikkeling*)"* (Couvreur 1914: 191). Thus for Couvreur, their capacity for development – learning Indonesian, citizenship, and civilization – was mediated by emotional and personality characteristics: their cheerfulness, their eagerness, their courage.

The *pánde* ("cunning") category is part of a Weyewa-language ideology in that membership in the category is based on the capacity to speak in certain ways to certain kinds of people, mostly people in positions of power. Related to the Indonesian word *pandai* ("clever, competent"), the Weyewa term also commonly suggests a social status rather than simply a personal attribute. Thus one may say of a person that he or she is an *ata pánde*, a "clever person," meaning that he or she possesses a skill, usually involving linguistic performance. Ritual speakers are, by virtue of their verbal skills, *ata pánde*, "clever persons." Where ritual speakers' cleverness is tested is in marriage negotiations, a setting in which the capacity to cunningly outwit one's opponent is the very definition of *pánde*. While it may also refer to non-verbal technical skills such as blacksmithing, weaving, or housebuilding, it is primarily focussed on areas of knowledge whose display is accomplished through verbal performance.

In the contexts of myth and ritual, *pánde* ("cunning") is not a notably high-status or noble characteristic. In Sumbanese oral tradition, orphans such as Mada Luwu prevail over cruel antagonists by being clever. After being beaten and left for dead, Mada Luwu is nonetheless able to win the hearts of his estranged sister and her family through song. In other narratives, an *ata pánde* ("clever person") is able to deflect the anger or hostile intentions of an antagonist through a clever remark or misleading statement.

The status of cunning and cleverness appears to have changed somewhat in response to the demands of Dutch presence. In nearly every *Memorie van overgave* ("Memories on the transfer of office") concerned with Sumba, there is a section devoted to describing and evaluating the various "rajas" (kings) of Sumba. Among the highest praises given to them by the colonial officers is that they are *flink* ("clever, smart, competent"). One meaning of *pánde* ("clever") which it did not possess before Dutch presence was that of "literate" and "bureaucratically competent."

In colonial terms, what did it mean to be *pánde*?[4] It did not entail mastery of magic or special arts so much as skill in speaking and writing Malay. Malay was the language of schooling, literacy, and administration. The language in which competent selves emerged was seen by Dutch and other foreigners as Malay/Indonesian. An often-mentioned factor in determining whether a native administrator was *flink* ("clever") was whether that person could speak Malay. This indeed was the policy of the Dutch East Indies: "When speaking to ranking Native Administrators, the *controleurs* shall as a rule use Malay" (Gorkom 1896: 20). The association of public activity with Malay was codified in the manual for colonial administrators quite explicitly as an interpretation of native affective sensibilities: "It is certain that the regents, for example, in public, in the earshot of their subjects, do not like to be addressed in their native language" (Van Gorkom 1896: 22). Thus, owing to a Dutch interpretation of "native" feelings, the local languages are banished to the private, personal, and individualized domains of interaction.

If Indonesian/Malay had become the language of formal and *flink* ("clever, cunning") public discourse, then by default Weyewa was the language of private and less cultivated speech. In particular, it was the language of anger, a discourse which was explicitly banished from modern settings. This is still true today: as anyone who has spent any time in an Indonesian bureaucracy knows, it is very important not to lose one's temper in public.

An experience from the summer of 1994 helps illustrate the way in which "anger" has become increasingly scorned, marginalized, and evaluated in Indonesianized aesthetic terms as *kasar* ("crude, uncouth"). In the course of negotiations over marriage payments, my friend Mbora Kenda flew into what might have once been described in Shakespearean terms as a "towering rage." In a way that reminded me of King Lear angry over a perceived insult to his status, he stomped off to sit by himself on the front porch. He was furious at how his niece's new in-laws were balking at giving her parents a gold ear pendant for her brideprice. In thunderous voice, he challenged the idea that they could not pay. "That you would even hesitate is a personal insult to me" he said, thumping his chest dramatically. His surprised in-laws quickly produced a pendant to mollify him and get on with the proceedings. His in-laws" response was interesting, however. While they complied with his wishes, they made it clear that they considered his outburst *kasar*, an Indonesian language word meaning "crude, rough," and that it was inappropriate behavior for "Christians" and "people of understanding." Angry behavior, they implied, belonged to the traditional world he had recently forsaken, not to the world of Christians he had recently joined.

As Mbora Kenda sat alone fuming on the porch, a young fellow – an unemployed recent college graduate – pointed to him and said to me ironically *"kabani-mbani-wa"* ("he's an angry, bold man"). Once a category of respect and prestige, an angry man in my young companion's world was someone out of date, crude, and uncouth. To him, calling his elder an "angry man" was like calling him an "old coot.'[5]

Just as the English phrase "towering rage" evokes connotations of another era, another time, the "angry man" in Sumba is something of an anachronism. Both presuppose a hierarchy, social status, and legitimacy that no longer exist. Within the world of "towering rages," only high-ranking men are entitled to this experience: children, subordinates, beggars, and most women were not. It suggests a certain autonomy of feeling from physical aggressive action: righteous wrath not fistfights. By contrast, the tight linkage of anger with aggressive action in contemporary Western literature, cinema, and indeed daily life makes such a notion hard to understand.

The young man described himself in Indonesian in sharply contrasting terms: as an *orang mengerti*, "a cognoscente, a person who understands," or in Weyewa as *ata pánde*, "a cunning person." Yet he himself has not totally abandoned traditional ways. Although his highest aspiration is still to land a government job, he prides himself on his ability to sing evocative songs in ritual speech. At night, by the kitchen fire, on request, or even spontaneously, he sings laments about lost love, jealousy (*kanggoula ngau*), humiliation, and sadness, and occasionally personal triumph through cleverness.

When Mbora Kenda's adult Christian son finally approached him on the porch, and told him that the ear pendant he demanded was received, the young man spoke to his own father in Indonesian. The young man chided his father gently for his outburst, and proposed that cooler heads should prevail. Mbora Kenda could not reply effectively in Indonesian, but accepted the admonition quietly. By speaking Indonesian, his son placed the discussion in a public, implicitly Christian framework, in which such outbursts of anger are "crude" and inappropriate.

Anger has not disappeared from Weyewa life, of course, but it is supposed to be linked to a narrower range of contexts. One day, a school-teacher friend of mine walked in to my house and sat down, having just arrived on the bemo (covered pick-up truck) from the town of Waikabubak. "I heard today that the Bupati [Regent] struck his driver" he reported. "What happened?" everyone wanted to know. "Well, they were out on a tour of a village and while the Regent and the [VIP] were out walking, the driver fell asleep in the car when the Regent was out touring with a VIP and when he found the driver asleep, he got angry and hit him in front of a lot of people." Since we had just been talking about anger, I broke in and asked "so, is the Regent a *kabani-mbani* then?" Everyone smiled but one of my friends dismissed the idea with a wave of his hand:

Ah no. no. no. The Bupati is a modern man, a Christian. When he gets angry, it's because there is a cause: for example, someone is making a mistake. Most of the time [the Bupati] speaks in a refined (*halus*) manner. "Angry men" did not do that . . .

Conclusions

I have paid particularly close attention to the history of "anger," "humility," and "cunning." As the contexts and relations between "anger" and "humility" gradually shifted (see Figure 7) circumstances created partly by the Dutch were seen to offer expanded opportunities for other kinds of emotional and personal experience, ones that many of my Weyewa friends summarized with the label *pánde* ("competence, cleverness, cunning"). Understood as "cleverness," *pánde* has resonances with a lively and vivid cycle of "orphan" myths in which a young boy

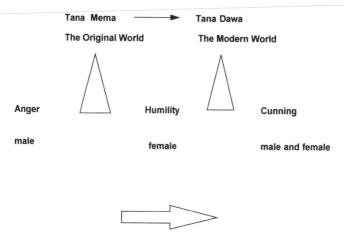

Figure 7   *Changing models of self expression in Weyewa 1900–1994*

overcomes his personal experience of "humiliation" (*milla*) and degradation at the hand of his powerful in-laws through clever, trickster-like
subversions, manipulations, and magic. The more recent connotations
of the term have to do with technical mastery of the symbolic and
technological resources of modern life. Proficiency in the Indonesian
national language, the written word, bureaucratic and legal rules, and
agricultural technology are examples of *pánde* ("competence") and
offer an alternative to "humility" (*milla*). Under the Dutch system,
only the children of elites had the opportunity to become *pánde*: only
they were sent to school, offered jobs in the civil service, and learned
to speak Indonesian. As the Dutch and Indonesians gradually inter-
vened in the Sumbanese political economy, Sumbanese language
behavior has been partly mediated by these shifting conceptions of self
and identity.

Unlike the emotional shifts described by Kulick (1992b: 20) among the
Gapun in New Guinea, among the Weyewa this emotional shift is not
couched in terms of individualism and collectivism, and only secondarily
in terms of gender; rather the prevailing idiom of discourse about
emotional expression and selfhood privileges status, hierarchy, and
agency; gender differences tend to be assimilated into these differences in
prestige, renown, and dominance. Currently, both Weyewa men and
women describe themselves as either "cunning" or "humble" (and
occasionally both at once), depending on their circumstances.

What is striking about the Weyewa case is the specific semiotic process
by which this transformation occurred. As Judith Irvine (1990) has
shown, emotionally expressive features can be seen as an essential

attribute of certain social classes. Drawing on her fieldwork among the Wolof of Senegal, she argues for closer attention to the organization of diversity in a given community's conventions of affective communication. In the Wolof case, for instance, there is a "cultural association between social ranks and affectivity" (1990: 152). High-status nobles are seen as laconic, while low-status griots are noted for their loquaciousness and more volatile affectivity.

Analysis of Dutch colonial reports and memoirs shows that the *kabani-mbani* figure was perceived as having an important social status, one which was threatening to Dutch control. His threats were partly accomplished through verbal means, often poetic ones. These displays were seen as essential attributes of the kind of leadership which the Dutch most wished to control. With potent performance construed as an icon of despotism by Sumba's elite, the Dutch contained it by separating the performance from the actual use of force. The "angry men" could perform verbally but not display their potency through violence: that was the role of the Dutch army and police. Thus "angry" but exemplary speech was no longer complete and total: it no longer had the spiritual, social and practical linkages with legitimate force, violence, and social action that it once had.

4

CHANGING FORMS OF POLITICAL
EXPRESSION: THE ROLE OF
IDEOLOGIES OF AUDIENCE
COMPLETENESS

There is a distinctive kind of cheer that even a casual visitor to the island of Sumba is likely to witness. The cheerleader (usually a young man) leads with a high falsetto yodelling cry that falls in tone, like a whistling bombshell hurtling towards earth, which then explodes into a thunderous, concussive "*yawao!*" from the audience. In Weyewa ritual ideology, such hoorahs indicate a kind of ceremonial assent towards the proceedings. In a society where the recruitment of labor and human capital was historically a paramount expression of power, such seemingly inarticulate noises are crucial, if unacknowledged, indications of involvement and participation on the part of the conscripts.[1] A series of three (or sometimes seven) of these shouts of applause are traditionally performed before setting off on some challenging group activity, such as carrying a pig to a feast, harvesting a rice field, or dragging a tombstone. Such shouts not only express the "spirit" on the part of the audience, to some extent they define the collective, if ephemeral, unity of the group itself.

These cheers are now used in campaign rallies, soccer matches, and to greet dignitaries and government officials. Such borrowing from the domain of work and "tradition" into the domain of politics is a hallmark of Suharto's New Order Indonesia. Bowen (1986), for example, has carefully shown how the metaphor of *gotong-royong* ("mutual self-help") was imported from the vocabulary of agriculture into the realm of national politics and development. What have not been fully explored, however, are the implications of this borrowing process for the process of linguistic change. This chapter discusses the linguistic ideologies by which ideas about political and economic participation are recursively projected on to ideas about community and communication from one level to another. According to Gal and Irvine (1995), linguistic ideologies "claim and thus attempt to create shifting 'communities,' identities, selves and roles at different levels of contrast within a cultural field." In this chapter, I argue that Weyewa ritualists, whose efforts to convene ceremonially complete audiences in a Dutch-dominated world seemed increasingly hollow, nonetheless succeeded in projecting concepts of the work group and the orphan spectator on to the realm of state politics.

The study of the politics of language change in Indonesia

Most studies of the politics of language in Indonesia, have, as Errington (1986) observed, been either "modernist" or "historicist" in orientation. The modernist group (e.g. Alisjahbana 1976) tends to stress the new, developing, contemporary, and progressive aspects of modern Indonesian discourse as a break with its feudal and traditional past. The historicist style of writing (e.g. Anderson 1990; Siegel 1986) emphasizes the ways in which modern Indonesian political discourse is strongly continuous with its traditional and colonial past. Errington argues that neither orientation sufficiently accounts for the ways in which Indonesian is actually used in context. On the one hand, for example, only a little observation in contemporary Indonesian society makes clear that the national language is not, in practice, the instrument of social and political equality that its planners envisioned. Wide variations in use exist in ways that divide the population by class and ethnicity. On the other hand, modern formal Indonesian in actual use has not simply supplanted the old and overtly hierarchical Javanese *krama* respect language, either; unlike *krama*, modern Indonesian and street slang are never exchanged non-reciprocally between speaking partners as a way of showing status differences.

Like Errington, I wish to base my arguments on the role of language in political change on observation of use in context, not just on the role of the producer, speaker–hearer, but also the audience and hearer. Following those who examine politics in its interactional context (Scott 1990), I examine political relations in communicative ones, situated in verbal and expressive exchanges. By looking at changing genres of ritual speech through which relations of power are expressed – from *oka* ("chant") to *lawiti* ("lament") – it is clear that a reorientation of political expression has occurred in which most Weyewa now figure as spectators to the modern Indonesian state apparatus rather than convenors of audiences.

A traditional linguistic history of the Weyewa highlands might miss important facts of political change in the region. Among Weyewa, the story of the politics of linguistic shift is not happening on the level of dialect – a code that defines a regional group – but on the level of register – a code that defines a special situation and roles within that situation. While Weyewa are not changing what they consider to be their native language, their ways of using it and of using ritual speech are changing rapidly.

To understand how this shift could occur, I will sketch first the ideology of reception as audience completeness, exemplified in the practices of Lende Mbatu, a renowned "angry man" highly skilled at convening audiences for ceremonial purposes. While early Dutch administrators initially stepped into audience roles of this sort, their Calvinist iconoclasm, combined with their growing military and political power in the region, led them to be increasingly impatient with the theatrical, elaborate, and indirect forms of communication that Sumbanese leaders required. Although the Dutch did make an effort to support local forms of political discourse, their attempts must have struck a hollow note to most Sumbanese, for these ventures to create a hybrid but authoritative form of ritual discourse have not gained popular acceptance. When the Japanese colonial "state" arrived in force in 1942, any attempt at imagining the colonial state as an audience all but disappeared, but local forms of political communication as response, such as *lawiti*, began to develop. These new forms of ritual-speech response amount to an emerging form of spectatorship, in which citizenship is represented as a relation of ratification, emotional support, or humble resentment.

Audience completeness in Weyewa ritual ideology

Although Sumba never possessed a specifically Indic "theater state," its nineteenth- and early twentieth-century polities appear to have placed similar importance on hierarchy, spectacle, and rhetorical performance embodied in the person of a ritual leader. Part of the potency of the *kabani-mbani* ("angry man") for Weyewa derived from the way in which he made use of symbols to mediate the relationship between himself and audience, through speech, symbolic exchanges of food, cloth, and valuables, and with spectacular displays of ritual drama. Speaking of the more specifically Indicized state, Geertz's description applies well to the more marginal polities in Indonesia's Outer Islands: "The [Indic] state drew its force from its imaginative energies, its semiotic capacity to make inequality enchant" (1980: 123). For the ruler, historian Anthony Reid writes that "religious festivals provided an opportunity . . . to display himself before his people in all his majesty" (1988: 174).

During the late nineteenth and early twentieth centuries, the political and ritual centers of Sumba were fortified ancestral villages (Weyewa, *wanno kalada*) in which most Sumbanese lived or claimed affiliation (Kapita 1976). At the political center of these villages was a charismatic ruler (often a *kabani-mbani*), who embodied and protected the security of the entire village "like a leafy banyan tree" and who exacted loyalty, labor, tribute, and sometimes servitude, in return. Conceived of as a social and indeed cosmic center and source of status, the "great villages" of such men spawned lesser, pioneer villages that radiated outwards, whose inhabitants were obliged to return periodically with ceremonial tributes in spectacular feasts in exchange for continued agricultural prosperity, blessings, and protection.

One of the earliest observers on the island in the 1860s described his experience of the importance of speech in Sumbanese politics:

at each opportunity, in which it appears that discussion will take place, the orators try their best to let their "arts of blather" shine forth. For hours on end, they can talk on and on with great speed *and try to amaze their audiences.* They never speak directly to the issue, but indirectly, and they finally come to the point they had intended to make in the first place. The one who speaks most beautifully and lengthily wins the case.   (Roos 1872: 74, my emphasis)

The significance of the audience for the meaning of the center was construed in terms of "completeness." That is, the center was not complete, whole, and undivided unless the full audience was there to witness and admire its theatrical display. The most prominent image of the ritual audience is expressed in the couplet,

> *mattu mata*   the eyes are complete
> *tanga wiwi*   the lips are paired

As members of the audience gaze on the main performer, their eyes (as metonyms for attentive audience members) are judged to be "complete" in that everyone is there who needs to be there. Likewise, the "lips" – a metonymic image of participants as speakers – are all "paired," which in Sumbanese ritual ideology is an image of completeness and totality (cf. Needham 1980).

Lende Mbatu: a *kabani-mbani*

Lende Mbatu was a masterful convenor of audiences, a renowned ritual speaker, and a man who considered himself (and was widely regarded by others as) an exemplary citizen of an older kind of polity in Sumba. Gifted in poetic oratory, capable of projecting a fierce, yet likable persona, Lende Mbatu was widely respected for his knowledge of ritual lore, his economic acumen, and his ability to organize and carry out large-scale ceremonial events in fulfillment of his obligations to his ancestors, including his own father. In bearing, appearance, performative style, he was a *kabani-mbani* ("angry man") *par excellence.*[2] Yet his authority was severely restricted by the watchful apparatus of the Indonesian government and military.

His reputation had much to do with his verbal skills in ritual settings and in informal negotiations. While he did display aggression in his oratory and in his efforts to recruit labor for ritual tasks, he only rarely resorted to physical combat or fighting. There are allegations that he purchased the services of a mercenary to attack one of his enemies some years ago. For most Weyewa today and in the past, and indeed most Indonesians, military service is a privileged, but not widely shared, attribute of citizenship.[3]

Plate 7   *Lende Mbatu* [Photo: Edward Parker]

Lende's progress: an example of convening an audience

As Tsing (1990) has noted for the Meratus, power can be understood as the ability to "convene an audience." Lende Mbatu's extraordinary ability to get people to come and contribute to ritual events comes from his memory for detailed history of personal relatedness and genealogical connection, and his ability to place economic and labor obligations in a more general moral framework using ritual speech. He is good at explaining kinship duties and then forcefully holding people to their commitments.

I once accompanied him as he approached a neighbor extract to such a commitment. To get the man and his family to agree to help pull a 20–ton stone out of a quarry, Lende Mbatu began by telling the history of the stone and how he got interested in pulling it out:

pa-dana-ba-nggu-ni pa-willi-ni	[my father] got me to take over his work
ba-na pa-tukka-na ngara ndukka-na	and he ordered all
ne ana-na zamme-ba-na a pa-willi	of us children to work on it
ka-nyaka dukki-ni ba wa'i-ni	and so here we are
na eta-wa ondi ba na-manippi	and [my father] dreamed of the tombstone
"ka-ndana tanga-ki-wa ondi-nggu	"why isn't there a mate, a pair
na ro'o watu-ngge?"	for this lid here (i.e. a stone base)?"

As Lende Mbatu makes his plea for help, he begins by stressing that his request is based on his sense of filial duty, a leftover obligation from his now deceased father. By phrasing it this way, he deflects a possible cynical criticism that he is simply seeking a name for himself. By mentioning his father's dream about the lack of a base for the tombstone lid, he suggests that there is an emotionally charged, and somewhat ominous urgency to the fulfillment of this promise, since dreams are thought to reflect a troubled spirit, and to forecast future events.

Lende Mbatu's host wonders how soon he will have to assemble his men to help:

ippa tengi lolo-ba-mu	are you almost ready to drag it?
	he asks.

Lende Mbatu continues, however, on the theme of the moral basis for the request:

ka nyakka ba-ku baba-do-wa	"so that I can complete [my obligations],
ka-nyakka tengi-wa lunggu-ni	that's why I'm pulling it," I say to him

With a flourish of modesty, he self-deprecatingly suggests that,

nda oro-ki-na-we	it is not because
pa-wizzi- dou pongu	I myself am so strong
ka nya-we hitti pa-tau-we ne loddo	thus when we do actually carry it out
nya mema-do-na	it will be due to the efforts of
duu-dadi-nggu	my relatives and kinsfolk
ne ba nda'i-mo a wa'ingga zauwa	if you weren't there I wouldn't be where I am now . . .

He suggests that he is really nothing without the help of his kinsfolk, and somewhat disingenuously deprecates himself before his host. He quickly reminds his host, however, that this is not simply a gesture of kindness; it is an "exchange of favors." He leaves ambiguous who owes what to whom, however: whether he is calling in a favor due from help delivered in the past, or whether he is offering to help his host in the future.

ne ndowo-na nduwa pa-menne-nggu	I'm hoping for the exchange of favors
monno ndowo-na pánde	and the exchange of expertise
ba wa'i-do-na a mbei-ngge	and if someone wants to
ndowo-na	exchange favors
monno ndowo dengangga pánde	and exchange expertise with me
pa-mbei-ko-na duu	it is up to those relatives

Almost instinctively composing a couplet ("exchange favors/exchange expertise"), Lende Mbatu makes a persuasive pitch to his host, who then agrees to supply labor for the stone-dragging event. As a result of the negotiations recorded in this encounter, nearly forty young men were recruited for the event, which took place the following day.[4]

Commanding the spiritual audience

In Weyewa linguistic ideology, the rules for asking for help and convening an audience are slightly different when communicating with outsiders, in this case, dangerous earth spirits, across whose territory the quarried stone must be dragged. Although he needs their help, Lende was more forceful and commanding. Indeed, these "outsiders" are the focus of his wrath and "anger" (*mbani*). In this brief performance, he shouts his commands to the outside nature spirits before giving the order to hundreds of men to begin pulling a 20-ton tombstone from a quarry. Although it is the surrogate world of the nature spirits who are the immediate targets of Lende Mbatu's forceful commands, the hundreds of young men lined up to pull on the 100-meter long vines also hear these messages, and they communicate intensity and urgency.

Nggaika kalete wole woza	Ride that stone [that stone] like a
na ndara pakalete mu	crocodile spirit[5]
ba zolo a mboto	haul the heavy load
a leita lomba	cross the steep ravines
ba dai dawua mbiduka	shore up the weak
hari a kandatu	who depend on you like people hanging from a rope
yemmi a tawora pinda lete	You are the Messenger Spirit who climbs the mountains
yemmi a karaki pinda namu	You are the Guardian Spirit who dives into the ravine
a mandi'i ndara ndende kikuna newela	You sit astride a fine, high tailed horse here and now
Nggoo . . .	Nggoo . . .
a langga lolo kamba	You guide us with trail of yarn
nggaika a lolu likke	You show us our limits!
Yow!	*Yow!*
lalalalalalalala!	lalalalalalalala!

As soon as he commands the spirits to "haul the heavy load," it is in fact the hundreds of men who burst into a collective "*yawao.*" Moving as one, they give the ropes tied to the tombstone a huge jerk. The massive thing lurches forward and a cheer rises from the crowd.

The ideology of audience completeness

On a spiritual level, the completeness of the audience is a central factor in the effectiveness and potency of an event. Conversely, a key reason cited for the failure of ritual events to achieve their stated spiritual or political goals is incompleteness of the audience; only rarely is it blamed on errors in the production of the ritual itself. For example, when a calamity occurs (e.g. fire, flood, death, injury) and a reason is sought for the wrath of the spirit who caused it, most often it is because a spirit (and the descendants of that spirit) was not "invited" to a feast, i.e. it was not complete, and thus felt left out (see Kuipers 1990). Or if an invited participant suddenly withdraws out of anger or a sense of indignation over perceived inappropriate treatment, this can throw the entire ritual proceedings into jeopardy. Even today, one of the major causes of misunderstanding between foreign visitors and their Weyewa hosts concerns this sense of audience completeness: when visitors do not remain at the ritual long enough to eat and receive meat, this important sense of audience "completeness" is placed in jeopardy, and often the host finds himself pleading with his foreign guests to wait a little longer.

When Mbora Kenda's two-year-old daughter died, he asked his brother to conduct a divination. His brother determined that a spirit from a neighbor's field was angry because he had not been invited to a key feast held three years ago. The reason for the failure to invite the spirit to the feast was that the neighbor and Mbora Kenda had had a dispute over the land that the spirit guarded and so the issue was simply avoided. Because the spirit was not invited, the audience was not "complete," its words were not heard and the performance was not authoritative.

In political terms, a key image of one's social influence, prestige, and status is the capacity to create a "complete audience." Ability to include everyone in an appropriate way, to serve everyone according to their due, is an essential attribute of those who have traditional power in the Weyewa highlands. When praising the feasts of a particular "big man," it was common to hear a guest say, "when I brought an animal to his feast, I was treated right." Or: "When I came to his feast, he received me appropriately." This refers not only to economic reception (i.e. the countergift), but also the verbal expressions: the appropriate spirits from the guest village were addressed, their descendants were appropriately acknowledged and addressed during the ritual-speech performance, and so forth. Failing to address and acknowledge the audience in a ritual performance appropriately is not simply an aesthetic fault; it seriously diminishes one's power within the community.

Power was indexed not only by the number of people who received meat, and were thus somehow obliged to reciprocate eventually, but also by the number of people one was able to recruit to produce such a collective activity. In general, the more people recruited, the more prestigious the event. The value of a pig, for instance, and the prestige of its owner, are measured in terms of the number of people required to carry it. Receiving an "eight-person pig" is high prestige indeed. Expressive genres parallel these economic and political practices.

The value of material goods (rice, water buffaloes, horses) is thus closely related to the expressive practices that accompany them. One agricultural officer shook his head explaining the problems he faced in getting the Weyewa to plant rice in rows:

The "big men" (*paama*) do not want to use the smaller work groups required for planting in rows, because no one could hear [the planter's] *yawaos!* Even though smaller groups are more efficient (*efisien*), the old men fear that they will be thought poor and low status because their work group doesn't make enough noise.

The number of workers one could recruit for a task was an indicator of the number of people who felt themselves obliged to the "great man." Women, too, were expected to ululate (*pakallaka*) in support of men's physical exertion if they were not themselves taking part in it. Much as the value of a gift is related to the amount of labor and time required to produce it, so also the value of an oration or other ritual speech production has to do with a volume, amount and frequency of response.

A list of what might be called "audiencing practices"[6] is shown in Table 2. Structurally akin to what conversation analysts call "back-channel cues," these "audiencing practices" are listed in order of the degree of contingency of response. For example, the *kabuara* "cheer" (which is another word for the *yawao* "cheer" described above) is almost entirely predictable and only slightly contingent in structure, volume, or timing on the particulars of whatever provokes it. The same *kabuara* or *yawao* is used regardless of whether the event is a stone dragging, election, or a soccer match. Although *pakallaka* ("ululation") often accompanies the same sorts of events in which *kabuara* is used, it involves somewhat more discretion on the part of the women who perform it, and they can select their timing, and modulate their form and volume depending on the moment of the performance they are seeking to support. Women voice their support of "placation rite" proceedings by ululating in a more muted way than they do in support of stone draggings. They never ululate during Indonesian public speeches. The *mala* ratification response is uttered by a designated responder. The

Table 2. *Audiencing practices in Weyewa*

Expressive form		Performer(s)	Occasions
kabuara	"cheer"	usually men	collective exertion
pakallaka	"ululation"	adult women	collective exertion
mala	"ratification"	usually adult men	narrative performance
lawiti	"lament"	adult women and men	following, or as an aside to, performance

performance of *mala* – which means something akin to the English "amen!" in African-American sermons – is contingent on the utterer's recognition of paragraph-like thematic unity to the discourse he is witnessing. It is quite possible to make mistakes: I have seen a young man utter *mala* at the wrong time during a speech and be roundly criticized for it. *Lawiti* "laments" are performed as a more personal response to large-scale events and authoritative performances. They are emotional, relatively spontaneous, non-obligatory, and highly discretionary. All these audiencing practices tend to occur in the context of feasts or economic exchanges, and all are more less direct: one does not typically hire a surrogate to express *mala* or *lawiti* on one's behalf. As we shall see below, more than phonological, morphological, or syntactic shifts, shifts in these forms of audience response provide clues as to the direction and nature of linguistic change among Weyewa.

Colonial containment: Dutch pacification 1906–1912

When the Dutch began intensifying their presence on the island in the late nineteenth and early twentieth centuries, they actively sought out audiences with charismatic leaders similar to Lende Mbatu. They did not, however, see themselves as participating easily in one of the categories of audience response. Their iconoclastic Calvinism made them impatient and uncomfortable with the richly mediated and indirect forms of communication favored by the Sumbanese. The Dutch sought direct communications with Sumbanese leaders, not ones embellished with ritualized displays, mediated by spokesmen or elaborate exchanges. One early Dutch administrator expressed his exasperation over the tendency of Sumbanese leaders to delegate the speaking role to a middleman: "the influence of Ama Nia is great. If we want to approach the rajas about anything, we must continually speak with Ama Nia first. We are totally dependent on this man!" (Wielenga 1912: 302). Samuel Roos, another early Dutch administrator of the island, from 1860 to 1866, put it in more general terms: "anyone who has any claims to renown [on Sumba] has at least one spokesman and *Radjas* have even more" (1872: 73).

Plate 8   *Women are an integral part of a complete audience*
[Photo: Herman May]

Although Roos depicted himself as a "guest" when he visited the houses
of the rajas, it must have been increasingly apparent to the Sumbanese
that the Dutch were not simply another audience.

When the Dutch attempted to short-cut the mediation process, and
tried to force the Sumbanese to communicate directly on a face-to-face
basis, the rajas became extremely uncomfortable and uncooperative. In
one notable encounter in the late nineteenth century, when the Dutch
assistant Resident Van Heuckelum, an envoy from Kupang, presented a
defiant Sumbanese raja named Umbu Tunggu with a chair, the latter
replied "it is forbidden to sit in a chair!" When Van Heuckelum
presented him with a cigar, he said "It is forbidden to smoke a cigar! It is
pemali [forbidden] for a European to live in [Sumba]!" (reported in
Wielenga 1916). If Van Heuckelum wished to trade horses, and do so
according to the indirect protocol of Sumbanese culture, that was fine,
but as a representative of the government, he was unwelcome.

The Dutch had very little success establishing an effective administration on the island until circumstances required a much more immediate

and direct mode of interaction with large numbers of Sumbanese. In 1869 and 1870, a smallpox epidemic struck the island and whole villages were wiped out. In this setting, the Dutch assistant Resident directly vaccinated over 20,000 people in 1870 alone. It was Dutch control over this devastating illness, and the abject subordination that the public clinical encounter required – quite literally permitting oneself to be shot – that Wielenga and others admitted began to place Dutch Sumbanese relations on a different footing in this early period. Wielenga reported, for instance, that he had very little success in communicating the gospel to the Sumbanese until he opened up a clinic for vaccination. He reports that he and his helpers administered several thousand vaccines in a six-month period (Wielenga [1904] 1987).

Instead of restructuring forms of political communication altogether, the Dutch sought to contain the circle of power in which the rajas operated, and to position themselves as the recipients of those indirect forms of communication: they wished to become the silent authority behind the (native) powers, even handing out scepters to the local leaders as a sign of their legitimating role. When the Dutch did begin to consolidate and shore up their authority on the island in the early 1900s, they did not try to create a direct kind of citizenship for the Sumbanese in the Dutch East Indies. All encounters with the Dutch government were to be mediated by Dutch-appointed "rajas" or *zelfbestuurders* (literally, "self-governors'). Couvreur, in an essay on the establishment of government on the island, wrote in 1917 that

once we know who and what these leaders are, we understand that we can only rule with and through them. The rajas, noble chiefs, and heads of descent groups (*kabisu*) must have our full attention, and also the *ratu*. The first three to be used in governmental administration and information, the *ratu* only as a source of information, since he can play no direct role in government.   (1917: 219)

Citizenship as spectatorship in Sumba

Although the Dutch hoped to maintain the appearance of a "self-governing" polity on Sumba, the notion of a colonial "state" as a strong, indeed brutal, governing body arrived in force with the landing of the Japanese occupation force. With their arrival, any efforts at imagining the colonial state as a part of a complete audience all but disappeared. However, during this period, local forms of political communication as response began to appear. The new forms of ritual-speech response amounted to an emerging form of spectatorship, in which citizens represent and depict their mode of participation as applause, cheers, ratification, emotional support, or humble resentment.

To understand which forms of speech were elaborated and developed –

without outside efforts at sponsorship – it is important to understand the ways in which Weyewa construed their relationship to state authority. In Sumba, citizenship – in the broad sense of membership in a polity – was more akin to a form of "spectatorship" than the contractual relationship between an individual and the state in modern republics (Pateman 1988).[7] As Geertz (1983) has argued, a semiotic – indeed theatrical – view of the relation between the state and the individual is required to understand Southeast Asian politics. Drawing – for the moment – on the theatrical metaphor, "spectatorship" is a useful way of understanding the marginality of Weyewa ritual speakers as political actors (see Rafael 1990; M. Hansen 1995; Johnson 1995). By spectatorship here, I do not mean the specialized role of viewer/audience that developed in sixteenth and seventeenth century Europe, where the theater, marketplace, and courts all developed separate spaces and roles (Agnew 1986). However, I do mean to suggest an intensification and elaboration of the role of the participant as experiencer: beholder, witnesser, and observer. As Weyewa audiences in formal, village rituals lost some of their power to create authority in the Dutch East Indies, individual observers began to reshape existing laments genres to comment on the doings of those in power from the perspective of an experiencer, a witness, and a bystander.

Unlike the *kabani-mbani*, whose charismatic appeal was ratified by the elaborate symbolic expressions of gifts and expressive shouts as part of overall dramatic ceremonial displays, in the early period of Dutch administration on Sumba, a primary expression of citizenship was material: the payment of head taxes (*welli katowa*, "price of the head"; in Dutch, *belasting*), or labor in, for example, roadbuilding and school construction (see Versluys 1941). Expressive audiencing practices began to lose some of their multivocal meanings as acts of political partici-pation were gradually specialized to realms of taxation and corvée labor. Between the Dutch administrators and ordinary Sumbanese there was little direct verbal communication, largely because there were so few Dutch on the island at any given time, and partly because the adminis-trators spoke Malay and Dutch, and most Sumbanese did not.

While severe restrictions were placed by the Dutch on the expression of anger (e.g. no more open warfare, headhunting, or cattle rustling), Sumbanese humility was to be interpreted in state-based terms. Part of establishing a new sentiment of *milla* ("humility") among the Sumbanese was to get them to understand that they had to be humble to Europeans, who controlled the regional heads, who in turn had control over district heads, subdistrict heads, village leaders, and so on. Being humble meant not just a general attitude, but in relation to the proper hierarchy of relationships. The focus of the administrators was on changing the consciousness of the Sumbanese. "Rules that are not understood are just paper regulations. Only through *understanding* can they take on life among the people" (Groeneveld 1931: 14) .[8]

The expressions of citizen–spectatorship: Japanese occupation 1942–1945

We are like rats that never sleep, we are like cats that never stop prowling.
(from a Weyewa *lawiti* composed during the Japanese occupation)

The state as such first became a truly powerful force with the arrival of 8,000 Japanese and their (largely Javanese) laborers in 1942. At this point, ritual speech appears to have been a kind of poetic refuge for expression of personal identity in the face of an increasingly powerful and coercive state. Some of the wonder, terror, and desire that mingled during the early often brutal encounters with Japanese in the period from 1942 to 1945 can be glimpsed in this brief *lawiti* composed upon seeing Japanese warplanes over the island in 1943:

White flying ships (1943)

yauwa na milla-ko-we ate-nggu	As for me, my heart feels weak
ba kuéta kapala lera kaka	when I see the white flying ships . . .
ammemundi ziddami	here they come
pa-lolo ya kamurangge	in a roaring formation
ho wali kere langita.	from the buttocks of the sky.
peikonawe patanawe	What are the ways of the world
na mbali mbonnu?	across the water?
na zuza lángu takka-po-we	Hardship will surely follow
yammengge	for us
lakawa bua mane	young boys

The man who sang this was an accomplished ritual spokesman, but he said he felt the *lawiti* was the best way to express his feelings of "fearful watching." Like an orphan, he sang of how his "heart felt weak" and profoundly *milla* ("humble, miserable"). Like an orphan, he could not communicate with, or engage in exchange with, the powerful individuals whose actions he observed. Like an orphan, he found himself on the outside looking in, forced to observe, watch, and wonder. Although he was an adult at the time he composed it, he represented himself as a wide-eyed child.

When I asked him whether they ever tried to perform "cursing *zaizos*" to cast out the Japanese, or to confront the Japanese with angry rhetoric, he looked at me with a bitter smile: "What use would that be? They had guns. They would have killed us." The only genre by which they tried to express their contemporary experience in ritual speech, he said, were *lawiti*: the songs of lament.

As the war became increasingly desperate for the Japanese, the moral standing of the official state declined even further in Sumbanese eyes. Since most of the civil servants collaborated with the Japanese, most state apparatuses were severely compromised in the eyes of the citizenry by the end of the war. Resentment of persons closely associating with Japanese was widespread. One song, for instance, was about a man who "benefited from Japanese occupation" (*"ata a uttu denga-ngge tana Nipo-na"*):

Doing "well" in the Age of Japan (1944)

Manu wolu na dede ndenga-ngge	He's a rooster who's doing well
tana Nipo-na	in the Japanese Age
Na dappa jadi di mata Kempena	He's the apple of the eye of the Kenpetai
di tana Nipo-na	in the Age of the Japanese
nggarro oro	Does he leave a trail?
nggarro wewe	Does he leave a trace?
na tollu-wangga lele	He's nesting his eggs
tandyonga laingo tana	in the smooth sandy office floors
na tenda-we . . .	he kicks his feet . . .
tanggollu tana lelingo	on their cool cement floors
na mbuka-we pintu lolo kawatu . . .	he can open the doors of barbed wire . . .

Once the province of charismatic Sumbanese men, the power of the Japanese was identified with "anger" (*mbani*). Unlike towering figures such as Lende Mbatu or Mbora Kenda, who were identified with the stability of the village and a certain legitimacy through kinship ties, Japanese might was construed as external, foreign, and entirely coercive. Most felt little connection to the Greater East Asian Co-prosperity Sphere (*Asia Timur Raya*) that Japanese propaganda told them they were soon to be part of. Since the Japanese military planned to use Sumba as a jumping off point for an attack on Australia, much work had to be done to build airstrips, bunkers, and roads. An extraordinarily large number of "foreigners" descended on the island (8,000 according to Kapita 1976). Many young Sumbanese were also pressed into forced labor (*kerja rodi*). Working in open fields with little food or water, with virtually no shelter during the day or night, many succumbed to exhaustion and disease. Those who did not die of illness were constantly under threat of beatings from the Japanese or Japanese-trained foremen. Word spread quickly in Sumba that conscription into the Japanese workforce was tantamount to a death sentence, and parents, spouses, and children all grieved to see a loved one carted off to work on the airstrips.

The following song was performed for me by its seventy-two-year old composer in 1988 as he recalled the *Tana Nipon*, "The time of the Japanese." It illustrates both the sense of intense personal feeling and the extreme detachment from the objects of observation that many survivors experienced. Note how the song's protagonist describes gazing upon the entire East Sumbanese city of Waingapu, then occupied by the Japanese, from a high mountain promontory, as his heart "turns inside out."

Working for the Japanese

"kako" ne ba hinna-nggu	"Go," I was told
wakelu paraingu	by the village headman
kapala dawa mbani	the leader of the Angry Foreigners
Londo ndoku takkanggo	I'm perched on high like one
ne lewatu mandatti	in a swidden guard house
na billaku takokoya	that glitters on high
Elo-po-we bawa	I gaze below at
Kaninggo Tana Darro	Kaninggo Tana Darro
na kaballeka ate raino	and my heart turns inside out
Elo-po-we dete	I look up at
Kamanggaminggitu Madyangga	Kamanggaminggitu Madyangga
Pangaddu We'engapu	As we approach Waingapu
we'e mata nda ma wara	my tears flow without stopping
Elo-po-we deta	As we look down upon Waingapu
touda kilo We'engapu	from three kilometers" distance
kambodda zonggu-na-ngga alu	we are herded with a stick into a circle
na ama dyawa mbani	by the Angry Foreign Father
Arro, ndewa raino-ku-ni	ah, my love, my soul,
yemmi-langge	all of you
nona, inna, amanggu	sweetie, Mother and Father!

In the face of the overwhelming might of the Japanese, the emotional response was that of "humility" (*milla ate*) and intense watchfulness, like "cats" and "rats" who do not sleep at night.

Wali ba-na male-ngge	returning late at night
na pikiru padyangu lebaru	he thinks long and hard:
hitto ole	We my friend
mata	have eyes
inda ndura-wi	that never sleep.
hitto ole	We my friend
ta-tudda-wa wodo	are like cats
inda mbeika-ngge	that never stop prowling.
hitto ole	We my friend
ta-ngenda-wa malawo	are like rats
inda ndura-kangge	that never sleep.
ta-pato'o manu maro	We listen for the distant cock crowing.
roo tutu rekka milla rekka	Alas, these are the considerations of a humble person
darra-na-we ate-na	with a meek heart.

Although the tone, tune, and general "meekness" and "humility" of the song strongly evoke the traditional "orphan," the composer immediately signals his audience that this is a hybrid genre by opening with the (Sumbanized) Indonesian phrase *pikiru padyangu lebaru* "think long and hard" (Indonesian: *"pikir panjang lebar"*). The entire song is thus framed as a reflection from within this foreign perspective. By positioning himself as a "humble person" with a "meek heart," the composer is clearly evoking traditional orphan imagery. The references to "eyes that never sleep," and the furtive watchfulness of cats and rats evoke a marginality, elusiveness, and quick-wittedness that are also an important part of the orphan's persona.

Increasing independence

After the Japanese departed in late 1945 (legend has it that they all departed overnight), efforts to encourage expressive participation in political affairs began again, including the sponsoring of ritual-speech oratory. The Sumbanese elite began to describe the previous colonial period in terms of a style of deference – *Ya Tuan, Baik Tuan*, "Yes sir, fine sir" – which they now rejected. They first announced their declaration of independence from the Netherlands church with an evening of oratory (*tau-na li'i*) (Krijger [1948] 1987: 512–513), singing, and feasting. They used a *zaizo* placation feast format complete with ritual oratory, in which church leadership and Christian deities were substituted for indigenous markers of audience participation and wholeness (cf. also May 1979). In another case, in 1966, festivities surrounding the inauguration of a small hydroelectric dam were accompanied by a ritual-speech performance of the history of the sacred spring on which the dam had been built. Although there were many disagreements about who was most qualified to perform the ritual, the final version has attracted little notice and few people can now remember it, even though it was composed in the style of an authoritative genre known as "words of the ancestors" (*li'i marapu*), a supposedly fixed and unchanging genre of ritual speech. This was apparently a one-time event, and there has been no call for this genre ever to be performed since.

Instead of traditional ritual-speech oratory, songs seem to have been the preferred mode of expressive participation in emerging Indonesian politics. Even today, ability to sing the Indonesian national anthem is taken as an important citizenship skill. In December of 1949, when a great procession was held in the West Sumbanese town of Waikabubak to celebrate the Renville accord, the end of fighting with Indonesia and the emergence of the United States of Indonesia, Luijendijk, the oldest of the Dutch evangelists present, was asked to give a speech to bless the newly independent republic, after which the national anthem of Indonesia was sung. Luijedijk could not resist a swipe at Sumbanese competence in their ability to act as citizens:

We feared that we would be accused as oppressors. But nothing happened; on the contrary . . . we were asked to join in the great meeting . . . I heartily and honestly congratulated them on their freedom. Indonesia Raya [the national anthem] was sung. Since my wife and I learned it by heart we could sing it much better than many of our Sumbanese friends. (Webb 1986: 122)

If the national anthem was a sympathetic means of participating in political affairs, a more oppositional form of verbal performance emerged in this period that attracted large crowds, the *kompanye*, "the campaign": usually consisting of Indonesian language, bullhorn-assisted monologues from the back of a truck or jeep on market days, these became increasingly commonplace in every subdistrict of the island in the years leading up to the elections of 1955. For most Sumbanese listeners, this represented a kind of oratorical spectacle that was novel and exciting. Although it was often carried out in Indonesian in the cities, many of the ideas were translated into songs and stories in the local languages. By 1959, in West Sumba there were six parties actively campaigning, Partai Kristen Indonesia (*parkindo*), Partai Nasional Indonesia (PNI), Partai Katolik, Partai Komunis Indonesia (PKI), Nahdatul Ulama (NU), Ikatan Pendukung Kemerdekaan Indonesia (IPKI) (Dapawole 1965).

All quiet on election day (1955)

On election day in 1955, the sudden silencing of expressive acts of citizenship – cheering, campaigning, and debating – was one of its most remarkable features. By all accounts, the atmosphere was extraordinary. Whole villages walked together as if moving towards a feast, yet there was no gong beating, no ululating by women, no noise; an atmosphere of eery solemnity pervaded the district headquarters as people congregated and waited for their names to be called.

The turnout was also remarkable. Why? Some argued that villagers feared reprisals if they did not support their candidates. Others said that they simply wished to exercise their new rights. Still others said that villagers were simply responding to the instructions of the village leaders. Whatever the case, on election day itself, the songs, cheering, and oratory ceased and men and women, some suckling their children, some old people with walking sticks, filed into the polling places one by one.

One of my close Weyewa friends helped organize this event in his subdistrict, and composed a song which describes in almost painstaking detail the experiences of proud and charismatic local leaders as they were made to walk in groups to the polling place, where they were instructed to sit quietly (without whispering). Each person kept an attentive ear for when his or her name was called off. They were then each led into the booth by the members of the election committee, who held the voter by the hand and waist. After they make their choice, the ballot is "folded in three," and "swished" into the box.

The Election (1955)
lurruta palona:	we sit straight:
"illa mbutti-mbutti kau!"	"don't you whisper!"

tamangga wóro mangga-ndi	we keep watch for one another
tarema wóro rema-ndi	we wait for one another
ngara pa-ka-tekki-na	for the names to be read off
ketua mbaita zurata	by the election chairman
na téngi-nda-ndi límma-nda	our hands are held
na waitondawe kendana	we are escorted by the waist
Palisi jaga keamana	by the police who protect the safety
kalíbbowanda kóro dana.	of our space in the polling booth.
Ta-wúkkemowe zúrata	We open the ballot
patírromúndi matanda	we scan it with our eyes
ta-líppata ka-tóuda-we	we fold it three times
zewwa-ku-we patti dana.	it swishes into the [ballot] box.
peiko-nda-we óle	What now my friend
tana merendeka?	of our free country?
tana índa líndaka	The landscape is not yet
ngara ndúka Indonesia.	smoothed out in Indonesia.

Experiences such as these do not seem to have inspired narratives organized around the more authoritative genres, such as *zaizo* or *li'i marapu* ("words of the ancestors"). The tale is being told in ritual speech, but via the melancholy genre of *lawiti* laments. What brings smiles to the listeners' faces when they hear this song is the excerpt which describes how everyone "sits straight" (*lurruta palona*), which echoes the words used to command little children to sit in order. Like little children, their hands are held as they approach the ballot box, but this time by police. Although this is a national ritual celebrating private choice, the clearly guided, and rather public nature of the event prompts the singer to echo ironically the words of the government by wondering about their use of the phrase *tana merendeka* ("free country"). It should be noted, however, that the singer is self-depre-cating in his use of the term, because although he knows Indonesian fluently, he deliberately over-Sumbanizes the pronunciation throughout the song, in a self-parody of their lack of sophistication. The laughter evokes an image of the hopelessness of Weyewa identification with the nation state. The lament, *peiko-nda-we ole*, "What now my friend?," is a characteristic line from orphan tales, in which the singer bewails his or her lack of control over the situation.

The "communist" coup and *milla* humility (1966)

Political campaigning continued unabated in the early 1960s in Indo-nesia, despite the fact that elections had been suspended by Sukarno's Guided Democracy, and frustration grew. This was a period of intense song development: not many of these songs are willingly performed today for fear of reopening a painful chapter in history. As in the rest of Indonesia, it was strongly ideological: accusations of *feodalisme*!

("feudalism!") were leveled at the ruling party while counter-accusations of *ateisme* ("Atheism!") were hurled back at the communists, with no apparent political means of resolving the growing tensions. While the Communist Party did in fact grow in influence in Sumba over the period 1955–1965, far more important to the experience of most Sumbanese was the powerful reaction against it in the aftermath of the attempted coup of September 30, 1965.

The number of communists (PKI) on Sumba was never really very large. Most of the key individuals in local party politics were from other islands in the east, such as Sabu, Roti, and Ambon, although most were Christians. According to interviews I had with people in West Sumba, organizers held meetings in the villages to talk about allowing the free use of "sacred" forests, providing land to the landless, freeing people from debt slavery, and widespread access to tools such as shovels and hoes.

While it is sometimes suggested that illiterate farmers in Indonesia in general and Sumba in particular had little understanding of the ideological agenda of communism, I think this oversimplifies the situation. Class differences in Sumba, particularly in the eastern districts, are in fact sharp and defining, and the class critique offered by PKI struck a resonant chord with the poor and alienated farmers and seriously frightened the elites. "They planned to kill us and take our land" one old aristocrat told me. So why weren't the killings and retribution worse on the island? For one thing, the bulk of Sumbanese still retained a sense of spectatorship regarding all levels of politics. To many of them, it was all a form of spectacle, since the economic integration with the center was so tenuous, they saw little motive for getting involved.

What the violence and backlash did communicate, however, was that the native elites and Christian leadership were firmly in control, and in many ways the traditional hierarchies had been restored. Christianity and elite control were OK; atheism was not. A new twist was added, however; it was not enough to prove one's affiliation by singing the national anthem, one had definitively to exclude other possibilities. To be a full citizen, one had to swear not to be a communist. By the early 1970s, to obtain an identification card that identified one as an individual and as a Warga Negara Indonesia (*WNI*), for instance, one needed a letter of "non-involvement in g30S (the September 30, 1965 coup attempt; *surat bebas g30s*).

In the middle of 1966, a judge was appointed to try the suspected communists. A list of suspects was prepared, consisting of A, B, C, and D categories. The A category reportedly consisted of the leaders (*pelopor*) who were said to have actively worked for the overthrow of the current regime. These people were to be arrested and executed; the B category consisted of those who were still active members of the party, but not leaders; these people were to be tried and exiled (*buang*; literally, "tossed away"). The C and D category were reserved for the Sumbanese who were more or less passively implicated in the activities of the PKI. For instance, those who had attended meetings, signed their names to lists, or even belonged to a village where PKI meetings were held. These individuals were in some cases rounded up in the village square and beaten publicly, sometimes while strung up upside down. Some thirty years later, they are still required to report to the police on a regular basis.

At least six PKI leaders were executed on a beach in Memboro, in northern Sumba, and 13 more on the beach in the south at Rua, but many more were imprisoned, permanently branded "traitor," and publicly vilified, stripped, and beaten. One victim of public ostracism composed this song. He describes how, like monkeys and wild pigs, he and other accused PKI supporters were rounded up and brought to what appeared to be a festival. After being beaten and exposed to the sun for two days and three nights, the singer asks a question that echoes ironically the young orphan girl's lament discussed earlier: how can he complain, since the government calls itself the Mother and Father, and Improver of the Sumbanese land and people? How can you criticize your own parents? Better just to accept one's fate, he concludes.

The reprisal (1966)
we were hit as our heads were ducked
this is surely a complicated cloth
they hit us till we fell face down
this is a yarn of extraordinary length
we were held there two nights
and three days
like
rice piled up in the sun
we were held there two nights
like
corn piled up in the sun;
well, how about this?
it was our own Mother cuddling us
well what can be said?
it was our own dear Father dandling us.

While the irony here is sharp, it is also complex. If the government is to claim for itself the title of Mother and Father of Tradition, then its actual behavior seems far from nurturing and parental. While this song appears as one of the boldest forms of sarcasm, none of the songs attempts really to engage the Indonesian government or state officials directly, or implies an alternative.

Festivals of Democracy: a local GOLKAR campaign rally in 1982

The work group becomes a discourse of citizenship

In the 1960s, when the central government of Indonesia was experiencing a crisis of legitimation fueled by runaway inflation, political unrest, and foreign intervention, the Sukarno and Suharto regimes gradually suspended many of the features of constitutional democracy. For those who experienced the relatively free and open – albeit flawed – elections of 1955, this posed, and indeed continues to pose a profound question as to the meaning of elections. If they were no longer going to be "LUBER" (Direct, Public, Free, Secret)[9], then why have them at all? The GOLKAR (Golongan Karya ["Functional Group"]) ruling party came up with a brilliant explanation: they would be "festivals of democracy" (*pesta demokrasi*).

The speaker in the following passage below expresses well this ritualistic understanding of citizen participation. He is appealing for 100 percent of the voters to support GOLKAR and implies that anything less will be an embarrassment to the village. To drum up support, he somewhat awkwardly asks that the audience acknowledge him with a *kabuara* before he continues any further. It is notable that not a single person attending this event was not a native Weyewa speaker, yet the speaker uses Indonesian to speak.

Tempat di sini untuk kami menyampaikan appa yang di tugaskan dan appa yang perlu kami sampaikan kepada bapa lingkungan PuuMawo ini, maka pertama-tama	we are here for us to convey what our tasks are and what we need to tell the head of the neighborhood of PuuMawo, so first of all
saya bertanya kepada semua yang hadir pada hari ini, appakah kamu semua yang hadir pada saat ini adalah orang, orang GOLKAR atau tidak, [hoo] kamu coba jawab. Orang GOLKAR semua? [golkar!] betul. Kalau orang GOLKAR, marilah kita sambut sebelum membukah kompanyinya kami pada hari ini lingkungan Puumawo ini. Kita *kabuara* dua dua kali dan disambut oleh seluruhnya	I ask everyone here on this day, are all of you attending at this moment Golkarians? or not? Go ahead and answer. Golkarians, all of you? [GOLKAR!] Right. If you're Golkarians, let's welcome the launch of our campaign today in the neighborhood of PuuMawo. Let's cheer two times with everyone responding.
larlarlarlarOOOOOoooo yawaoo	hip hip [audience] hooray!
larlarlarlarOOOOOoooo yawaoo	hip hip hooray!
Terima kasih kepada baba-bapa atas kesempatan dan pernyataan	Many thanks Gentlemen for this opportunity and the kind word

bapa-bapa dalam lingkungan PuuMawo.

Pertama-tama, kami datangi bapa dalam lingkungan di sini, dasarnya apa? sehingga kami sampai di tempat bapa-bapa mengiringi (?) bapa.

Dasar pertama adalah karena bapa-bapa pada kampanye di Elopada tida seluruhnya hadir . . .

Dasarnya kedua adalah kompanye di dalam desa Ombarande sendiri, bapa-bapa dan mama-mama ada yang tidak sempat hadir dan tidak sempat mendengar penjelasan appa oleh-oleh yang diberikan oleh bapa-bapa kita dari Tingkat Kabupaten maupun Tingkat Propinsi.

Dasar ketiga adalah tanggung jawab kami yang menerima suatu sirih pinang daripada Bapa Bupati pada tanggal tigabelas malam di desa WeiRame, pada waktu itu, saya mewakili desa Ombarande, menerima sirih pinang dari tangan Bupati, dan telah berjanji, bahwa rakyat desa Ombarande menusuk GOLKAR seratus persen.

Dan perjanjian ini berat bagi saya, karena saya sendiri yang menerima atas nama rakyat desa Ombarande.

Oleh sebab itu, sesudah kompanye pada tanggal duapuluh, kepala desa menyatakan lagi bahwa rakyat desa Ombarande "seratus persen," berarti tanggung jawab kami sudah dua orang, yang memeka.. meme . . . beban berat atas seratus persen pengakuan rakyat desa Omba rande.

kemudian lagi, pada pengakuan kepala lingkungan dan kepala oma, di dalam kompanye tanggal dua puluh empat bertempat di Ombakei di

of the gentlemen from the neighborhood of PuuMawo.

First of all, we've come to your neighborhood here, for what reason? Why have we come to mingle with you gentlemen?

The first reason is that in the Elopada campaign not all of you attended.

Second, in the campaign of the subdistrict of Ombarande itself, not all gentlemen and women made it, and there were some who didn't hear the details about what benefits will be given to us from our friends at the Regency and Provincial levels.

The third reason is my responsibility as one who received betel and areca nut from the Regent on the evening of the 13th in the WeiRame subdistrict at that time, I was representing the subdistrict of Ombarande and took the betel nut from the Regent's hand and promised that Ombarande would vote GOLKAR one hundred percent.

This promise weighs heavily on me because I took this oath in the name of the people of the subdistrict of Omba Rande.

Because of that, after the campaign on the twentieth, the subdistrict head said that the people of Ombarande would vote one hundred percent [GOLKAR], thus we bear a heavy burden [of delivering] 100 percent of the votes in the subdistrict of Omba rande.

Furthermore, with the approval of the subdistrict and hamlet heads, in the campaign of the twenty-fourth of May in Ombakei in

desa Ombakei di dalam desa
Ombarande, menyatakan satu
kebulatan tekad lagi bahwa
mereka itu menyatakan akan
seratus persen munusuk GOLKAR
di dalam tanggal empat mei
seribu sembilan ratus delapan
puluh dua nanti.

the subdistrict of Ombarande
they expressed their
commitment again that they
will come out with one hundred
percent votes for GOLKAR
on the date of May 4,
1982.

Sekarang adalah tanggung jawab kepala
sekolah, kepala desa, guru-guru
dan kepala lingkungan
dalam bertanggung jawabnya
seratus persenya GOLKAR, di
dalam kemenangannya adalah
satu-satunya jalur, suara kita yang
kita sampaikan, kita dapat
menyampaikan aspirasi kita
di dalam menyampaikan
segala keinginan kita kepada pihak
atasan atasan baik ketempat yang
jauh maupun ketempat yang
dekat maka untuk kita bertanggung
jawab ber-sama-sama lagi, dari
rakyat sehingga kepentigan untuk
rakyat dan kembali pula
kepada rakyat kami . . . datang . . .
lagi . . . pada . . . hari ini khususnya
rakyat PuuMawo

Now it is the task of the school
principals, subdistrict heads,
teachers and neighborhood
heads to responsibly deliver 100
percent GOLKAR
votes, for winning there is only
one way, and the word we
convey here we can tell you of
our dream to convey all of
our wishes to our superiors
who are both far and near
so for us to be responsible
all together, [we give] from
the people thus the needs of
people [are met] and it
returns to our people this day,
here in this especially the
people of PuuMawo.

inilah dasar-dasar kunjungan kami di
dalam kompanye kami pada hari ini.

These are the reasons for our
campaign visit today.

Formal democracy reception

In this text, the speaker describes the reasons for the meeting as (1) the
poor attendance at Elopada; (2) poor attendance at Ombarande; (3) the
explanation of obligations incurred by the head of the neighborhood
towards the Regent and Governor to vote 100 percent GOLKAR. Like
Lende Mbatu, and other orators, he is preoccupied with the problem of
audience completeness: if everyone does not attend, and the vote is not
"100 percent GOLKAR," then his authority is not assured. It is clear
that the problem of "completeness" is one that exists from the standpoint
of the leadership, not what it might mean for the local people. It is only
in the eyes of the party leadership, for example, that the number of
people in attendance were "insufficient": one man listening to this tape
suggested the leadership had wanted more people to *yawao*. The speaker
also stresses the importance of his obligations to his superiors, the
Regent and the Governor, with the silent assumption that the audience

will identify with his responsibilities and therefore support him by voting GOLKAR. His effort to explain why anyone should vote for GOLKAR rests on the party's premier status, not on anything the party might actually do for the citizenry *per se*.

Pemberton (1994) has suggested the "festival of democracy" could also be translated as "formal democracy reception": an event that presupposes a "reception" of something that has occurred prior to the ceremony, and whose purpose is largely to invite spectators to experience the largesse of the state in permitting them to endorse it. It suggests a formal event which the state is staging for the benefit of the citizens, an act of generosity and munificence, not an empowering institution by which the people get to select their own leadership and representation.

By insisting on the cheer "*yawao*" from its Sumbanese audience, GOLKAR functionaries effectively create an unstated image of the audience as "workers" and the government as labor recruiter, and the terms of their collaboration, *gotong royong*, "mutual self-help," which is a key platform of New Order legitimacy (Bowen 1986). As Reid and others have noted, the ability to mobilize populations for labor has long been the paramount expression of power in Southeast Asia, and this is especially true in Sumba, with its rich history of large-scale collective ceremonial activities such as stone dragging, house raising, and feasting (cf. Hoskins 1985).

Discussion

One Weyewa friend somewhat bitterly suggested that in fact the *yawao* was in some ways the only real form of political participation they had had in a recent election process:

Let's not bother any more with elections. Why even hassle with them? What, if I run for president, am I going to be elected? There's not even the slightest chance of that happening. Whatever's going to happen is going to happen. We might as well just *yawao* "give a collective cheer" and just go home [i.e. and not bother going to the polling booths].[10]

With biting irony, the Weyewa commentator places ritual responses – the *yawao* – at the very center of the political process for the West Sumbanese citizenry, and suggests that the process of actually casting the ballots themselves has little meaning. But his example – the *yawao* – suggests that while these elections may be quite predictable and have little value in determining leadership, the communicative relations expressed in the campaign process are far from meaningless.

If we view citizenship, for the moment, not as a legal and political relationship, but as communicative relation between individuals and a polity, then in Sumba the exemplary citizen in what they refer to

Plate 9   *Since the late 1980s, police (at right) are a routine part of the*
audience of many large-scale ritual speech events

somewhat nostalgically as "traditional society" was the *kabani-mbani*
("the angry man"), whose elite status and prestige was related to his
ability to recruit labor and animal sacrifices for large-scale feasting, ritual
performance, and ceremonial exchange. Subordinate citizens not only
communicated through participation in food and labor exchange, but
displayed their involvement through "audiencing practices" – acts of
ratification of speakership, acknowledging listenership, and elaborating
one's sense of spectatorship through laments and songs.

As the Regent's office restricts large-scale ceremonial exchange and
ritual spectacle, the Department of Agriculture, with the help of the
Army, has also successfully restricted the size of planting and harvesting
work groups by requiring new agricultural techniques. As economic
activity has become narrowed, specialized, and separated from religious
ritual, political expression, such as campaign oratory, has become
increasingly secular. It is now carried out in the Indonesian language.
Like oratory in the past, it tends to be elite, but the economic functions
are less public and open. Economic obligations resulting from such
oratory are increasingly covert and viewed as illegitimate, and are
described as bribery (*sogok*) and embezzlement (*makan uang*). But ritual
speech has not disappeared. It is no longer a primary vehicle for the

Plate 10   *Oration by the subdistrict head, 1994*

production of political meanings, but rather for the reception of them: in
this case, through the *yawao* and the *lawiti.*

Studies of political communication in Indonesia, such as those by
Pye, Karl Jackson and others, tend to focus on those who are producing
political meanings, not on how the meanings are received, evaluated,
and responded to. Even experienced political scientists such as Liddle
(1970) who study local reactions to political events employ standardized
political-science tools such as survey questionnaires, government statis-
tics, newspaper articles, and other academic and scientific devices for
interpreting local sentiment, rather than examining the native forms of
popular response and expression. Reception of political meanings in
Sumba is not a silent, passive activity, however. Political assent,
approval, and evaluation are often expressive acts mediated by local
genres of communication. While they may be dismissed by political
scientists as unreliable indicators of local political will, such audiencing
practices are a very real part of the political landscape in many parts of
Indonesia.

From the standpoint of studies of language shift, the example here
suggests the direction and nature of linguistic change have been crucially

mediated by linguistic ideologies about the importance of audience completeness. These beliefs have been projected from the domain of agricultural and religious ritual on to the realm of national politics in ways that reveal and create new sentiments and structures of marginality. The fundamental character of this change could be missed, however, if one fails to recognize the functional diversity of speech forms in a language. Second, despite government efforts to support ritual speech – through missionary sponsorship of hybrid forms, government establishment of "*bahasa daerah*" as a curriculum item, there has been little interest in it. However, the *lawiti* and *yawao* are important because of the way in which they are mediated by an ideology of linguistic reception. Hearers have an impact on the direction of linguistic change.

5
IDEOLOGIES OF PERSONAL NAMING
AND LANGUAGE SHIFT

Samuel Roos, Sumba's first Dutch administrator in the nineteenth century, was struck by the fact that even friendly Sumbanese would not directly tell him their names. "If you ask a Sumbanese his name, he laughs and gives no answer. If others are present, then he says, 'ask him,' and points to that person." (Roos 1872: 70). Even though the names are not secret, and they are proud to have their names mentioned by others, it is somewhat awkward for a Sumbanese to tell you his or her name. Roos, as a European outsider, assumed that the function of names was to refer to particular individuals. The names for him were primarily a linguistic tool for individuating particular persons. Sumbanese – particularly the high-status ones with whom he describes his early encounters – assumed that the role of a name is a more social one, in which names are actually in the custody of others, who use them for address and classification.

The problem Roos encountered is not unique to Sumba. Proper names pose special problems for studies of language change in general: should they be considered a narrowly personal, linguistic possession or a more broadly social and collective phenomenon? What is the relation, if any, between name changes and linguistic marginalization? In some cases of language shift, personal names seem to answer to a different call, as it were, from the rest of the language. They do not necessarily change in the same way, or at the same rate, as other features of language. For example, Allan Taylor described how among the Native American Gros Ventre people attach great value to "possessing an authentic Indian name" (1989: 171) as a way of socially classifying themselves, yet very few of them have extended their competence in the language to other areas of the lexicon and grammar. By contrast, in the case of the Gaelic speakers described by Watson (1989), the English naming system has, for several generations, already had a "massive influence" on the "naming system in Irish and Scottish Gaeltachts" which, in the long term, Watson speculates, "is bound to have had an adverse effect on attitudes of speakers of the Gaelic languages to their native tongue" (1989: 58, n9).

In this chapter, I examine the role that proper names play in linguistic shift in the Weyewa highlands. As in previous chapters, I argue that focussing on ritual speech reveals and highlights the crucial role that linguistic ideologies have in organizing these changes. Beginning with a description of prestige naming, I analyze the varieties of native naming practices and show how they reflect not only a preoccupation with renown, but also with social distance and affiliation rather than simply the identification of unique individuals. In the second section of this chapter, I explain the adoption of the more highly differentiated and individuating Christian naming practices, a shift I associate with a process of "indexicalization" whereby a sign once viewed as designating a cultural category comes to be viewed as functioning ostensively and pragmatically: akin to an act of pointing. While prestige names have lost some of their classificatory functions as exemplary categories of prestige, their individuating, indexicalizing functions – as in the names of race-horses, pick-ups, and businesses – have taken on an additional connotation: that of autonomy.

The ethnographic study of proper names

Although the study of proper names has a long and distinguished history in philosophy, these linguistic phenomena pose special problems for ethnographers (Searle 1958; Kripke 1972; Bean 1980). Allerton (1987) has observed that it is difficult to know what to do with proper names analytically: are they individual possessions? Or are they social, collective, and conventional? In a paper in 1983, Mertz developed an argument that recasts these issues in a new way. She argues for the need to appreciate the relation between the pragmatic and semantic functions of names. On the one hand, names are semantic in that they serve to classify people into categories. For example, Geertz, in a famous study (1973), argues that the Balinese system of teknonymy – naming oneself after one's offspring (e.g. "mother of so-and-so) – is such a powerful social-classification system that it gradually erases individuality, even a certain perspective on time. It results in the individualizing, personal name of the parent being forgotten altogether, thus producing a shallowness of genealogical knowledge that is flexible and strategically manipulable in times of successional crises.[1]

On the other hand, since at least the time of John Stuart Mill, it has long been customary in linguistics and philosophy to stress the pragmatic functions of a name as a relation between the sign and the interpreter. Lévi-Strauss criticizes C. S. Peirce and Bertrand Russell for such views: Peirce for "defining proper names as 'indices' " and Russell for "believing that he had discovered the logical model of proper names in demonstrative pronouns." For Lévi-Strauss, "this amounts in effect to allowing that the act of naming belongs to a continuum in which there is an imperceptible passage from the act of signifying to the act of pointing" (1962: 215, quoted in Mertz 1983: 55). In this view, carried to its extreme, names are a device for pointing and reference. While this perspective has its appeal, it erases all consideration of the role names play in what Geertz calls "symbolic orders of person definition."

What is needed is a way of understanding the relationship between these two functions. To appreciate this, Mertz argues that it is crucial to understand that "personal names play somewhat different roles in address and reference" (1983: 56). Based on her fieldwork in a formerly Gaelic-speaking community in Cape Breton, Nova Scotia, she observes that "in accordance with a community ideal of solidarity, the Cape Breton only allows familiar names in address. Thus a speech situation is always defined as an exchange between intimate equals" (1983: 70). However, the use of names in reference is changing significantly: Gaelic names are disappearing. The kinds and direction of the disappearances can be attributed to "changes in community boundaries and notions of 'insider' and 'outsider' definition. The more classificatory names – those that require community cooperation and 'insider' knowledge for formation and use – are falling out of use" (1983: 68). Thus while in address, familiar names were always used, the complex and evocative system of descriptive, classificatory, community, and kin names are dwindling, largely because they presuppose too much knowledge from the speakers, who are increasingly unfamiliar with the personal particulars of the individuals in the community.

In the Weyewa highlands, speakers are moving away from naming practices that require extensive insider, background, and ceremonial knowledge and toward names that uniquely identify individuals – names that point them out of the crowd, as it were. This process, which I call "indexicalization," has not eliminated all forms of local naming. One of the most classificatory and presupposing areas of the naming system – the prestige names, such as "horse names" – no longer involves the obligatory use of a situation-specific name as an alternative way of classifying a person in address. Now, such prestige names are everyday ways of *referring* to businesses, bemos, and racehorses (available for use on any occasion) in ways that are supposed to evoke their special, individuated nature as an indication of their autonomy.

As the Dutch imposed their ideas about bureaucracy on the island of Sumba, drawing on principles developed for the urban, complex societies of Europe – where if you say "ask him," "he" might not be able to answer – the responsibility for the custody of the name gradually shifted back to the owner, and literary proof had to be offered of ownership (in the form of ID cards, baptismal records, driver's license, marriage records, etc.). Sumbanese describe such names used primarily for reference as their *ngara pajak* ("tax name"), i.e. the names used on their census records (see Ventresca 1995). This reflects a shift towards more European-type language ideologies. As Silverstein and others have often observed, European speakers reveal a tendency to see language as essentially a device for transparent reference and making propositions about the things referred to (1979). Rumsey, for instance, argues that Australian aboriginal languages do not dichotomize talk and action, or words and things (1990). M. Rosaldo (1982), also argues that Ilongots think of language in terms of action rather than denotation and reference. Christian names (*ngara Keristen*), when Weyewa began to adopt them in large numbers in the late 1980s and early 1990s, came to be seen as primarily a way of referring to the person, and were not seen as a vehicle for address or for classifying a person in relation to prestige-linked behaviors, such as feasting, oratory, and ceremonial exchange. It classifies a person implicitly as "modern" and a subject of the state.

Traditional name-seeking: Rato Kaduku

As a way of telling the story of the transformation of the Weyewa ritual naming system, the case of Ngongo Kaduku figures in the "early" and "traditional" part of the narrative, and thus is a logical place to begin. Ngongo Kaduku was a man with a distinctive name, fierce, "angry" eyes but an impish smile, and a beautiful, gravelly voice that produced some of the most eloquent ritual speech in the Weyewa highlands. His demeanor, appearance, and reputation exemplified Weyewa ideas about "tradition," and provides a glimpse of Weyewa ideas about "name-seeking" behavior in the past. The only son of a wealthy "angry man," he was often simply known by his father's "horse name," *Kaduku*, (literally, "foreleg"), but he preferred it when the extra label, *Rato* ("priest") was added, as in *Rato Kaduku*. Draped in distinctive black cloak, leaning on a staff, with his peaked red headcloth, and smelling of fresh coconut oil (he insisted on daily massages), he was always inspiring to see, hear, and smell! He had a wicked sense of humor about almost everything, but he really cared how he was addressed.

He had spent much of the previous fifty years "seeking a name" (*wewa ngara*) in anticipation of his death, which occurred in 1992. Name-seeking was a process that in Weyewa signified economic, ritual, and political risk-taking and display. He boasted that when the Dutch East Indies army (KNIL) arrived in Wai Dindi in 1906, he had already made a name for himself as a farmer by filling ten grain "silos" (*kapettela*) with rice in one season. Stimulated partly by the need for cash to pay the Dutch-instituted "head tax," he began a career as a gambler, and made a

Plate 11   *Kaduku: an angry man who made a "name" for himself*

name for himself, winning and losing his inheritance several times back and forth. "I had five wives, but I lost all of them due to gambling. One day I'd win the cattle for the brideprice, the next day I'd lose it again, and the negotiations would fall apart. I lost five wives this way."

When he finally settled down, in the 1950s, his only wife bore him three children. He began "seeking a name" in ritual and spiritual matters. He was a sought-after ritual speaker, and he used his knowledge of ceremonial and genealogical lore to justify his claims on the wealth of distant relatives. Because he had sponsored a "house building" renewal of his ancestral home, dragged a tombstone for himself, and carried out a *woleka* "celebration feast" – all highly public, visible, and expensive events that attract much attention – he was, until his death in 1992, widely addressed as *Rato*, an honorific title glossed broadly as "priest" but which is less a designation of a social function than an indication of respect for ritual achievements.

In August of 1989, he was at the center of controversy when a jeepload of police drove into a Weyewa village and abruptly brought a ritual-speaking event to a halt. As in the police raid on a Balinese cockfight described by Geertz (1973), local officials stopped a contest over status and masculine identity requiring the slaughter of animals. In this instance, the competition involved not cockfights but notorious water buffalo feasts accompanied by poetic oratory, prayers, and recitations. As it happened, no one (myself included) ran in panic as the police jumped out with their guns drawn.

Instead of running in fear, the crowd surged forward to watch as the police – poorly paid young men from neighboring islands in starched military uniforms – loudly and condescendingly lectured Kaduku in the Indonesian national language on the importance of conserving one's cattle so as to make a better life for all Indonesia. Like parents admonishing children, they scolded the proud man for feasting in ways that are "wasteful and backward"; they observed darkly that while no crime had yet been committed, excessive slaughter was against the law. The already rendered pig meat could be distributed and taken home, but after that, the ranking officer explained to the crowd, everyone should "disperse," and go home.

To make sure that no more animal sacrifice occurred, the police sat themselves down on the veranda of the host's house and waited as they were served a meal of rice, boiled pork and coffee. Much scurrying around accompanied this abrupt turn of events, and all eyes were on Kaduku for his response. Everyone knew that this charismatic, powerful, aged man and renowned ritual spokesman was expecting to receive a very large tusked hog in exchange for the dramatic slaughter of a water buffalo in the square. Kaduku was trying – unsuccessfully it seemed – to hold back shouts of "anger" (*mbani*) and frustration at the police intervention, I learned, because he had already planned to keep this large and renowned animal, give it a name, and if possible have it slaughtered at his own funeral.

One official later shook his head on hearing this story, "that's just the problem with all these traditional leaders, they're only trying to make a name for themselves, they don't care about the future." By giving the pig a special couplet name, Kaduku would increase his own renown, and the name would live on after both he and the animal were gone. The official said he did not object to Weyewa seeking prestige in "modern" ways, such as buying a Honda, a Seiko or Rolex wristwatch, or Gudang Garam cigarettes. When I wondered aloud whether this wasn't also a kind of name-seeking, he conceded that these were also prestige items, but it is not their names that are important, he felt, but the objects they referred to, which are seen as offering benefits to the consumer – transportation, time, and individual enjoyment. In contrast, he regarded the seeking of prestige and a name as an overemphasis of one's "name," renown and other rather flashy superficialities.

The feasting system now facing official criticism has its cultural and psychological roots in what Weyewa call "seeking a name" (*wewa ngara*; in Indonesian, *cari nama*) by which one bestows on oneself a couplet name for an object – a horse, a dog, a pig, a knife, an ear pendant – acquired in a feast. One can also inherit such a name from one's father or other agnatic forebears, although the name is usually bestowed in a feast marking a transition of some kind: for example, the overcoming of hardship, an abundant harvest, a successful marriage, the establishment of a new homestead village. The owner was then entitled to be so addressed, or sung about in praise songs, using the names of the objects. These names not only established indexically the wealth and status of the owner, but also the inalienability of the object and thus spiritual connection with the owner. In an example discussed below, an angry man who died in 1971 liked to be called, among other things, *kamilla la moddu wawi*, "Midget the pig."

Since the launching of Suharto's New Order in the wake of the events of 1965, the emphasis has been on economic development and spiritual alignment with the nation/state. Names are a little investigated but revealing way to examine the shift in language use from ritual speech to more Indonesian-based usages that reflect profound shifts in individual identity. This chapter examines the ways in which ritual-speech names were bestowed as an integral part of the exchange-based identities of "angry men." Christian names, on the other hand, signify more individual membership in a confessional community. Couplet names have not disappeared, but are used for place names (e.g. Nyura Lele Mayongo, We'e Paboba Yarra for Weyewa), bemos, businesses, and racehorses, and not to the owner himself.

To understand the political economy of "naming" in Weyewa, we need to understand first how the naming system, to borrow Geertz's succinct phrase, is "historically constructed, socially maintained and individually applied" (1973). Modes of address vary according to several factors, including situation, rank, intimacy, gender, education, and genre of speaking. Sobriquets (*ngara lemba*) are commonly performed as part of ceremonial songs, and are expressed as part of couplets or ritual speech. As the feasting system declines in importance in social life, Sumbanese have increasingly begun to adopt Biblical names for people and Indonesianized words for economic goods. These shifts can be understood not only in relation to economic development, but also shifts in personal identification: as Christians, and as educated (*pánde*) people.

Weyewa native naming practices

In the 1960s, the vast majority of Sumbanese were still ancestor worshippers and not affiliated with any world religion. Their native system of personal naming was a dynamic one, and affected by the history of economic and political changes, but only slightly by Christianity. Since one of the functions of naming in both modern and traditional society is to indicate status, it is important that the class structure of the new Indonesian society was beginning to emerge. The traditional elite were converting to Christianity, and adopting new names too.

One of the crucial semantic, classifying functions of the traditional naming sytem was to create boundaries between in and out groups. One of the ways in which this is accomplished is through the system of "hard" and "soft" names, which is based on a distinction that roughly coincides with "public" and "private.'

Personal names: the "soft" and the "hard"

Ngara ("name") in Weyewa refers primarily to a verbal label that is conventionally established (given or taken) as legitimately denoting an object through a culturally recognized act of bestowal. If the Balinese naming system emphasizes the classifying and ceremonial functions of naming as a system of person definition, the Weyewa system suggests an openness to the potentially problematic relationship between name and individual, and a general encouragement of individuating nomenclatures associated with status and prestige. Although it is more unstable, and allows for more changes, it also permits individual embellishment and particularizing, especially later on in life, in conjunction with the feasting system.

Unlike Balinese personal names, which are highly individualized and unique from birth, Weyewa babies are traditionally given personal names from a rather limited stock. In a computer count of the names used in the 1992 census records for a subdistrict, I found that the vast majority of men (72 percent) possessed one of just six forenames, and nearly the same was true for women (79 percent possessed one of eight names). Second names were only slightly more differentiated. Such names are usually drawn from the same pool of names during a short ceremony held eight days after a child is born. Agnatic relatives and the mother's brother (*loka*) are assembled at the house of the child, and a pig is slaughtered. A green coconut is opened up, and a finger is placed in the milk, and then put to the mouth of the baby. Names of appropriately gendered ancestors are listed first, and if the baby sucks the finger (or in some cases, the mother's breast) while a name is uttered, then that name is chosen; it "fits" (*na moda*). To "revive an ancestral name" (*pa-kedde-we ngara umbu-waika*) is regarded as particularly desirable. To arrive at the second name, the process is repeated. The child is then said to have a "namesake" (*tamo*) relationship with whoever shares its binomial, but particularly to that ancestral person. However, if the child later becomes sick, a divination may be conducted, and one possible cause may be that the child's *tamo* does not agree to having his or her name used. Because of their individual characteristics, and particular personality features, they "do not fit" (*nda na modda-ki*). The assumption is that name and referent should be virtually inseparable (Forth 1983).

Table 3 shows how traditional personal names are typically two-syllable, and generally different for men and women. Names are typically binomial, with the last names selected at the naming ceremony also. In many common names, the same vowels are used in both first and second syllables: for example, *Ngongo, Mbulu, Mbili, Lende, Wini*; women's names seem somewhat more likely to end in *i* – *Wini, Lali, Soli, Koni* – but there are men's names that do also, for example, *Dadi, Bili*. The first name is more closely associated with the individual's identity, and may be used when addressing people of one's own age and status, and younger. Personal names are more commonly used by peers, age-mates, and elders. When addressing an older person, it is more appropriate to use a teknonym, title, or avoid direct address altogether.

Most personal names are considered *ngara ndakke*, or "soft names," and each has a "hard" or "crude" name (*ngara katto*) associated with it. Much as Henry has Hank as a nickname, so *Ngongo* is conventionally associated with *Ngila* as a "hard" name.[2] These hard names are only used in address by those with whom one has the most intimate relations: one's wife of many years, and perhaps reciprocally among elderly siblings. Furthermore, the very use of the name presupposes a situation of familial, in-group intimacy among the hearers and is otherwise awkward. Thus in most settings, "people get angry when they hear their 'hard names'." I was told to be especially mindful of this when I was learning to speak Weyewa so as not inadvertently to offend anyone. Regardless of one's intentions or who the audience is, all speakers are responsible for not uttering a person's "hard" name in the earshot of the owner in public settings; such an act is cause for offense. It is said to be a provocation used in battle or in wild boar hunts. On the occasions when I have heard such names used, bearers respond with embarrassed laughter; but I have seen them occasionally get quite irritated, as when a child uses such a name in the presence of his or her parent to be disrespectful or deliberately insulting. On the other hand, older adults who know each other well sometimes address one another reciprocally with such names, and older married couples speak to each other in this way in domestic contexts. Children sometimes devise ways of using these names indirectly as taunts, deliberately violating the boundaries of inside and outside. I once heard a boy tease his friend named Ngongo by playing on the homonymy between the "crude name" for Ngongo – *Ngila* – and the word meaning "to whinny': He mocked his friend by calling out to him repeatedly – "Hey, *Ngongo*, don't listen to that horse *whinnying*," "hey Ngongo, *don't* listen to that horse *whinny!* etc. [*E Ngongo, ndu rengekana na ndara a* **ngila**. *E Ngongo, ndu rengekana na ndara a* **ngila**! etc]."

Using palatalization to distinguish between address and reference

The Weyewa, Lauranese, and Kodinese languages use palatalization to distinguish between the name of someone being addressed and someone being spoken about. In these cases, the initial consonant of the proper name is palatalized.[3] Thus the names of the heroes of a common folktale, *Ndelo* and *Kazi*, are typically pronounced as *Ndyelo* and *Kyazi*, since they are being spoken about. This creates a boundary between in and out groups in the sense that defining a name as being spoken in reference by definition denotes someone *not* in the speech situation, and thus as someone classified as an out-bounded other (Mertz 1983: 70)

Namesake system

People who share the same name address one another as *tamo* ("namesake"), not by their respective names. They are thought to have a special bond, as between a person and her ancestral namesake. Although neither women nor men change their names at marriage, both are expected to identify with the spouses" name in important ways. For example, two women whose husbands have the same name are said to be *tamo* ("namesakes"). The same is true for men with wives of the same name. Thus if, for example, Robert and Paul both have a wife named Barbara, they call each other "namesake" (*tamo*). A male child who is named after a living grandparent is called *tamo ama* ("namesake of father"), and a girl is called *tamo inna* ("namesake of mother"), until the grandparent passes away, after which time the name may be used. It is interesting that the construction of namesake label is from the perspective of the namer, not the named. For example, a small child labeled *tamo ama* ("namesake of father") is *not* the namesake of its own father, but the father of the child's parent; to be accurate from the child's perspective, the label would have

Table 3. *Men's and women's personal names*

Men's names		Women's names	
"soft name"	"hard name"	"soft name"	"hard name'
Malo	*Mette*	*Peda*	*Roki*
Zairo	*Zokke*	*Ninda*	*Rede*
Lende	*Rua/Ngedo*	*Leda*	*Ponne*
Mbulu	*Mbennaka*	*Dada*	*Tiala*
Ngongo	*Ngilla*	*Koni*	*Mbiri*
Mbili	*Kurri*	*Zoli*	*Lawe*
Dairo	*Lade*	*Wada*	*Lew*
Mbora	*Tyalo*	*Lali*	*Pindula*
Mete R	*angga*	*Winni*	*Tannge*
Lelu	*Atu*	*Louru*	*Ladde*
Dowa	*Kelo*	*Mbuta*	*Ngapu*
Mali	*Keba*		

had to be *tamo ama kaweda* ("namesake of grandfather"). The namesake system thus assumes a sociocentric (rather than egocentric) perspective to meaning as a form of classification that decenters the individual.

Teknonyms

Teknonyms are used by both men and women upon the birth of a first child. Thus a woman becomes *inna Lende* ("mother of Lende") and her husband is *ama Lende* ("father of Lende"). The eldest child is usually selected as the source name of the teknonym, regardless of whether it is a boy or girl, or whether it survives to adulthood. This unites the married couple in address; they are thus identified publicly in terms of the child they share. Since there are literally thousands of *Lende*s in the Weyewa-speaking region, however, teknonyms are not particularly helpful in differentiating identity. It does occasionally happen that a parent will take on the name of a younger child to show disapproval of the eldest, or to show particular favor towards a younger child. Teknonyms are also used in conjunction with Christian names; thus one can be called *Ama Ester* ("father of Esther"). They are most commonly used as names of address for adults of childbearing age; occasionally, if the child becomes famous, an older adult may retain the teknonym into old age. The Weyewa do not normally adopt teknonymously the names of their grandchildren.

Ngara Lemba ("sobriquet")

Sobriquets, or assumed names, are an arena of personal labeling that permits individual differentiation. This general category may include the sorts of names mentioned above, but may also include some other unique names that have to do with some peculiar feature of the bearer's personality, biography, or wealth. As relatively undifferentiated human beings, "without a liver" (*nda pa-ate-ki-po*), children rarely possess a *ngara lemba*. For most adults, a teknonym serves as a term of address. But if a person stands out in some way, a differentiating term may be applied.[4] For example, Petrus stands over six foot tall. Although I have never heard it applied in his presence, he is commonly referred to as *Malo Mandeta* ("Malo the Tall"). The husband of my housekeeper during my stay from 1978–1980 came gradually to be known as *Mbili Dawa* ("Mbili [of the] Foreigners") not only because he stayed with me, but because he often spent time in Waikabubak working for and staying with the Chinese. Mbora Kenda was for a time referred to as *Mbora Umma Potto* ("Mbora with the bamboo [roof]") because he made an unusual-looking roof out of those materials. A notable Dutch *controleur* "civil administrator" was known as *marommba wawi mbolo* ("gentleman [who eats] whole pigs"), for his prodigious appetite.

Prestige names: *Ngara ndara* ("horse names")

While names referring to attributes of one's body or behavior are not always embraced by the recipient of the label, names referring to possessions, particularly horses, dogs, ear pendants, water buffalos, pigs, spears, or swords, are honorifics. Sometimes generically described as "horse names" (*ngara ndara*), they are used for addressing individuals on formal occasions, and for praising them indirectly in songs, and in eulogies. Such names typically have a trinomial structure to them:

> Attribute 1 (Adjective) + Attribute 2 (Nominal) + Head Noun:
> *Dappa Doda, Karambo*, "Swift Conqueror, the Water Buffalo"[5]
> *Pera Dangga, Bongga* ,"Trading Escort, the Dog"[6]
> *Mette Ngora, Bongga*, "Black Snout, the Dog"
> *Ropa Lara, Numbu* ,"Spans the Road, the Spear"[7]
> *Kaweda Ngara, Keto*, "Ancient Name, the Knife"
> *Ndende Kiku, Ndara*, "Upright Tail, the Horse".

Attribute 2 (nominal) may sometimes be derived from a verb, as is common in some Native American naming traditions (Mithun 1980). In "Swift Conqueror, the Water Buffalo," *doda* is a verb meaning "to flatten, crush, vanquish." In this context, however, it functions like a noun. Such names may be inherited from an ancestor, or they may be acquired as a result of some special meaningful occasion accompanied by feasting.

Onvlee, in an essay on the "Significance of livestock in Sumba," sheds some light on the meaning of personal possessions:

> personal possessions are singularly linked with the life of their owner. They are not impersonal; rather they are part of the person who owns them and are related to his life in a particular way. A person's betel-nut case is a good example. In west Sumba when someone leaves behind his betel-nut case, his parang [knife], or cloth, his *ndewa* ("vitality") is affected: *nakoba dengangge ndewara* [*sic*].
> ("His ndewa becomes powerless") (1980: 196)

He notes further that there is a "certain opposition to the sale of anything associated with the land or with the personal identity of the owner" (1980: 199).

I would also add that personal objects such as betel pouches, knives, cloths, horses, and buffalo are used as resources for the personal autonomy for boys in particular and a source of differentiating oneself from one's mother and father.[8] Boys first acquire a cloth and a knife at around age thirteen or fourteen; at about the same time, they begin to chew betel and areca nut and so need a pouch. In an insecure world, differentiating one's identity and declaring one's autonomy from the nurturing environment of one's "house" (*umma*) was seen to require some "anger" and "boldness" (*mbani*) on the part of the boy. One of the ways in which this is done is through the acquisition of objects through trade and negotiation, contexts that presume a potential for conflict.

Powerful and rich men and some women in Weyewa are set apart from the rest of their peers by their names, their goods, their words, and their capacity to influence others and control their world. Their charisma comes partly from their "anger, boldness" and its capacity to motivate, attract, and repel people. Having a horse and dog name is part and parcel of this influence. To be truly *mbani*, it is not enough simply to possess animals, one must be named after certain selected ones. When one acquires sufficient wealth that one can devote valuable livestock and goods to the sole purpose of furthering one's prestige (since such animals cannot be traded), then these animals are given evocative names (e.g. "razorgrass, the spear"). Once bestowed, the names are the preferred form of address on ceremonial occasions. For the interlocutors of the name-bearer, on ritual occasions, it forces them to position themselves by how much respect they show.

Having oneself named and addressed with the label of certain personal objects is one of the highest forms of prestige; in the past, some men were named after their slaves, although this is no longer done (but see Forth 1981).[9] Sometimes these names are handed down from a male grandparent on the father's side; one can also give oneself a horse or dog name, often as a way of commemorating a feast or a particularly good harvest, or some successful event.

Horse or possession names are more than a way of denoting a person, they are a means of conjuring the memory of the individual. Listening to Weyewa talk about a powerful man or woman, one does not often hear connected, temporally organized biographical narratives about events during a lifetime; instead one hears about clusters of belongings, radiating out, as it were, from a charismatic center. These powerful nuclei both attract and cast a shadow on social inferiors. The life histories are organized as tales about personal objects, flowing in and out. Powerful men – *ata attu* ("core person") as such men are sometimes called – are idealized as never alone, as always accompanied by their possessions, slaves, prancing horses, barking dogs, and elegant clothing. Like gigantic banyan trees, big men take care of those who are beneath their protective canopy.

From the standpoint of an addresser, by invoking the name of a prized possession, one avoids directly mentioning the name of the individual, which is regarded as too impolite. Plainly and openly speaking the name of revered individuals or spirits is forbidden: indeed, a common way of referring to the Creator Spirit is "whose name cannot be uttered, whose title may not be mentioned" (*"nda pa-zuma ngara, nda pa-tekki tamo"*). By naming a person in terms of a possession, one mediates the relation between speaker and the addressee.

A central part of the identity of these men had to do with their belongings. When great men and women died in Sumba, their lives were eulogized with lists of their belongings. The following song (*matekula*) eulogizes a charismatic angry man named Mbaiyo Pote, who died in 1971 and whose remains were reburied and moved to a grander tomb in 1984 in a ceremony I attended.

Wu Mbaiyo-o la Pote Paza	Oh Mbaiyo, braided mane
Pote-o-ngge Paza Ndara	"braided mane" the Horse
Padiera-ngge Lombo azu	"Forgive me Lombo" the Dog[10]
Kadienggi-ola Mbolu alli	Watchful, his little brother
Wu Mbaiyo-o la kako enggo	O Mbaiyo you went everywhere in joy
Kako-o la Enggo Keto	"Go in Joy," the Knife
Puwa la Tana-o, Mane	Crush the Earth, the Water Buffalo[11]
Kamila-o la Modu wawi	Midget, the Pig

The song continues to describe other named objects such as "Razorgrass the Spear," "Whiteplume, the Sword," "Impenetrable, the Shield," "Renown, the Scarf," and so on.

When I heard this song performed – late at night, prior to a feast for the descendants of the deceased – I was initially very puzzled when I heard people weeping: why would they cry over a list of objects? Why didn't the song say anything about Mbaiyo Pote as a person? How could this song have been powerful enough to have evoked any memories of the man at all?

These names are highly evocative of Mbaiyo Pote as a person, not only because of Weyewa beliefs about the connection between a name and its referent but because the act of naming such goods is an important and distinctive act of self-definition, a way in which Mbaiyo Pote differentiated himself. The name not only described his distinctive identity, it constituted it by positioning himself in the Weyewa moral economy. He is addressed as "braided mane," and the next line elaborates that "braided mane" is the name of his horse. He is then addressed as "Forgive me Lombo," and the next line elaborates that this is the name of his dog. Mbaiyo is described as someone who went everywhere in joy, a name that he gave to his knife.

In another eulogy I heard, a man sang of his mother and father:

wu Lende Tollu Lena	O Lende Floating Egg
Pandiende-o Lawi bendila	"Rests Upright" the rifle
wu inna-o Ngota	O Ngota, my mother
mbia kaka wawi	"White Tusk" the pig
mazewa-ngge mara Rua	We part like the low tide at Rua
ta woleka ta Wone	We disperse as after a feast at Wone
ne diangga-o dadi numbu	"Created Long" the spear
kyambu baru, teko	"New Goals" the sword
toma-na padou-mu-ngge ndende ndara	you've reached the horses" water hole
dukki-na pangazu–mu bongga mette	you've arrived at the bed of the black dog

In this song, the singer laments the loss of both his father, Lende, and his mother, Ngota. He refers to both of them indirectly by mentioning their possessions, "Rests Upright" the rifle, and "White Tusk" the pig. The rifle, associated with aggression and anger, is an exemplary "male" object that stands for his fathers" boldness as a *kabani-mbani*. The pig, "White Tusk" is an emblematic "female" object, since it is typically women who must carry out the labor-intensive task of feeding these animals each day. He bids both his parents farewell, likening their departure to the receding tide on the beautiful sandy beaches of Rua in southwestern Sumba, and to the conclusion of a feast at dusk across the open, lonely plains surrounding the village of Wone, where dispersing guests seem to disappear over the horizon as they leave. Since men are the ones with most of the wealth in the family, when he continues to eulogize his parents, he concentrates on male objects. He sings of "Created Long" the spear – no doubt a spear of prodigious length – and "New Goals" the sword – probably a sword that was named following some major accomplishment.

Personal relationships to belongings are constituted by the naming relationship. The act of bestowal results in a personal relationship that requires the owner to take the object out of circulation. As a person grows and becomes more of a unique individual, with more and more control over their environment, part of their identity includes the objects that they control. It is as though a person's identity radiates outward and gradually comes to encompass valued objects metonymically associated with that individual, such as spears, knives, horses, dogs, etc. The image of a potent center, surrounded by a constellation of valuable and indeed magical objects, is one that resonates with descriptions of the classical Indic kingships, in which power is associated with an exemplary center.

As Onvlee suggests, such a personal relationship with possessions is seen as incompatible with sale or exchange. When Weyewa name their horses, dogs, and cloths, for instance, they take them out of circulation. Selling (*batta*) or exchanging them is regarded as taboo (*erri*). That is not to say that it cannot be done, but it is not approved of, and there may be supernatural sanctions for doing so. Ideally, named goods are no longer available for exchange or slaughter at any feast other than the funeral of the bearer of the name. In Sumba, in which material exchange is a central idiom of sociability, this act of removal from circulation is itself regarded as a bold and daring act.

Named animals may be sacrificed upon the death of their owner. When Mbaiyo Pote died, his burial was depicted as a return of his body to the ancestral mother and father. The named animals still alive (in this case, the horse and dog) were slaughtered at the funeral and in order to accompany him as his body and possessions were reclaimed by the ancestors in partial repayment for the gift of life. Other named objects – pendants, cloths, knives – were also offered to the spirits along with his body as a gift to the spirits of the unseen world.

Why are these names in ritual speech? The act of bestowing a name – any name – is an act of taking control over reference, and distinguishing an object from a broader semantic category. The use of metaphoric elaborations provides semantic identity by adding a gloss on what is otherwise an opaque label. The use of ritual couplets for names takes a further measure of control by defining the audience as well. It establishes the names as part of a discourse that occurs in exchange with the ancestral spirits. An important part of the audience for such names is thus not only one's peers, but the ultimate authorities in Weyewa social life: the "Mother and Father" spirits. Having a special couplet name thus at once differentiates one's identity and expands the audience for the use of the name to include – at least implicitly – the ancestral spirits.

Tana dawa "The modern (literally, 'Foreign') world"

As the example of Ngongo Kaduku suggested, "seeking a name" is now discouraged by officials from the district- and regency-level governments. The opposition to name-seeking is framed in economic and developmental terms: it is regarded as wasteful and backward, and as impeding the progress of the Sumbanese people. In an interview in 1994 with the Regent, he pointed proudly to the success of his program, which he calls *eka pata* ("the new way") "[Fewer people are] feasting, wasting their resources; they are using their cattle, pigs and other animals [instead] for education and making a better life for themselves."

Name-seeking feasts do indeed seem to have declined. No one I asked in 1994 could think of any younger men or women under forty years of age who use or even seek such names, and most of the traditional feasts performed in the past few years have tended to be rather modest by historic standards – between one and four water buffalo slaughtered, and only slightly larger numbers of pigs. What is not clear is whether the Bupati can take any credit for this shift in priorities or even what role a shift in economic values may have played in this.

While one might argue that the decline of name-seeking might be a direct result of a recent emphasis on the development of the agricultural sector rather than animal husbandry, the rise in the pig population (see Figure 8) suggests that in fact pigs have become more important than they used to be, and certainly could have formed the basis of a lively feasting economy (cf. M. Lewis 1992). One might further argue that the decline of name-seeking is linked to the depersonalization of livestock among Weyewa as the market economy comes to play an ever-larger role in their lives. Colonial era reports show that approximately 5 percent of the population in Weyewa (1,400 out of a population of approximately 25,520) attended one of the biweekly markets; now the number is closer to 15 percent on a biweekly basis (Versluys 1941; Kantor Statistik Sumba Barat 1989). But as the pig population grows, and plays an increasing role in the Weyewa economy one might also expect that pigs would occupy greater symbolic importance in their constructions of identity. Yet pig names are rarely used or sought after among younger people. Still another argument might be that their new sources of income – rice and coffee – are less easily individuated, thus not easily named. It is difficult to imagine anyone naming a coffee tree or rice plant. However, Weyewa traditionally did name rice fields, occasionally with great acclaim and this could have, potentially at least, formed the basis of a new name-seeking status system. Yet name-seeking feasting has declined.

Recent patterns of naming (1980s and 1990s)

Economic reasons are only part of this picture of change; it is helpful to place the marginality of *ngara ndara* ("horse names") and *ngara wawi* ("pig names") and the changes in naming in relation to a kind of "historical ecology" of linguistic resources. By examining prestige sobriquets in relation to other verbal resources in Weyewa, we can see the way in which different labels index shifts in identity and affiliation.

Ngara Keristen, Christian forenames

Adopting a Christian name after baptism has a long history in West Sumba (Haripranata 1984: 124), but initially anyway, these names were not often used in everyday address or reference. Indeed, there was some anxiety in the late nineteenth and early twentieth century about the meaning of these baptisms, since the names did not seem to be used by any of their recipients. Missionaries began to worry that Christianity was very superficial among the Sumbanese. Especially among the Calvinist missionaries such as Wielenga, there was a growing emphasis that any name change had to be accompanied by a transformation of consciousness. To reflect this change, "we seek a renewal of the language" as well, declared the Calvinist minister Lambooy ([1932] 1987). In 1994, Christian names were more likely to be used for address in public settings such as schools, churches, and government.

As the number of Christians has risen (see Figure 9),[12] so also has the number of Weyewa bearing Biblically derived names. Based on a comprehensive computer listing of all the names in the 1990 census of Kalimbundaramane, I found that 67 percent of all Weyewa in that subdistrict now possess Christian forenames. Most Weyewa regard the possession of a horse or dog name as an indication of non-Christian leanings. Because they are acquired in the context of feasts, such sobriquets suggest pagan ritual, and the couplet names often used in horse and dog names imply the invocation of ancestral spirits.

There is a greater variety of Christian names than native names. Among 1,481 people in the sample in the subdistrict of Kalimbundaramane, there were 481 names in total, but only 14 of those were *ngara tana mema* ("native names"), names which nonetheless were shared among 33 percent of the population. Thus 467 names were *ngara Keristen*. Far fewer Christian names were shared than were native names and thus fewer people shared a spiritual "namesake" (*tamo*) connection

Plate 12   *A named racehorse*

Plate 13   *A named horse is sacrificed at the funeral of its master as a gift to the ancestors* [Photo: H. J. May]

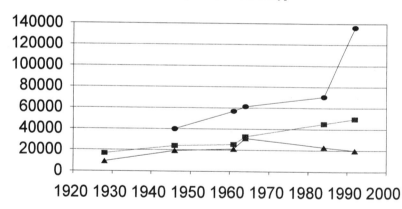

Figure 8   *Farm animal population in West Sumba*

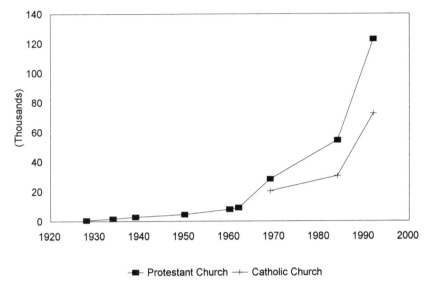

Figure 9   *Church membership in West Sumba*

based on first names.[13] It is true that the greater variety of Christian names does in some cases make it easier to identify unique individuals.

Another major incentive to adopting a Christian name is the desire to pursue schooling beyond elementary school. As of 1994, in order to register for continuing education in middle school (SMP) or SLTA technical school, students have to present a birth certificate (*surat akte kelahiran*) notarized by a clergyman. Many Sumbanese believe that the clergymen will refuse to do so unless the student gets baptized and adopts a Christian name. In 1994, high-level clergymen vigorously denied this, others called it a thing of the past, while still others have smilingly acknowledged that it still occurs.

Debora Lali Pora

Mbulu Renda's eldest daughter is a shy girl who seemed proud of her father's profession as ritual speaker. When I visited her father in 1980, when she was about ten years old, I once recall her quietly practicing some ritual-speech couplets from a recitation she had heard the night before. When I returned in 1984, I was surprised to learn that this girl – the daughter of one of the leading ancestor worshippers in Weyewa – had changed her name to *Debora Lali Pora*, the first name *Debora* a clear indication that she had been baptized as a Christian. When her sisters and brothers saw the look on my face as they explained this to me, her brother spoke up: "If you're not a Christian in school, the other kids tease you. Some times even the teachers ridicule you: "Why are you still Marapu? Huh? Still pray to rocks and trees, huh? No need for you to go to school, you're a pagan (*kafir*).'" She wanted to go on in school to middle school (SMP), and her teachers urged her to do so. At the time of registration, however, she was told she had to present a number of papers, a fee and a birth certificate signed and stamped by a clergyman. She had never visited any priest or minister ever before and so she was acutely embarrassed about the prospect. Finally she screwed up her courage and went to see the Catholic nuns who work at the health clinic near her house. When the nun asked the young girl her religion, and was told *marapu*, the sister simply asked the girl if she wanted to become a Christian. Debora said "yes." So the nun told her to come back next Sunday for some catechism classes with the priest, after which she could be baptized. At that point, although she had second thoughts about her decision, Debora did not feel she could get out of her obligation to attend the classes, and thus began the process of conversion.

When I asked how the name Debora was chosen, she said the priest chose it, and read from the Bible explaining why he chose that name as he welcomed her to the faith, but she could not remember what he said. She says she goes to church now because it is expected and if she does not go she will get teased by the other students in her middle school. Since no one else in her family attends, a neighbor child stops by her house before church to pick her up so they can all walk together.

What about ancestral approval? When I asked Debora's father, Mbulu Renda, about this, he said he was sure the ancestors approved of the name change. Why? Because "the ancestral spirits want her to get an education." By Debora's getting an education, "the whole family is strengthened and prospers." How does the spirit who is Lali Pora's namesake (*tamo*) feel about this change? I asked. "She approves. I held a divination [*urrata*] after she was baptized to ask, and I was told it was good."

The selling of named goods

Spirits are not always so happy about violating or changing names. Goods that were once named as part of a name-seeking feast are increasingly being sold off for cash. As a result of a vast improvement in roads and public transportation in the region in the past, bi-weekly markets (*parengga*; literally, "meeting place") have greatly increased in popularity and are an ever-present opportunity to generate cash in this manner. According to the Regent of West Sumba, the Sumbanese, and Weyewa in particular, have realized the economic benefit of a more rational attitude towards valuables. They have, in his words, "cast off psychological obstacles that hold them back." No longer personalized, valuables are increasingly regarded as assets that can and should be exchanged for education and other more modern resources. Although this has generated some controversy within the Ministry of Education and Culture, many Weyewa are selling *barang keramat* ("heirlooms") in order to pay for college education (see P. Taylor 1994). Surprising as it may seem, I would argue that this process of desacralizing objects is closely interwoven with shifts in identity and attitudes towards language.

In a struggle to acquire more cash for sending his nephew to college in Kupang, Petrus and his kinsmen decided to sell an heirloom Chinese bowl to an Arab "art shop" owner in Waikabubak. Since the bowl was named, and was featured in some songs I had recorded, I asked if it was forbidden to sell it. "No," came the answer, "we asked the spirits to release the prohibition." Anxious to hedge their bets against the possibility of angry ancestral spirits' exacting revenge for their selling of the sacred heirlooms, Petrus and his Christian kinsmen nonetheless approved of his "heathen" kinsmen's plans to perform a "pagan" ritual for desacralizing the object. In 1993, however, a string of calamities beset the family, including the death of a middle-aged man due to cerebral malaria, and the paralysis of a young woman due to a fall. The Christian and *marapu* factions immediately began to argue about the reason for these difficulties. The *marapu* spirit worshippers argued that the deities were angry about the selling of their goods.

Crucial to this process is an intellectual move by which Weyewa interpret the naming process as a kind of *weri* ("taboo") that can be lifted, thus permitting the object to be sold. *Weri* are temporally limited. Such taboos may be removed by asking the ancestral spirits to lift them, and permit their exchange, in return for an offering. *Weri* are commonly placed on the exchange of young girls, cloths, pigs, cattle, and other valuables for a period, in order to preserve them for future exchange or slaughter.

Uses of Christian names in address and reference

The difference between "hard" and "soft" names, and the palatalization function to distinguish between address and reference has not been carried over into Christian names. Nor does Christian naming system have a way of addressing someone poetically with descriptive names that classify them in terms of their valuables and other possessions.

While the name-created boundaries between public and private, for instance, have been elided through the dwindling of hard and soft names, there are boundaries emerging between social distance and intimacy that are enacted through the use of the titles versus the more personal *ngara Keristen* "Christian names."

Nama pangkat ("title")
Address + function, e.g.

	Pak Guru	"Mr. Teacher"
	Pak Camata	"Mr. District Head"
	Bapak Raja	"Mr. Raja"
	Ibu Menteri	"Mrs. Minister"
	Pak Dokter	"Mr. Doctor"
Title + personal name, e.g.	*Pak Joel*	Mr. Joel
	Dokter David	Dr. David
	Nona Janet	Miss Janet
	Pendeta Enos	Reverend Enos
	Guru Malo	Teacher Malo

Ngara fam ("family name")
Title + family name

	Ibu Dapawole	Mrs. Dapawole
	Pak Keremata	Mr. Keremata

Ngara sefe [C.V.] ("Enterprise Name [Limited]")
Title + company name

Mr. Edge of the Field	*Bapak Ujung Padang*
Mr. Good Hearted	*Bapak Dessa Ate*
Mr. Emanuel	*Bapak Emanuel*

These names, however, may be used in both address and reference.

Dede Bobo, a.k.a. Bapak Ujung Padang, "Mr. Edge of the Field"

Like Rato Kaduku, seventy-two-year-old Dede Bobo has spent much of his life seeking prestige and status, although the path of his life has taken a very different course. Much like the Dutchmen he so admired, he has retained the name he was baptized with – *Dede Bobo* – but like his elite Sumbanese colleagues, he has acquired a prestigious Indonesian name that refers to his accumulated wealth, *Ujung Padang*, literally "Edge of the Field," but in fact the name of his prosperous transportation and rice-polishing business owned jointly with his sons. Like Kaduku, Dede Bobo was born into a relatively wealthy family, but by the time he came of age, Dutch schooling was no longer regarded with suspicion, but a sign of prestige, something accorded only to certain elites, and so he and his family pursued it enthusiastically. His second name *Bobo* marked him as a scion of an important man, and he continues to be proud of this label as a sign of his heritage. It was the name he was baptized with as a child, and it is the name he retains. It is often used to refer to him. By the time the Japanese arrived in 1942, Dede Bobo could read, write, and speak Malay fluently, and had a position as a clerk. The military leadership quickly spotted him as a bright, well-connected, and enterprising administrator. He rose rapidly within the local Japanese administration, a matter of deep ambivalence not only for him but for his Weyewa kinfolk and neighbors.

When the war ended, because he had collaborated with the Japanese, his status was morally somewhat ambiguous, but a grudging respect nonetheless remained among the people, and his administrative skills were desperately needed after the war as the Dutch prepared to hand over their administration to a local elite. He was given the title of *raja kecil* ("little raja"), and people addressed and referred to him as such, at least up until the mid-1960s. His old-fashioned education and Malay speaking style bespoke earlier Dutch based norms, and younger elites found him to be too unabashedly *feodal* ("feudal") in his attitudes for the democratic world of modern Indonesia, and so he gradually found himself appointed to fewer and fewer committees and on fewer consultative boards. It appeared that his star was fading. Gradually, fewer and fewer people referred to him as *Bapak Raja*.

His faith in the importance of education and marrying well has served him well. At great personal expense, and drawing on outstanding debts owed him, he managed to get all but one of his four sons and two daughters through high school and college, a major achievement in any society, let alone Sumba. Three of his four sons live off the island, and are working in highly placed government and business positions in Jakarta, Kupang (Timor), and Ende (Flores). One of his daughters is married to a man who is being considered for a provincial governorship.

His name has evolved in the period from 1980–1994. No longer addressed as *Bapak Raja* ("Mr. Raja") when I first met him in 1978, he was simply introduced and addressed as *Dede Bobo*. Occasionally people would refer to him as *Paama Bondongaingo* '('Mr. Bondongaingo") after his clan name, an allusion to his vigorous defense of his claims on clan land, to the point that many people believe he and his kinsmen had murdered his opponents in land feud. Since the late 1980s, he has become less identified with his clan (indeed, he now often refuses requests to participate in clan feasts) and more with the plot of land that he and his sons are aggressively developing as a diverse set of enterprises, under the Indonesian label, *Ujung Padang*, a phrase meaning literally "Edge of the Field." He is now most commonly addressed as *Bapak Ujung Padang* ("Mr. Ujung Padang") and his wife is addressed and referred to as *Ibu Ujung Padang* ("Mrs. Ujung Padang"). He now has three bemos, two flat-bed trucks, a small retail kiosk, and a rice-polishing business, all labelled *Ujung Padang*. It signals a distinctly *Indonesian* (as opposed to "traditional") and enterprising orientation.

He does not seek "horse names," "pig names," or "buffalo names." To do so would be to defy the very national development programs and the system of authority with which he so identifies. His approach in setting himself apart in status and prestige is to embrace the symbols of modern Indonesia. Although he speaks Weyewa to his wife at home, and to his sons, his labels for himself are largely Indonesian-language ones, for example, *Ujung Padang*. Not unlike traditional elites in the past, such as Kaduku, he has gained wealth and power through connections with powerful outsiders from off the island; first the Dutch, and now the modern Indonesian elite with whom his children are associated. Although he has not used a traditional horse name or buffalo name to indicate his prestige, the use of the Indonesian name for his own personal address form conforms in many ways to the linguistic ideology of Sumbanese prestige naming.

Patronymics

Another recent development has been the emergence of Western style patronymics. Although this is still a minority practice, it is an influential minority, since it tends to be done by Western-oriented and educated Weyewa elites. For instance, *Sam Rewa*, a school teacher, has named all his children with the patronymic *Rewa* as well, which in fact is a *ngara ndara* ("horse name") from his male ancestors. Thus his son is named *Henk Rewa*.[14]

The survival of prestige naming

Partly because of the importance of the market, the meaning of personal possessions – particularly prestige items – has shifted. For Mbaiyo Pote, personal possessions expressed his individuality by the act of naming them. The most highly prized prestige items – for example, a *hardtop* ("hardtop jeep") – are not usually named to my knowledge. While in *tana mema* ("the traditional world") named prestige items were viewed in some ways as objects that not only stood for but were referentially and materially exchanged for their owner (i.e. by using the name of the object to address the owner, and by sacrificing the object to compensate the ancestors for the deceased), valued commodities in the "contemporary world" (*tana dawa*) – clothes, shoes, purses, wooden cabinets (*lemari*), television sets (*tifi*), and stone houses (*rumah batu*) – are usually not named at all.

One important area in which the tradition of prestige names has persisted, and indeed developed, is in the domain of "horse names" applied to "racehorses" (*ndara malle*), covered pick-up trucks used for transport called bemos, and local businesses. An important theme linking these three categories is the association with risk, and this is particularly clear in the case of racehorses. Most animals, if given names at all are given descriptive names such as "white," or "black," or "patient." Since many pets such as monkeys, civet cats, birds, dogs, and cats are not routinely given names, it is all the more striking that racehorses should be singled out for naming, and usually names in the native language of the owner. Most of the racehorses in the annual 1994 horseraces in the track outside of Waikabubak were given native language binomials that reflect sentimental themes, personal experiences or unique features or attributes.

Some recent racehorse names

"Prancer"	*Pangga Lewu*
"Soul Mate"	*Ole Ndewa*
"Close Resemblance"	*Reda Ole*
"Prince of Coffee"	*Putera Kopi*
"Knows How"	*Pánde Pata*
"Full Cottonwood"	*Rita Bewa*
"Guided Missile"	*Peluru Kendali*
"Heaven Field"	*Manda Elu*
"Glad First"	*Engge Belli*
"New Ways"	*Eka Pata*

The two Indonesian-language names "Guided Missile" (*Peluru Kendali*) and "Prince of Coffee" either were given by a non-Sumbanese-speaking Chinese who owned the animal, or in cooperation with a Chinese financier for the horse. The majority of other names were in Sumbanese languages, and in some cases strongly evoked the traditions of prestige name-seeking and indeed legendary "angry" men (e.g. *Ole Ndewa*, "Soul Mate"). Even more striking, this is an activity in which the Regent, as well as a number of Sumbanese-descent Indonesian officials participate and enter their own horses.

Another named valuable is the bemo, the small covered pick-up trucks with benches in the back used as public conveyances throughout Indonesia. In Sumba, these vehicles are always provided with names, which are spray painted on the side panels in often gaudy colors. Although the names are often in Indonesian,[15] approximately half of them are in Weyewa or one of the other languages of the island, and often use a line out of a couplet.[16] Like racehorses, bemos on Sumba are associated with the youthful autonomy and risk-taking of their drivers and ticket takers (*kornek*).

While both horse and bemo names are used as a way of differentiating the identity of the conveyance from others, the names are also often corporate labels and refer to the business that owns it. Occasionally, the name comes to attach to the owner as well, so that Weyewa will refer to the owner of a particular bemo by his bemo name. There is a diminished sense, however, of any special connection between the name and its referent; nor is there certainly any sense that the object somehow stands for or can be in some sense exchanged for the owner.[17]

Why has the tradition of prestige naming been applied to racehorses, bemos and businesses? Like the traditional horse names, these names are bestowed upon objects that represent risk. The act of naming – because of the link it establishes to the referent – offers a way of attempting to control that risk. While the feasts in which the traditional horse names were bestowed were risky to one's prestige (see Keane 1997b), and indeed to one's whole social, religious, political, and economic well-being, a racehorse, a bemo, or a business entails risk more narrowly, to one's financial well-being and personal reputation.

Bemo and racehorse names are different from the traditional prestige-naming system, however. The use of prestige names for racehorses, bemos, and businesses is indexicalized, in the sense that the name is viewed as primarily pointing to the actual referent – vehicle, business, or animal – and is not regarded as a metonym for the owner, a part of a verbal identity construed as a whole. No one has ever suggested – as far as I know – taking a named bemo out of service, closing down a business, or killing a racehorse, upon the death of its owner, as was customarily done for the objects named with traditional prestige names.

The prestige names in current use are more narrowly ostensive and indexical than their traditional counterparts. When Ngongo Kaduku embarked on a traditional name-seeking quest, to a significant degree, the fortunes of his whole village lay in the balance. If he failed in an effort to drag a tombstone, to carry out a risky marriage negotiation, or to draw the necessary audience and participants to a feast, such a failure might have serious implications for the capacity of village members who were identified with his efforts to recruit labor for agricultural activities, to keep angry ancestral spirits from causing misfortune, and to create and maintain alliances of mutual protection. Currently, if the Regent's named racehorse fails in its bid for first place, it's the horse that loses, not him, and he still has a job and his family can still eat.

Why haven't the "hard" and "soft" names survived? In most areas of the Weyewa region, this practice of maintaining tabooed names in conjunction with the names in everyday use is gradually dwindling. The most obvious reason is that the local names on which the system was based have been largely replaced by Christian naming practices. However, these names could have survived using some sort of binomial system in which the first name is a Christian one and the second is a local name. But even so, sensitivities about the use of "hard" names are on the wane. The reason for this, as Mertz (1983) has suggested for the people in Cape Breton, is that such names presuppose too much, and index too little. The "hard" and "soft" system places the custody of the "hard" names in the hands of others, along with knowledge about the intimate contexts and uses of such names, knowledge which may not be available to most interlocutors in a growing and increasingly mobile society.

But if the contemporary prestige names are more narrowly indexical in their usage, they have also acquired an additional connotation: that of autonomy. Activities such as horse racing and small-business enterprise (including the maintenance of a bemo) are seen by many Sumbanese as ones in which an ordinary Sumbanese person can triumph over wealthy entrepreneurs and powerful government officials. In 1980, for instance, the horse of a relatively poor man from a remote subdistrict of West Sumba defeated the horse of the Regent in a major upset. Although wealthy Chinese entrepreneurs and powerful government officials are able to purchase the best horses and pay for their grooming and training, such upsets occur with enough frequency that these events are a matter of major local importance.

These races offer a public, yet distinctively local means of challenging public authorities and wealth. By giving horses prestige names, the competitors not only evoke tradition, but they suggest a sphere of autonomy from officialdom that in this modest and self-contained way poses a challenge to it. Horses have long been traditional symbols of autonomy by which local males established their distinctive identities. The fact that horse races in Waikabubak have traditionally been accompanied by several other distinctively not-official-not-private events such as night markets (*pasar malam*), "traditional dancing" (*tarian adat*), and even gambling (*tau riti*) suggests that these events have institutionalized a domain of relative autonomy from both government and traditional familial spheres, and the emerging use of ceremonial prestige names are part and parcel of this.

Conclusions

Acquiring a "name" for oneself was once a central goal for Weyewa status and power seekers. The very word for fulfillment, completeness and encompassment *ngara ndukka* ("all, everything, entirety") literally can be glossed "name of the limit," suggesting the importance of naming in the process of constituting a totality. By "naming" something, one could define an entity as an autonomous thing, differentiated from the rest of its kind. What the powerful "angry" men sought was not only to be differentiated from the rest, but to be autonomous, complete, and exemplary. By acquiring names in spectacular prestige feasts, they established themselves as individuals surrounded by key symbols of material value in Sumbanese life: horses, buffalo, pigs, spears, and cloths.

As these name-seeking feasts began to run afoul of the Indonesian government's efforts at national development, and Christian names grew increasingly popular due to religious conversion, the prestige names have not died out altogether, but have remained in the realm of racehorses, bemos, and businesses. The surprising use of the ritual-speech system of prestige names for bemos and businesses points to an area of autonomy and risk. Drawing on the connotations of spiritual potency and autonomy associated with such names is particularly useful in arenas of endeavor as perilous and subject to chance as capital enterprise.

For students of language shift, the evidence is clear that these shifts were mediated by language ideologies about the meaning of proper names. For Weyewa, a key aspect of the meaning of a name was its semantic, classifying function: thus finding the right "fit" between the child and the name at birth was crucial, and could even affect the child's health. Seeking a name was a way to classify and establish oneself socially among one's peers as superior, potent, and exemplary: as a *kabani-mbani*. For the Dutch and the Indonesian bureaucracies, a key function of a name was to refer to a unique individual for statistical and counting purposes. Its local semantic and classificatory function was less important in terms of control and surveillance.

6

FROM MIRACLES TO CLASSROOMS: CHANGING FORMS OF ERASURE IN THE LEARNING OF RITUAL SPEECH

This final chapter examines the changing forms of erasure employed in the teaching and learning of ritual speech, changes that contribute to the ways in which ritual speech as a register has shifted in its uses. By selectively ignoring ("erasing") the diversity of speech varieties, the ideologies of language learning – both colonial and post-colonial – create an image of what ritual speech is ideally. Learning ideologies contributed to the shift in these ideals from "angry" to "humble," from exemplary to marginal, from sacred to secular. The practice of learning ritual speech was once described as a totalizing experience involving miraculous inspiration, an experience that designated the learner as central and exemplary. Ability to perform verbally alone was seen as an act of spontaneous anger and boldness that was central to one's identity as competent, but which did not acknowledge the contributions of teachers, nor did it recognize the gradual and systematic process by which learning was (and is) interactively accomplished. Classroom schooling, on the other hand, requires not solo performance or anger so much as respectful response; one must learn active audiencing practices. Teachers occasionally code-switch, and borrow between Indonesian and Weyewa, sending subtle messages to the children about the relative merits of each. When they switch into Indonesian they are implicitly suggesting to students what kinds of things are "better said in Indonesian." Ritual speech, seen as a variety of the local language, is relegated to a marginal area of the curriculum devoted to sports, regional folklore, and local arts.

Anger and learning

Prior to the massive implementation of school-based learning practices in modern Indonesia, the Weyewa system of learning exhibited a differentiation between acquisition of ritual and non-ritual knowledge, was sharply gendered, emphasized charisma, and miraculous inspiration at the same time that it obscured its own systematicity. It made use of expressions of anger in the form of corporal punishment and harsh ridicule in the ritual domains. Despite the risks, rewards for learning and

125

using ritual speech were considerable: ability to participate in, control, and to enact some of the most important economic, political, and religious events in their lives.

Proficiency in ritual-speech performance involved the mastery of what was viewed as a total system. Not only is each line "completed" by its rhythmic and semantic pair, but the audience must be complete, and each turn must be appropriately positioned on the "ladder" (*nauta*). Each line of a couplet has its precise pair: for example, the pair for the line *ndara ndende kiku* ("horse with a standing tail") is *bongga mette lomma* ("dog with a black tongue"). Together, the rhythmically and semantically parallel lines refer to a "good speaker" or performer. Failure to properly pair the first line with the second one is cause for fines or supernatural retribution. A performance must also be complete (see chapter 3). Each performance must be carried out in the presence of specific spiritual and human interlocutors, with particular sequences of actions, or "ladders" (*nauta*), to lead to true, authentic performance of the "words of the ancestors." Failure to follow these procedures properly can be a cause for a lack of completeness and ancestral disapproval. On the other hand, those who are effective, angry performers of ritual-speech are regarded as exemplary figures who in their behavior, words, and social position, reflect the source and structure of Sumbanese moral and social order. Such ritual performers tend to characterize "true" ritual speech as a monolithic whole: monologic, narrative, and authoritative. This attitude toward ritual speech is one that erases the actual diversity of more common, intermediate genres that lead up to the eventual performance of these sacred "words of the ancestors."

Learning ritual speech or other formal knowledge required an act of boldness. Among the approximately 100,000 speakers of the Weyewa language, *nunga* means to "learn, try" or "to attempt." When I was watching little six-year-old Agus play in the front yard with a long stick, pretending to throw it at his sister, his father described this kind of practice as "learning": "he's learning [*nunga*] to throw a spear." A related word, *nonga* ("to attempt"), suggests the act of pushing forward, protruding, jutting out, projection, extrusion; in Weyewa, the act of learning is a socially marked one that involves sticking out.

For children, the act of learning to speak languages such as Indonesian or ritual speech is an act of thrusting oneself forward in a social sense. As the language of schools, government offices, and formal settings of all kinds, the Indonesian national language (*panewe dawa*, "the language of foreigners') is especially marked when used at home, suggesting a public performance. Once, when sitting around in a kitchen in the Weyewa highlands, I heard three-year-old Irma give a cookie to her older brother Agus, and then tell him in Indonesian, "run along now" ("*pigi suda*"). It amused the adults listening to see such a tiny girl adopt an adult role, but also because it evoked a formal performance in a very domestic setting. By using Indonesian, she had defined the encounter as somehow public, which seemed quite funny to us as we squatted by the fire.

When children speak Weyewa to their parents, they are, in a sense, offstage, performing in what has come to be defined over the past several decades as an unmarked but intimate domestic space. Weyewa is the language of the home, hearth, and family; few Weyewa think about their language as an object of intellectual effort or contemplation. When I asked why twenty-eight-month-old Omi was imitating her mother's Weyewa-language answers to my questions, her mother laughed and said, "she's just playing"; only after some reflection did she think that Omi's behavior could be called "learning" (*nunga*). Weyewa do not think that children need "training" or "teaching" (*pa-nunga*) to learn to speak Weyewa; parents say children simply acquire it from listening. No one would consider punishing a child for ungrammatical use of Weyewa.

On the other hand, one "learns, tries" (*nunga*) Indonesian and *tenda* ritual speech, and these can be taught. Since one self-consciously "attempts" (*nunga*) to speak these forms, one must be prepared for failure and its harsh consequences. When children make mistakes speaking ordinary Weyewa, they are not beaten or scolded; it is assumed that "it will improve all by itself," as one father told me. Using Indonesian poorly or awkwardly, on the other hand, may result in ridicule, or even a box on the ears. Parents get "angry" at their children for incorrect usage of the national language. Likewise, young men are publicly humiliated, and may even be fined or receive supernatural sanctions for using ritual-speech inappropriately or incorrectly (Kuipers 1986). Both ritual-speech ability and Indonesian-speaking ability are acquired later in life, and are thus thought to be under more conscious control and responsibility on the part of the speaker.

Learning *tenda*

While some ritual-speech competence was important to adult male status in Sumba, first efforts at speaking ritual speech could be humiliating. As one who has attempted to speak several times in ritual-speech events, I can testify to the sense of bristling anticipation one feels as one takes the floor. Although Weyewa ritualists were polite enough never to direct their criticism at me, I have witnessed three or four such moments where outright derision occurred, and one I remember vividly and was able to record on tape. In this case, a fourteen-year-old boy attempted to take the floor as performer in a *zaizo* placation rite, an all-night long ritual-speech dialogue. It was a small event, attended mostly by close relatives and myself. As the *zaizo* began and evening dinner dishes were cleared away, Mbulu Renda, a well-known performer, began to beat the drum slung over his shoulder and chant an invocation to the spirits. After about fifteen minutes of a throbbing rhythm accompanied by tinkling gongs, his topic changed. He began to invite those attending to contribute "leaves to his tree, fruit to his branches": to offer blessings or comments on the proceedings.

Since I knew they expected me to contribute a short blessing on the event, I silently readied my much-rehearsed little speech. As was customary, I thought I would wait for someone else to speak first to set the tone for the evening. Suddenly, before any of the elders could speak, the air was pierced with a thin shrill cry of the singer's fourteen-year-old son, who had put on a headcloth and a waistcloth for the occasion: "Hail *zaizo*! I support your knees, I support your buttocks! I offer leaves for your trees, fruit for your branches! Why don't you wheel the horse about and bring the dog around, so that you can get to the trunk of the tree, source of the water? Amen!" In correct ritual-speech form, he had said: "Greetings, Singer! I support you! Why don't you now shift your discourse and get to the main point of the evening?"

The singer, glaring at his son, held up his hand to bring the orchestra of gongs and drums lurching to a halt. A tense silence followed. Instead of the gongs and drums starting up again so that the singer could put the question to music, the singer waved them off, scowled at his son, and exploded into a rage of expletives, curses, and vulgarity:

You blockhead! I'm going to box your ears! What! Are you the "one who speaks at dusk, the one who speaks at dawn"? How about it? So are you going to stay up all night now? If you speak first, you have to keep up with it all night long! Are you going to do that? You stupid water buffalo! [pause] . . . And you ask me to "get to the source of the water, the trunk of the tree'! Hah! I've only started! How can you ask me to "get to the source of the water, the trunk of the tree"! You fool! What am I going to do with you!

While the boy's face burned with embarrassment, the smaller children snickered. The boy's father was enraged over two things: that his son had spoken first and that he had asked him to "get to the point" so early on in the performance. While his speech was technically correct, whoever speaks first in a *zaizo* implicitly accepts responsibility to close out the ceremony and watch over the details of the proceedings for correctness. Apparently, the boy, in his eagerness, overlooked this fact. By asking his father to "get to the point" ("source of the water") so early on in the evening, the boy was already violating the very rules he was supposed to be watching over.

Weyewa depict the process of learning to perform as something that requires considerable boldness and assertiveness. First-time speakers are

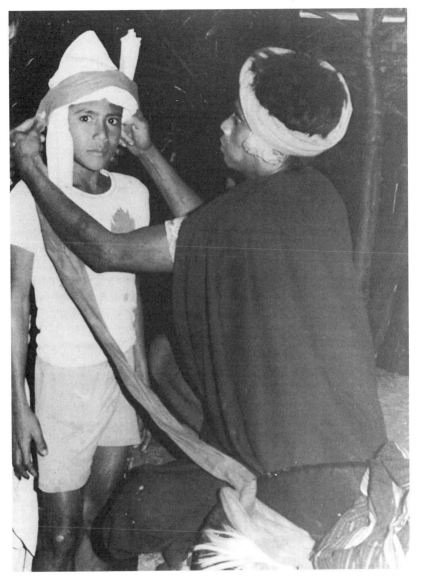

Plate 14   *Learning to perform in ritual events* [Photo: H. J. May]

encouraged to overcome shame and embarrassment (*"ndu makke-kana"* "don't be embarrassed," the bystanders shout), but must expect to be greeted with howls of derision and harsh ridicule. Even if the performance is flawless, the best they can hope for is a respectful silence. There is

no tradition of positive evaluation for specific techniques of performance.

Watching the treatment of the young boys, I often wondered how
Weyewa singers and ritual speakers got to be so good at what they do.
They speak fluently and eloquently for hours on end, rarely repeating
themselves, flawlessly assembling couplets till the early hours of the
morning. To understand the composition process, I sometimes practiced
quietly in my house, alone to myself. (If people hear you speaking to
yourself in Weyewa, they become seriously concerned for your sanity.) I
was alarmed at how often I found myself tripping up, stumbling over
words, especially when I tried to speak as quickly as is customary in
public rituals. Getting tongue-tied in a sacred event is not good. So how
do they do it?

When one asks the speakers themselves, they invariably minimize the
importance of technique, and will not discuss any systematic methods of
learning, memorization or practice. Like the Sumbanese mythical orphan
figure *Mada Luwu*, they claim to acquire such cunning through magic,
chance, or through supernatural gift. *Pánde* ("cunning") for them is not
something one acquires through hard work, repetition and unison
exercises of rote memorization, as in an elementary school, but in a flash
of insight, a divine intervention, and sudden display of angry bravado.
But unlike the venerable Asian traditions of education involving a flash
of spiritual insight, in Sumba there is not even a spiritual mentor figure
to guide one along the way. In most cases, ritual speakers say they were
suddenly required to speak by circumstances, and so they did. Lende
Mbatu said he first performed when a hired singer lost his voice; Mbulu
Renda first performed when the hired spokesman failed to show up; and
Ngongo Kaduku first performed when a singer was ridiculed and
stomped off the job. All claimed not to have any prior training, and to
have experienced initial fear, followed by the triumph of a successful
performance.

Off-the-record "echo" and "elaboration" learning: a kind of pragmatic erasure

Yet there is an unmarked, almost hidden, but quite systematic way in
which I have seen young men (seldom girls) try out their *tenda* skills in
front of an adult audience. It is a style one might call "echoing" or "echo
and elaboration." On a number of occasions, on the night before a
ceremony is to be performed, I have seen adults and children sitting
around the hearth fire discussing the ritual, social and moral background
to an upcoming event. While the main participants to such discussions
are the adult principals, younger adults and grown children listen and

contribute informally, via audible, but not conversationally recognized or ratified, repetition and echoing of adult conversation. Although in fact their contributions to the discourse may occasionally be considerable, their participation is not acknowledged. This amounts to what might be called a sort of "pragmatic erasure."

I have recorded several such instances of repetition. Repetition in discourse contexts – it turns out – is not a simple matter of mere duplication, and indeed can serve many different social and cultural functions (Ochs 1983: 31–32). In one instance, a few hours before a *zaizo* ("placation rite") performance was to take place, a young man was listening to his father explain to the hired performer the supernatural causes of a motorcycle accident that was the reason for the event. Each time the boy's father would confess to some neglect of religious responsibilities in the recent past that could account for such a calamity, the listening performer would nod and sometimes contribute a couplet or two that translated the event into ritual-speech terms. What I noticed was that the boy would then echo the performer's ritual couplets, although no one formally acknowledged these actions on his part. For instance, the father explained to the performer how he was coming home from his garden when he heard about the accident and he was shocked: *"Just as we were coming home – Ninda here was walking with me – Mbulu ran up and told me that Lende was in an accident [pause] Hoo!"*

The performer, looking at the man, gave a nod and said, *"Struck from behind, throttled from the tip,"* a couplet which depicts the surprise one feels when struck with misfortune. Just as the father was nodding back to the performer (presumably to indicate agreement with the poetic translation of this portion of the story), the boy piped up, but without looking at either the speaker or his father: "Ya, "struck from behind, throttled from the tip" so it was." No one acknowledged verbally or non-verbally that the boy had said anything, and the boy's father went on with his story.

In another case, an elder clan leader was sitting around the fire with his brothers talking about the history of his clan, while groups of men, women, and children looked on. As the clan leader looked at me, he narrated some snippets of clan history.

"We have the status of elder brother in this village. It's true. You can hear many other stories around here, and it's all nonsense. We are the ones who 'pioneered the fields and crossed the mountains.'" A young boy listening intently, repeated this couplet and added one of his own: "Who pioneered the fields, crossed the mountains, who maintains the land, who defends the territory." When I swung my hand held microphone toward him in the expectation that he might continue and speak further, he smiled shyly and covered his face and turned away. He was uncomfortable at having the spotlight placed on him during what was supposed to be an offstage speech.

Aside from a few titters among his age mates, there was no other acknowledgement of his unofficial turn at talk. In these utterances, the boy echoes his mentor's statements, and elaborates off the record. By echoing the mentor's statements, he is not making any claim to the speaking floor, he is simply supporting him. He indicates this continuity with the speaker's position thematically, intonationally, and non-verbally. There is little or no pause between the speaker's last phrase and the boy's continuing speech. If construed as conversational, such overlap is rude, and is considered an interruption; instead of being seen as an interruption, it is simply an unauthorized continuation of a monologic turn. The young boy shows that he is not interrupting by not making eye contact, not raising his eyebrows, or changing his body position. He may, however, nod gently in agreement as he speaks and look in the direction of the speaker. By thus not claiming the responsibility implied in a turn at talk, he is not drawing attention to himself, nor asking that his competence as a performer be assessed.

At the same time, he is allowing others to witness his skills as an orator. Adult specialists can hear him perform and be impressed (or dismayed) without being obliged to acknowledge this as a legitimate turn at talk. If there are corrections to be made, they can make them in a similarly-off-the record, and relatively unembarrassing, way. For example, the adult specialist may appear to repeat the novice's "elaborated" remarks, even though in fact he is slightly revising them in a more correct form. I once heard a young man attempt to "echo" his uncle's words in a way that was technically correct, but slightly awkward; his uncle nodded slightly an acknowledgement of his nephew's elaboration, and went on to revise the couplet slightly. Since this is all done informally, it preserved the autonomy and independence of ritual speech as a sacred, other-worldly style, not subject to explicit educational efforts.

The "echo and elaboration" method is actually quite systematic, interactive, and requires complex coordination between teacher and student, even though there is no overt recognition or interactional acknowledgement of it. The native Sumbanese "method" of learning and teaching requires accommodation by the student and teacher to the semantic, pragmatic, and overall thematic structure of the event. The student must master the content of the discussion in order to elaborate on it. Since it is not viewed as an official turn at talk, the learner has relatively greater freedom than a system that requires official accountability for "putting oneself forward." The Indonesian-language method described below, by contrast, involves relatively little semantic interpretation, and much phonological recognition and rote memorization.

Anger and knowledge in early schools: angry varieties are banished

Before the Dutch troops "mounted" the island for their pacification campaign in 1906, there were no formal schools on the island. The energetic young missionary Douwe Klaas (called "Deka") Wielenga was granted permission and a small subsidy by the colonial government in 1912 to set up schools, as long as the missions agreed to be mostly secular in their instruction.

As with American curricular disputes (e.g. Hirsch 1987), the Dutch missionaries in Sumba were involved in a national debate about many aspects of what the students should learn (Penders 1968; Groeneboer 1992). One of the biggest controversies was over how much of the Dutch language the children should learn. What they agreed on was the need to create loyalty to the Dutch, construed as a sense of familial obligation. To create "loyalty" they drew on distinctively Dutch Calvinist conceptions of voluntarism and free will. They tried to make Sumbanese pay for their education, on the grounds that if they thought it was valuable, they would want it more. Another important conception among the Dutch was reflected in the unusually prominent role of music and song in the curriculum: along with reading, writing, and arithmetic, all students were required to study, even at the most basic level, singing. They were taught national anthems (e.g. songs to Queen Wilhelmina) (Van den End 1987: 113), Dutch folksongs, and Indonesian-language songs.

Another important way in which learning was accomplished was through the creation of a total institution – a boarding house run on the model of a family with the missionary as the father at the head of the table. Missionaries would routinely accept Sumbanese children as boarders in exchange for help around the house. But Sumbanese parents were initially reluctant to let their children go to such an institution, because learning is closely associated with anger, and anger against the child of someone "else" is an offense, likely to result in conflict.

But the Dutch believed that anger as a form of discipline did not belong in the classroom, but in the home. Wielenga wrote back to his congregation in Holland that the main obstacle to getting Sumbanese elites to send their children to school was the belief that these children would become his personal possessions – a plausible concern on an island in which about 20 percent of the population were slaves or of slave descent, and could trace their condition to some sort of abduction or servitude. When he assured them that they could have their children back, they countered, "Our children are as stupid as water buffalos. Whenever our children don't understand something, they will of course get a whipping. You will be angry at them and angry at us. Now that we are friends, why should we get angry at one another?" Wielenga's response is instructive: "Precisely because they are so stupid, that is why they should go to school. Clever children should not be at home. And don't fear: they will not be struck at school." Lest one should think that Wielenga opposed corporal punishment altogether, he added: "When the schoolchildren are naughty they will be brought to their parents who can give them a thrashing" (Wielenga [1908]1987: 146).[1] Anger was not a pedagogical device in the Dutch classroom.

While the idea of parents' punishing children was not new, the moral framework of Wielenga's proposal was entirely novel for the Sumbanese. Wielenga was suggesting that parents bore some responsibility for their children's educational performance, rather than, as Weyewa native ideology saw it, children being largely themselves responsible for accommodating to the adult norm (see Ochs 1988).[2]

While they used a warm and inclusive "family" ideology to explain their educational practices, the Dutch in fact applied this only to an elite few. Nor did they expect the family to be a reflection of the classroom: the subsidy was given to the educational system on the grounds that the church agreed to provide an essentially secular education. In the cynical but frank view of one observer, this system would create relatively low-cost native leaders who could take the blame for colonial mistakes.[3] The joining of religious and class interests came together most clearly in the words of the evangelist Van Dijk, who was knighted in the Order of the Oranges of Nassau in 1924 ([1925]1987: 242), and who was of the opinion that Dutch-language pedagogy should be stressed (cf. Groeneboer 1992). On Sumba, the evangelists he felt should see the schools as a way of combating communism: "We need people," Van Dijk wrote from Sumba in 1925, "who know the importance of placing themselves in the breach against the entrance of revolution and disbelief" ([1925]1987: 245).

Rather than having students *nunga* "try, assert" instead they were taught to *respond*: to be a clever audience. In this system, anger and punishment were supposed to be avoided as disciplinary strategies. Instead the teachers – mostly young men and women from other islands – used a statement and repetition method, or occasionally a question and answer method. In both cases, it tended to reward those who were able to provide the correct *response*, and did not involve providing explanations for those who failed to understand or follow along. In one report on a Sumbanese school, the inspector is critical of teachers who failed to pay attention to the laggards:

A letter is written [on the board], its name is pronounced, and the children learn the letter. A teacher has them say in chorus after him *bee . . . a, ba; bee . . . oe, boe: baboe* "maid." There is no attempt at independent work. The result is that the nimblest among them learn the letters, and by frequent repetition memorize it. The less brainy among them do not memorize it, and fall quickly behind. One result of this method of education is that there are many who fall behind. The teachers do not use their free time to help those who fall behind. ([1914]1987: 184)

Once the children were admitted to this select group of students, the Dutch school examiner felt that the teacher had a responsibility to help everyone in the class to achieve.

The role of the vernacular languages in Dutch education

By law, the language of instruction in the Sumbanese *volkschool* was to be Malay. The missionaries, however, drawing on a model in which mind and emotion, brain and heart were separate spheres of experience, argued for the value of the *landstaal* "the local language" as being closer to the hearts and emotions of the people. Although Onvlee (1930) argued passionately for the importance of using the local languages in schools, and saw them as being an appropriate topic in the curriculum and even designed textbooks for this purpose (Onvlee n.d.), this was abandoned after the Second World War because the Japanese destroyed all the textbooks and told the Sumbanese that teaching local languages was simply part of a divide-and-rule colonial strategy.

Despite the formal support offered by some evangelists for the local languages, these languages were seen by some as incomplete, "difficult" (=unsystematic), even defective. According to Samuel Roos, the earliest Dutch administrator on the island:

The Soembanese have no script. The language they speak is very undeveloped. The princes and slaves speak to one another in the same way: they only have one expression for the personal pronoun *you* (*njomoe*) . . . Just as many children whose parents were born in the Indies confuse G and H sounds with one another, among the Soembanese this obtains between H and S: for example *Hoemba, Soemba; Savoe, Hawoe.* (1872: 36).

For Roos, the Sumbanese language was crudely incomplete in its differentiation of both the social and the auditory universe: it failed to distinguish sufficiently between respectful and less respectful forms of address; and like the much-reviled Indies-born Dutchmen (Groeneboer 1992), Sumbanese lazily blended together sounds (*h* and *s*) that, to Roos' ears anyway, were "meant" to be kept separate and distinct.

Missionaries had similar complaints. According to the Dutch Catholic missionaries in Laura, West Sumba, in the 1890s, the local languages were "difficult":

The local language is very difficult to learn, because there are several sounds that can only be pronounced properly after long practice. Besides that there is no one to teach me. Indeed there are a number of prominent figures who can speak Malay, but they only know a little, and they cannot translate all the words for me.. (Haripranata 1984: 128)

Another commented that

> to learn their local language will take quite a long time. Lauranese is fitting for someone with speech defects and a whiny voice. A person who cannot pronounce "r" and speaks through the nose will quickly learn to speak Lauranese. Too bad I don't possess those defects.   (Haripranata 1984: 122)

Despite Onvlee's enthusiasm for the study and use of local languages, several Dutch-trained Ambonese and Sabunese school teachers employed by the missionaries were known to have chastised and even beaten Sumbanese students for speaking "monkey language" (*bahasa kera*) – i.e. Sumbanese languages – in school. This was seen by teachers as a sort of secret code that students would use when they were not paying attention, and its use signaled a lack of classroom discipline.

Malay/Indonesian on the other hand, was a language of the wider world, used by the Dutch, the Ambonese, Sabunese, and Timorese visitors from other islands, and a language of writing, knowledge, and rational commerce. The romantic nationalist Alisjahbana – a linguist and the head of a national commission to develop and promote the Indonesian language – argued along similar lines for the rational character of the Indonesian language, as against the more ritualized character of speech in more "feudal circles" of Indonesian society. He goes so far as to claim that the structure of the Indonesian national language was a reflection of its position as the language of modernity. Citing the Dutch scholar Berg:

> That the Indonesian language does not know changes of nominals, conjugation of verbs or congruence, is not burdened by unnecessary nominal and verbal classes, forms degrees of comparison analytically, and only knows one form of adjective, and in general is free of irregularities, all this places the Indonesian language in respect to her inner form among the most useful languages of the world. Had Jespersen [a well known structuralist linguist] only known the Indonesian language, it would have been the closest to his heart's desire.
> (Berg 1951: 19-20)

Alisjahbana contrasts the useful, complete, and rational character of modern Indonesian with the courtly polite and ritualized styles of language common throughout Indonesia:

> Since the decline of Indonesian culture,[4] the language in feudal circles and even in the sphere of ritual life tends toward what Robert K. Merton (1949) called "ritualism', people uttering words without being convinced of their meaning. In establishing a new language as the basis of a modern culture in Indonesia, care should be taken that spoken words are as close as possible to the idea formulated and to the action resulting from those spoken words and thoughts, so that a strong ethical sense of responsibility emerges.   (1986: 47–48)

Like other modernists, Alisjahbana embraced the idea that referential functions of language are paramount for the development of language. Language should be a transparent window on the truth (cf. Reddy 1979; Silverstein 1985: 248). Ritualized styles of speaking that do not seem to have a referential function are not conducive to the "strong ethical sense of responsibility" he associates with citizenship in a modern nation state.

If Indonesian was to be constructed as a modern language, the other languages of the archipelago could then be represented as somehow non-modern, in a way that legitimated their position as "regional," and thus non-national, languages. A key ideological move on the part of nationalists such as Alisjahbana was to represent the Indonesian language as a language of democracy, and contrast it with the "feudal" languages of an old colonial order, despite the fact that it was the Dutch who in many ways promoted the use of Malay as the language of the Dutch East Indies bureaucracy (Hoffman 1979). Vernacular education, cast by the Japanese as part of a divide-and-rule strategy of Dutch imperialism, was seen as something to be transcended as soon as children were old enough to understand Indonesian.

Code-switching in the classroom

When I arrived on Sumba in 1978, only about 20 percent of school-age children actually attended school, but by 1994, nearly 100 percent of the eligible children attended school (see Figure 10). Much of this had to do with a massive school-building program, better roads connecting the schools, more available public transport, and a genuine desire for knowledge about the outside world. After Indonesian independence, the family ideology was used in educational practice in a different way: all Indonesians became part of a family in which the Indonesian government was the parent and the student-citizens were the children. Suharto is "father" and is referred to as "Pak Harto," "Father Harto"; his wife is referred to as Ibu Tien, "Mother Tien." Suharto's picture adorns each classroom. Although education continued to be a powerful mechanism for class differentiation in Sumba, by 1994, it was at the secondary and university levels where this took place (see D. Hansen et al. 1989). At the lower levels of education, now available to everyone, it was no longer an elite mark of distinction.

Yet in the classroom itself, there is little emphasis on continuity between the informal methods of learning among peers and with parents, and what goes on between the teacher and student. There is

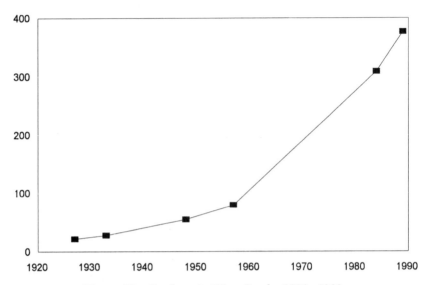

Figure 10   *Students in West Sumba 1920–1992*

instead a strong emphasis on repetition and correct interactional style, in a way that is more reminiscent of the unacknowledged "echo and elaboration" strategies of ritual-speech learning than what goes on in the home. Since neither questions nor partial repetition are normal parts of informal pedagogical practice in the home, the routines are more attuned to teaching students to understand, and appropriately respond to, forms of authoritative speaking. Such pedagogical practice socializes childen into patterns of accessing knowledge and services.

When the local language is used, it is employed in a negative context, signaling the fact that the children did not properly understand the question. The use of the local language indicates that the student requires special accommodation on the part of the teacher to help them understand. The students know that they have answered a question incorrectly if the teacher responds by asking the question again in the local language. In the example below, the teacher rephrases a question in the local language to get the children to understand. Unfortunately, Weyewa is not the native language for the teacher, and her effort to use Weyewa requires additional contextualization on the part of the students.

Plate 15   *Math lesson for seven-year-olds*

Plate 16   *A second-grade teacher pinches the ear of a boy who is not paying attention*

First-grade math lesson, August 1994:

sekarang ada lima, yah?	Now there are five, yeah?
yah!	Yeah!
Sekarang sebelah . . . itu ada sini	Now over on this side . . . there are how
berapa?	many?
tiga!	Three!
Pirra hidda?	(W) How many are there? 5
Dua!	Two!
Pirra hidda?	(W) How many are there?
dua!	Two!
berapa ini, Bahasa Indonesianya	How many are there, in Indonesian?
dua!	Two! 10
berapa ini, Bahasa Indonesianya?	How many are there, in Indonesian?
dua!	Two!
jangan lihat dulu di sana . . . berapa?	[aside] Don't look over there . . . how many?
dua!	Two!
du___?	t___? 15
Dua!	Two!
Sekarang di sini ada berapa?	Now there are how many over here?
tiga!	Three!
Sekarang kita gabung . . . ada	Now we put them all together . . .
dua disini dengan ada berapa disini?	There are two plus how many here? 20
Tiga!	Three!
Ti___?	Th___?
Tiga!	Three!
Mai yemmi ne*, mai yemmi ne*	(W) Come here* you, come here* you[5]
berapa kembali (W) ne?	How many are there back here? 25
tiga! lima!	Three! Five!
hah?	Huh?
lima!	Five!
(W)pirra hidda?	(W) How many are there?
lima!	Five! 30
betul lima?	Is that right, five?
betul!	That's right!
bahasa sini, berapa?	In the local language, how many?
(W) limma!	(W) Five!
li___?	F___? 35
lima!	Five!
li___?	F___?
lima!	Five!
li___?	F___?
lima!	Five! 40
bahasa Indonesianya apa lima?	What's the Indonesian [word] for five?
lima!	Five!
. . . duduk	. . . sit.
[pause]	
sekarang kita lihat ibu . . .	Now we'll turn our attention to the teacher.

Note: (W)= Weyewa language.

In this interaction, the teacher directly poses questions to the children and then waits for a response. Notice how the children are not called on to express their answers individually – answers are regarded as a collective responsibility. If a child gets the answer wrong, that child is not singled out by name. The responsibility for getting the right answer lies with the children, the teacher simply repeats the question until she gets the answer she wants, she makes no attempt to rephrase the question or reframe it, or to accommodate the children's state of knowledge other than using Weyewa. The clues to the desired answer lie not only in the knowledge of the referent, but in the phonetic form of the desired response – she gives partial clues to the phonetic form she wants and the children fill it in. On lines 15, 22, 35, 37, and 39, the teachers gives the first syllable of the word, and the children collectively fill it in. This is an archipelago-wide strategy, and is very common.

Unlike the indirect style of interaction in the echo and elaboration form of verbal learning, the classroom style is relatively direct, and the children as a collective whole are formally ratified as respondents. No single individual, however is recognized in either method of instruction. In elementary schools in Sumba, very seldom does a teacher ever use the name of a young student, or use it to single that child out as a designated respondent in a classroom exercise. If a child raises her hand in order to be recognized, the teacher typically acknowledges the child as a designated respondent by nodding, or by gaze. In general, however, the teacher poses a question to the "class" as a collective entity. This posing of questions, however, puts the teacher in an awkward position in terms of local ideologies of authority, because asking questions (*tuwa*) in Weyewa is tantamount to admitting that one does not know the answer, an admission of subordination (see Goody 1978). Teaching strategies in Weyewa do not normally involve questioning, but often make use of directives and negative evaluations. Positive evaluations place one in the debt of the respondent, an awkward position for an adult. There is little familiarity with the three-part system described by Mehan (1979) for United States classrooms consisting of a closed cycle of initiation, response, and evaluation.

In her comparisons of how African-American children use language at home and at school, Heath has pointed out that "methods of inquiring – seeking and extending information, confirming hypotheses, clarifying meanings – determine access not only to knowledge, but also to services" (1984: 263). In Indonesia, as in some other societies, the relation between verbal and non-verbal expression is crucial for interpreting their responses (see Philips 1983), although it has rarely been studied carefully, especially in the classroom. The central means of communicating confusion and seeking more information is remaining silent in response to a question by a teacher. The failure to respond, however, is likely to elicit a negative evaluation by the teacher, before any clarification or explanation. In those cases where the student does directly seek information, there are two ways in which this is typically done: one way is to cast eyes down, raise the hand, and very softly, almost inaudibly, request clarification, by saying, for example, *"Tidak tahu"* "[I] don't know". Another, bolder, but similarly stylized method, is for an individual to shout out, *"Tidak tahu!"* ("[I] don't know!") as though it were a collective response, without looking directly at the teacher. Students generally do not look directly at the teacher's eyes when making a response, since this is considered rude, even a challenge.

Detailed contextual knowledge was required of these seven-year-old children in order to produce the correct answers to the questions the teacher poses. When she begins by holding up some hats and suddenly, without any prior explanation, saying "now there are five, yeah?" the students were required to recognize that a verbal genre of questioning is about to follow in which they will be quizzed about their knowledge of some decontextualized problems. To complete their responses, the children need to understand that the goal of this query is not for purposes of social distribution or any other immediately apparent purpose, but to determine the quantity of the items she is holding, which is initially five. When she took three hats away, and then asked how many there were, one little boy initially answered "three" (line 5), thinking that there *should* only be three hats up in the front of the classroom, one for each of the class leaders, who each had a special hook. The children also need to know something about the interactional routine of morphological cueing, in which the teacher gives the first syllable of the correct answer and the children are expected collectively to shout the complete word. The apparent decontextualization of the semantic content of the questions obscures the richly contextualized nature of the interactional knowledge required of the children.

Once the unspoken inferences are clearly understood, the answer to the referential content of the question as posed is quite straightforward, indeed simple: How many is she holding up first? (5), then after that? (2). By contrast, the semantic, syntactic, and pragmatic content of the "echo and elaboration" routines in ritual-speech events in which a child seeks to elaborate a couplet is complex, but highly verbal, symbolic, and formal. The production of appropriate meanings depends not so much on unstated assumptions and interpretations of non-verbal cues, as on explicit verbal cues. Like the morphological cueing used by the teacher in the classroom, the adult ritual speaker provides a kind of verbal cue, but which the young novice then is expected to elaborate in thematically appropriate ways. Unlike the math lesson, the novice ritual speaker does not try to guess the unspoken meanings of a person who holds all the answers, but rather he becomes a collaborator, an assistant, a co-producer of meanings.

Teachers express anger at students in the classroom over a number of issues. Wandering attention, talking, fidgeting, and failure to follow instructions correctly are frequently causes for punishment. Aggressive behavior among the children is relatively rare, but when it does occur, the teacher often quickly decides who is at fault, and rapidly metes out justice to the offending party. In the one classroom I attended, the teacher was simply counting in Weyewa, and having the children chant after her. When one of the children failed to pay full attention and looked around the room, she walked over to him while continuing to count and hit him on the side of the head as punishment [see Plate 16]. One's bodily attitude (*sikap*) is seen as an expression of one's relationship to authority.

Ritual speech as aesthetic "culture"

There is a slot in the curriculum of the elementary and junior high schools for the teaching of local languages. Unlike other parts of the curriculum, which are rigidly prescribed from Jakarta, this slot is one that permits local discretion. While on the face of it, it would appear to make sense that the local administrations be responsible for this them- selves – after all, does it make sense for a Javanese official in Jakarta to tell a Sumbanese administrator in the Weyewa highlands how to teach Sumbanese? – on the other hand, in this highly centralized bureaucracy, without directives from the center little seems to get accomplished. Although local-language materials have been produced with central government funding, their distribution and use is poor (Kridalaksana 1993). This may have to do with the local administrators'' emphasis on national (as opposed to local) testing results, and on the legacy of orality associated with local languages.

Elite interest in the local languages and cultures has come from the universities, local scholars and the church. In Kupang, Timor, the Universitas Nusa Cendana, or UNDANA, has established a Research Center (Pusat Penelitian), which has carried out a number of documen- tary research projects devoted to the description of cultural diversity in the Province of Nusa Tenggara Timor. These books can be purchased at the university, and are also available for consultation at research libraries around the world, but are not generally available to the local population.

Plate 17   *Nggollu Sapi Dance Team with trophy*

A local scholar from East Sumba, Umbu Hina Kapita, has written several books in Indonesian on Sumbanese culture, which are sold in an East Sumbanese bookstore, but at a cost of approximately US$8–10 per book, these are out of the reach of most Sumbanese. Finally, the Catholic and Protestant Churches have developed some native-language materials, with subsidies from missionary organizations. Some native-language hymn books and a local-language New Testament have received a certain amount of acceptance. However, the distribution and reception of these materials has been poor. Most people who can read are more accustomed to reading in Indonesian, and find the reading of their native language to be a struggle.

The only arena in which ritual-speech use has acquired some more general currency among the wider, non-elite population has been in connection with school performances. Many schools have formed dance and music clubs to perform at school, church, and government functions. The elementary school of Gollu Wawi in West Weyewa is an example. The head of the school, thirty-seven-year old Johanis Malo, took over the post in 1992. A native Weyewanese, he was born in a village not far from his school to a family that is well respected in the area although not wealthy. With a steady income from his teaching position, three healthy children, and a solid position in his church, Johanis had ambitions to make a greater aesthetic statement with his life. He tried painting,

Plate 18   *Performing "ritual speech" from script*

practicing on paper during the long hours of school recess, and during vacations and breaks. Some of his efforts now adorn the walls of the elementary school he heads.

But when two of the women teachers in his school said they wanted to enter the dance competition organized by the local head of the "culture" section of the ministry of Education and Culture in the district of Wewewa Timur in West Sumba, he was interested. He got donations of gongs and costumes from several families, and the teachers began working on putting together a performance. Since they did well in the contest, which was judged by the head of the culture section in the regency (also from the Weyewa region, it turns out), they have been asked to perform on other occasions. Recently, they have performed for the provincial governor's wife in Kupang, Timor, at the horse races in Waikabubak, for weddings and Christmas celebrations at his church, for a political rally of GOLKAR, the government party in Waimangura, and twice for Western and Japanese tourists based in Waikabubak, for which Johanis Malo was paid about US$10.00 by the tour leader.

In the performance, the costumes, dances, and gong music were the featured portions of the presentation. While a woman sings in ritual-speech couplets, she stands near the back of the stage, and acts more as a kind of accompaniment to the dance and gong than as a "melody" or a situational focus of the event. These hybrid performances combine features from *woleka* ("celebration feasts"), *zaizo* ("placation rites") and *lawiti* ("songs"). Like celebration feast dancing, boys are costumed in headgear, shoulder cloths, and ankle bracelets as if preparing for battle. Young girls wear sarongs that go up over the breasts, but expose the shoulders, something ordinarily forbidden by current norms of modesty in schools and government. They also wear decorative headcloths, ivory bracelets, and necklaces.

Unlike traditional celebration performances, the more modern dance performances of boys and girls have a specific referent. They are *about* something, usually something quite specific. For example, several recent modern dance performances I have witnessed depict "rice planting." As part of their effort to represent something iconically, the dancing of the boys and girls is precisely coordinated. Whereas boys" dancing in particular usually consisted of relatively spontaneous and individualized prancing, hopping, and feinting motions (*kaba-na*) that reflected on the personal state of excitement of the performer, in these more recent performances, the boys follow a rigid choreographic regime. The girls' dancing differs from traditional *nenggo* dancing, which were slow gyrations of the wrist, arms, and hips, displaying mostly the female form; the more modern version is designed explicitly to model and depict iconically certain activities, for example, planting of rice. At a precise moment in the dance, all the girls mimic the motions of transplanting rice seedlings from the hands into the muddy soil.

Unlike the traditional dances which sometimes lasted over an hour, these modern presentations (*pertunjukan*) tend to be brief, usually only about three to four minutes long. This is because the performances are designed for competitions in which time is limited. Comparable units of time are allocated for pop songs on cassettes and radio, and for hymns in church. Like celebration feast dances, it was held in an area that permitted focussed attention, but it was not held amidst a circle of ancestral megalithic tombs and gravestones: it was the stage of the church.

Like *zaizo* placation-rite performances, the singer is accompanied directly by the drum and gong. The performer, however, is not quoting the words of an orator, or the ancestral spirits, but is responsible only for the narrative depiction contained in the song. The singer is not responsible to the ancestral spirits, but rather for evoking an image of the "traditional" in the audience. In all the events I have witnessed of this kind, the performer has been a woman, not a man, although I'm told there is no restriction against men performing in this way. The woman reads from a text to remind herself of the words to the song. Like hymn-singing in church, ritual speech in these performances resembles other such forms of specialized knowledge in modern Indonesia that are associated with literacy.

The performers were not chosen because they had family connections, or otherwise related, they were chosen largely because of their interests, their skills and physical attributes. In the performances I studied, many of the participants had no close family connections – a distinct contrast to the kinds of relationships that occur in village-based ritual-speech events. The goal of the performance was not to placate ancestral spirits but to please judges, government officials, or, in some cases, paying (Western) tourists.[6]

When Johanis Malo's "team" of dancers and singers performed on a stage at the horse races in 1994, several people pointed urgently in the direction of the woman singer, who was accompanying the dancers. "Look, Mr. Joel!" they said, "Ritual speech! Traditional speech! Go on! Record it!" Since I had already recorded several such events, I hesitated to pull out my equipment, but then I noticed an official from the Ministry of Education and Culture urging me to record. As I stood there obediently holding my microphone towards the singers, I asked myself why I was somewhat reluctant to record this event yet another time. I knew they were no less "authentic" than any of the other events I had recorded in the villages. On further reflection, what bothered me was the loss of the diversity of the verbal repertoire that this represented. For the official and those who quite sincerely were urging me on, this *was* ritual-speech. It had come to stand for, in some ways, the full range of what was in fact a diverse and complex system of performance.

It is here that its ideological function guiding language shift becomes especially clear. It is only through the *erasure* of the wide variety of performance forms that the local language – *bahasa daerah* – even becomes acceptable as a category of intellectual contemplation (cf. Keane 1997b). If the full range were to be considered – including authoritative performances of ancestral narratives, founding myths, etc – it might pose uncomfortable questions about the legitimacy and authority of the current *status quo*.

Conclusions

Irvine and Gal have noted that among the kinds of ideological processes at work in language differentiation is the process of erasure, whereby certain characteristics of language are selectively overlooked, ignored, and disregarded, thus potentially contributing to their decline. One of the areas where this kind of erasure is most prominent in Weyewa is in beliefs about learning.

Erasure is probably a necessary part of all ideologies of language learning: after all, the only way to learn speech is selectively to block certain parts of it out. Among Weyewa, performers of ritual speech in village settings deny the learning process takes place at all: most claim a miraculous inspiration by spiritual sources, and supernatural legitimacy for their "angry" verbal interventions. This denial permits learners to carry out extensive offstage, unratified gropings toward competence in performance, using stratEgies that I call "echo and elaboration." These unacknowledged interruptions by learners consist of an unratified turn at talk whereby the learner echoes a line of the speaker and then elaborates on it, and then withdraws from the conversation unacknowledged by the ratified speaker, who then repeats the statements of the learner and continues.

Since Dutch colonial *volkschool*s did not permit or reward anger as a form of verbal competence, ritual speech was of course marginal to the emerging educational institutions of the empire. Local languages were also seen as incomplete, relatively unsystematic and indeed defective. Dutch-trained teachers used it mostly to correct students when they made a mistake. Although linguists such as Onvlee and others attempted to ensure that some forms of ritual speech (mostly songs) were taught in schools, during the Second World War most of the pedagogical materials were destroyed as examples of Dutch "divide and rule" imperialism. Recently, however, ritual speech has sporadically reappeared as part of "local culture" competitions and performances. Framed as examples of Sumbanese "culture" (*kebudayaan Sumba*), what are most often displayed – and win the most trophies – are "laments," performed by women as an accompaniment to dancers and gong and drum orchestras.

7
CONCLUSIONS

Languages do not just "up and die." They do not grow old, wear out, get sick, decay, or rot. It is true that we speak of language mixing, borrowing, and code-switching, terms which seem to imply images of purity and pollution, wholeness and partiality, completeness and fragmentation. However, languages are not organisms with lives of their own, apart from the actors who use them. Languages – and the boundaries between them, their dialects, and their styles – are just as much "imagined" as the "Imagined Communities" that speak them (cf. Anderson 1991; see also Heryanto 1989).

An important point of this book is that languages differentiate, change, grow, decline, and expand not because of "natural" life cycles but because of the way that linguistic ideologies, held by interested actors and speakers and those who hold power over them, mediate between features of linguistic structure and socioeconomic relations. Ritual languages, special prestige registers, and respect languages – widely found throughout Indonesia – are a particularly good place to look for such ideologies, since they are the focus of some of the most strongly held beliefs about what language is *for*, why it exists, how it should be used, and how it should change or be preserved (see Adriani 1932; Fischer 1934; Fox 1988; Grimes and Maryott 1995; Kern 1913).

In contemporary Indonesia, the official story of linguistic change is one of "development" – the tale of the establishment, cultivation, modernization, and standardization of the national language Indonesian, often portrayed as a relatively unitary phenomenon, a single vigorous body of words and rules (Errington 1992). When local languages are factored into the national history, they are cast as potential agents of disunity and national fragmentation (Alisjahbana 1976; Fishman 1978), or as (grateful) recipients of the ever-modernizing vocabulary of Indonesian, or, more recently, as a resource for cultural heritage (see Errington 1992: 421). In scholarly discourse about language change in Indonesia, local languages are often depicted as passive victims, prey to a predatory, homogenizing national-developmental juggernaut (e.g. Kridalaksana 1993; Florey 1993). Most of these analyses implicitly support a standard

149

narrative of techno-economic development, one articulated most clearly by figures such as Gellner (1983).

Although, in Sumba, ritual-speech performances are regarded as wasteful and backward, and not in line with the goals of national development, they have not died out, or disappeared. They are still being used, but in different, more marginal ways. The particular direction and character of these changes cannot be simply reduced to political coercion, economic necessity, or religious commitment. Instead, these transformations can be placed in the framework of shifting communicative ideologies about setting and place, emotional expression, audience participation, naming and learning as a way of interpreting the particular *ways* in which ritual speech has moved from the (exemplary) center to the social and moral peripheries of their communicative world.

Although it appears that, in the course of the 1980s, there was a sudden "tip" in the decline of ritual speaking – i.e. a rapid shift away from the use of this ceremonial speech style – closer inspection of the data reveals that this phenomenon had its roots in the past (see Dorian 1989). While many Weyewa themselves attribute this loss to the increasing number of converts to Christianity, if one then asks "why are they converting to Christianity?" the answer becomes somewhat less obvious. There has been no substantial increase in missionary efforts during this period; nor has there been focussed government pressure directed toward producing converts; while the banning of large-scale ritual feasting has had some effect, this only directly affected the largest and most elaborate ceremonies.

To begin to tell the story in Weyewa terms, we must begin with the "place" of place in Weyewa ritual ideology, and examine how it was transformed from one based on the idea of an exemplary center of ritual-speech performance and authority – the ancestral villages – to one in which such places were components of the secular Dutch *onderafdeeling* ("districts"), defined by colloquial speech use. The notion of "hierarchic inclusion" is useful here because, rather than simply explaining this transformation as a purely foreign, coerced imposition, or viewing these changes as superficialities cloaking the continuity of the ancient Indonesian polity, it shows how a spatial and logical idiom was utilized by both Weyewa and their colonial masters as a way of naturalizing, regularizing, and neutralizing the disruptions of change. As Sumbanese moved out of their ancestral centers of authority and established pioneer settlements, they were free to talk about their religion as they had in the past. Performatively, however, the local discourses were necessarily incomplete, since as a lower rung of the hierarchic structure of inclusion, village leaders always lacked a key member of the audience: the Dutch. This process of hierarchic inclusion has been crucial to the transformation of language ideologies in Sumba, and quite likely in other areas of the former Dutch empire.

At the center of these places were "angry men," a charismatic category of ritual spokesmen whose towering, expressive rages were central to their authority. These men and their verbal styles were marginalized not by force so much as a collaborative process whereby these angry, emotional performances were agreed on as being *essential* to authority – indeed, the very *icon* of traditional leadership. This image played well with Sumbanese rhetoric about the "core" and "central" social position of these men, but damned them in Dutch eyes as natural, full of primitive passion, and suited to a less civilized world. In place of anger, the Dutch sought to cultivate "respect" and "cleverness"; what they got instead was "humility" and "cunning."

In the new and developing world of politics, where Sumbanese were either humble or cunning citizens, their communicative role was one of *response*; more specifically, ratification. Skills in convening an audience and then using ritual speech to enact one's central status for the assembled throng – long considered a central feature of authority in Sumba – gradually came to be relegated to an increasingly narrowed ritual domain. Political activity was becoming a matter of simply *responding* in ritually appropriate ways. Thus some Weyewa feel that the ritual cheer *yawao* has become an example of the limits of ordinary Weyewa participation in national politics.

Before they learned to be humble and clever, most high-status Weyewa were concerned with "having a name." To achieve this goal one held feasts that resulted in one's being addressed by the names of the valuables one acquired in those events. As the government cracks down on "excessive" feasting, and Christian conversion increases, naming practices and the identities that go along with them, are changing. While traditional Weyewa names distinguish between address and reference, soft and hard, and classificatory sobriquets and more strictly referential "tax names," the increasingly popular Christian names – adopted with baptism – make no such distinctions and largely tend to assume that the function of a name is to individuate particular persons and to *refer* to them. Race horses, bemos, and businesses have retained ritual-speech names, suggesting zones of autonomy and risk, but also marginality.

Learning a complex form of poetic speech like *panewe tenda* in Weyewa has never been easy, but the process was once shrouded in mystery as well. The truly proficient masters of ritual speech would not admit to ever having learned it, instead arguing that they acquired the knowledge through sudden inspiration. Ethnographic observation shows that more subtle methods of repetition and elaboration are also involved. As more and more Weyewa attend schools, ritual speech is now systematically taught in some elementary schools, in a part of the curriculum reserved for local languages. In these, only songs are taught, thus erasing the most elaborate, authoritative, and potentially challenging forms of speech from the repertoire.

What are some more general conclusions that one might draw from this research? One important result of this research is the finding that linguistic marginality can be explained with reference to *linguistic ideologies*. These ideologies seem to operate according to at least five semiotic processes.

1. *Essentialization*, whereby a linguistic feature that *indexed* a social group or category comes to be seen as *essentially* or *naturally* linked to it. Among Weyewa, the "angry" character of ritual speech, a feature that indexed the social category of "angry man," came to be seen by the Dutch as a "natural" and inherent feature of Sumbanese leadership, and part of the *essence* of the savage condition of Sumbanese authority, from which the "people" must be delivered (see Gal and Irvine 1995). Processes similar to the essentialization described here appear to be at work in Java, where the *basa* respect speech form, and its attendant features of soft delivery and emotional equilibrium have come to be viewed as essentially linked to people of elite statuses (Errington 1985a).

2. *Spectatorship* is a process in which the relation between performer and audience has come to be projected on to other communicative relations in society, such as that between state and citizen. Ecklund (1977) describes the special, couplet-based courting poetry associated with the *nyale* sea-worm festival among the Sasak of Lombok. In what was initially an opposition between boy and girl, the *nyale* dialogue has been projected on to the broader realm of religious and national politics. As governmental authority extends its reach and parental authority is loosened, *bau nyale* becomes a forum for talking about moral dilemmas concerning degrees of autonomy from parental control in mate selection. Among the Angkola Batak described by Rodgers (1979), a wedding oration, initially designed as "advice for the newlyweds," has come to be projected on to the realm of national artistic performance, in which audiences are more distanced as spectators. Bowen (1991) has also described a similar process in Gayo verbal art by which the audience acquires a more distanced role of detached experience.

3. *Erasure* "is the process in which ideology, in simplifying the field of linguistic practices, renders some persons or activities or sociolinguistic phenomena invisible" (Gal and Irvine 1995: 974). By only teaching "laments," Indonesian schools render the more authoritative

and potentially challenging forms of ritual speech invisible. Increasingly, laments are coming to stand for ritual speaking as a whole.

4. *Hierarchic inclusion* is the transformation of ideas about speech in which a language, or language variety, once seen as complete and integral by virtue of its relation to a locale comes to be viewed as included in a larger grouping. Thus Weyewa ritual speech came increasingly to be seen as a part of the Weyewa language, which was in turn a part of the larger set of languages in Indonesia.

5. *Indexicalization* is a changing attitude toward language in which the function of a sign once viewed as semantic – i.e. as designating a cultural category – comes to be viewed primarily as ostensive and pragmatic, i.e. as an act of pointing. Thus Weyewa names, which once served to classify people in terms of address and reference, soft and hard, and as high and low status, are increasingly giving way in both address and reference to Christian names used to refer to people on tax forms and in all state and personal functions. These names have little in the way of semantic functions – other than to indicate one's religion and gender.

There are other broad implications to the findings discussed in these pages, particularly for studies of *linguistic shift*, on the one hand, and *sociocultural marginality*, on the other. One of the important criticisms of studies of language shift and other related fields interested in diachronic approaches to dialectology, onomastics, and language socialization has been the failure to account for the agency of the actors in the changing communicative system (see Kulick 1992b). In this study, I have addressed that issue in several ways. First, and most broadly, I have made use of the concept of linguistic ideology as a phenomenon that mediates between linguistic structures (patterns of use), on the one hand, and socioeconomic patterns, on the other. As ideologies, they are beliefs and attitudes that reflect the *interests* of their bearers. The processes of essentialization, spectatorship, erasure, hierarchic inclusion, and indexicalization – as they were played out in the Weyewa highlands – all suited the interests of various groups, some of whom had some power and authority over others.

Second, by focussing my analysis of language change on a special style, particularly a highly valued one like ritual speech, one can witness the operation of ideological interest with striking clarity. Attitudes toward change and preservation, structure, and performance – when it comes to evaluating a form of speaking that harks back to an earlier period seen as one of revelation of truth – can all be highly charged.

Third, I have introduced key cultural models of subjectivity and selfhood through which Weyewa organize their ideas about change.

"Anger," "humility," and "cunning" are all crucially linked to, and indeed defined by, forms of ritualized expression that have been in dynamic tension with one another over time.

Fourth, I have shown that the very idea of a geographically bounded ritual language as a total, whole and complete entity has to be understood in terms of the ideological, political, and economic interests of the Sumbanese big men and their territorial control over fortified "ancestral villages." Linguistic geography can be linked systematically to ideologies of place.

As for sociocultural studies of marginality, the linguistic approach adopted here provides crucial data otherwise overlooked. For example, without examining the sociolinguistic context in which *yawao* cheers occurred, it might be difficult to explain why these forms of ratification contributed to the Weyewa sense of expectation, on the one hand, and marginality, on the other. Likewise, only by examining the actual patterns of turn taking in classrooms is it apparent that Weyewa teachers denigrate the importance of their native language by only using it as a way to correct wrong answers. Finally, only by closely attending to the patterns of semantic classification at work in the Weyewa system of proper names it is possible to see the power of the state-imposed ideology of names as identifying labels.

Kulick has usefully outlined some general factors that render a community "open" to language shift, based on his experience in the New Guinea village of Gapun (1992b: 261–4). In the present case, however, the factors giving rise to the marginality of a speech variety cannot be attributed only to community itself, but rather to the ideological dynamics created by changing institutional arrangements:

1. *Close association with other aspects of the society deemed problematic by authorities.* Since ritual speech was central to the feasting system, which the Dutch and later the Indonesian government took it upon themselves to curtail, this close connection immediately put its future in doubt.
2. *The intimate link between ritual speech and negative aspects of the self –* e.g. *anger.* The authoritative posture of ritual expression was conceived of as being "angry." But many ritual speakers, such as Mbora Kenda, recognized what came to be defined as the anti-social and negative implications of this linkage, and decided to forsake the role of ritual speaker.
3. *The weakly institutionalized methods of social reproduction.* Since ritual speakers themselves did not even acknowledge the methods by which they learned it, and relied heavily on unstated methods of learning in ritual settings, it became extremely difficult to transmit it to others

when the ceremonial context was altered. With few explicit guidelines for teaching, the new forms of institutional reproduction in schools now have a freer hand in fundamentally transforming the basic character of ritual speech.

4. *Ambivalent support in modern institutional contexts.* Though official support was provided periodically for ritual speech, it was provided in ways that undermined its own goals. In churches, while they occasionally sponsored hybrid forms of ritual performance for particular celebrations – e.g. Indonesian independence day and Christmas – it was always clear that the truly authoritative messages – such as sacraments, scriptures, and spiritual obligations – were to be articulated in Indonesian. In government contexts, when ritual speech performances are sponsored, it is usually to send a message that the very traditions represented in ritual-speech must be set aside in favor of modern ways. Finally – and perhaps most crucially – because of the indirect methods and minimal administrative staff assigned to the task of socializing Sumbanese in new ways, such innovations progressed very slowly.

In order for this form of speaking to survive, four things would need to happen:

1. Textbooks need to be produced, distributed, and their use explained.
2. The teaching of local languages in the curriculum needs to be clarified and explained to local teachers, and made compulsory at the national level, not only at the local level.
3. Teachers need to be trained in the methods of teaching the local languages, and its importance explained to them.
4. Modes of assessment and evaluation for the effectiveness of the teaching need to be constructed.

Most Weyewa, teachers and pupils alike, believe it would be a shame to lose this precious resource. As one of the defining features of their culture, its loss means no less than the loss of a key trait of their identity as a people. So far, ritual speech remains an ideologically charged way of displaying both exemplary features of selfhood and the boundaries of social, moral, and political obligations. In this sense, it continues, albeit in vastly different form from that which anyone anticipated, to enact and exemplify a Weyewa inner state.

NOTES

1. Introduction

1 The multiple-choice tests were administered in classrooms in the Weyewa ward of Kalimbundaramane to sixty-three sixth graders in 1979 and seventy-one in 1994. Although the number of students who claimed to be "Christian" in 1994 was much higher, non-Christians did not do significantly better on the tests. For more on this survey, see Appendix.

2 In at least one Internet chatroom (http: //www2.inforyoma.or.jp/~bm7/crin-fo.htm) – a space where the race, gender, and even nationality of one's interlocutors may not be immediately apparent – the fractured nature of English syntax has become a source of identity: CRIBE (Chat Room In Broken English) "is a cyber chatroom system for users of English as a foregin [sic] language and anyone tolerant of misspelling, mistyping, system lag, and diffrent [sic] culuture [sic]."

3 Cf. here also Freud's speculation about the source of religious sentiment in the "oceanic feeling," an infantile state of oneness with the mother (Freud 1961: 11–12); See Jay 1984: 21–22.

4 For Koentjaraningrat, a key structural feature of these people is that they "roam": mengembara. He suggests that the term "marginal peoples" should be avoided because of its negative connotations, and that we should instead use "people that are urged to develop" (masyarakat yang diupayakan berkembang). He suggests there are two hypotheses about the origins of marginal peoples in Indonesia: (1) they are remnants of an ancient civilization who were left behind because they inhabited a place where others rarely visited; (2) a group of people who isolated themselves when, "because of some event, they were chased, and escaped to a remote place, and thus they did not participate in the development and progress of contemporary peoples" (1993: 10). He cites the case of the Raja Ubi community in North Sumatra, a case of 850 people who isolated themselves from others when they were chased into the hinterlands in 1948 by opposing armies of Islamic fighters. If they are left alone, they will become "marginal peoples" whose customs will differ from others in the region.

5 See Wolff (1959).

6 The great Dutch ethnologist Wilken believed that "generally speaking, [Indo-nesian] languages distinguish themselves through a particular impoverishment of words for expressions of generalities, while they are rich in words for particulars" (1892: 141).

156

3. Towering in rage and cowering in fear: emotion, self, and verbal expression in Sumba

1 C. E. Lansz, in his memoire of 1919, also mentions this loquacity rather irritably: "the Sumbanese has a big mouth, and makes a big impression, but is in fact quite cowardly" (1919: 27).

2 Roos, for instance, rarely mentions encounters with women, but, when he does, they are often positive: "Oemboe Daij is married to a Melolo princes who is very friendly and kind . . ." (1872: 107).

In accounts by Dutch missionaries and travel writers, Sumbanese women do not exhibit "anger" but rather a blend of shy humility and clever coyness. For instance, Ten Kate, a connoisseur, Orientalist scholar, philologist, and travel writer, visited the island in 1890. His writing style – like a verbal postcard:

> With great pearls of sweat on their faces, half shy, half defiant coquettes, they stepped forward toward the foreign master (*maramba djawa*), whose judgement they did not fear, for they were beautiful: beautifully in harmony in form and proportion, bordering on the ideal, the canon of human shape that the artists search for. (Ten Kate 1894: 587, quoted in Hangelbroek 1910: 50)

Under Ten Kate's gaze as "foreign master," the women are not threats but admirable aesthetic objects. It should be noted that it is only the Sumbanese women who receive positive descriptions by the Dutch.

Women are not a sexual or military threat, they are a threat to hygiene and purity. Another traveler, the missionary Hangelbroek, quotes the passage cited above with approval, adding:

> It is good that the Creator has endowed [Sumbanese women] with a good deal of natural beauty, and that when spoken to, they excel through a friendly and merry personality. For these women are dirty in the extreme! (1910: 50)

While such verbal and interactional autonomy was encouraged, their hygiene and sexual behavior was troubling.

3 Hollan and Wellenkamp note that their respondent, Ambe'na Kondo, distinguishes managerial anger from "real" anger: "Very often [I am angry at the meat division]. But I'm not really angry. It's only anger of the mouth! If we are angry at the mouth, that's so that people won't bother the distribution [of meat]" (1994: 114). In Toraja terms, many Weyewa displays of angry men would be "anger of the mouth."

4 The rise of the *pandai* "cunning" male was not restricted to Sumba: it took slightly different forms in Java, but Anderson describes the Raden Pandji figures and the Ken Angrok figure in Java, and the *parewa* figure in Minangkabau as "they live by gambling, experts in cockfighting, experts in *pentak* and *silat*" (Hamka 1987)

5 In a notable scene in Janet Hoskins and Laura Scheerer's film *Feast in dream village*, a renowned ritual spokesman in the Kodi region of Sumba, named Piro Pawali dramatically stomps off to another house to protest a perceived slight to his status, thus separating himself from the rest of the ritual activities in the village. Sitting on the porch and yelling at the other participants, he not only

has the complete attention of the ritual sponsors (and the filmmakers), but is able effectively to underscore his autonomy, and his status, in a way comparable with what Mbora Kenda sought to achieve in the earlier example (see p. 63).

4. Changing forms of political expression: the role of ideologies of audience completeness

1 Cf. Tsing's related observation that "power means . . . the ability to convene an audience" (1990: 122).
2 He was such an impressive figure that he was the main subject of the Indonesian portions of the PBS television series *Millennium* that was shown in May 1992.
3 It is not now required, nor was it a ritual requirement in the past for young men, for example, to prove themselves in battle or headhunting in Sumba. While military prowess and bravery have long been regarded as important, actual combat against enemies seems to have been delegated in many cases in the past to Endenese mercenaries, who were the hirelings of, or worked side by side with, the "angry man." Soldierly skills were valued and accorded prestige, but were not essential to full membership in the ritual cults serving ancestral spirits, or various tutelary spirits of the forests, streams, and fields.
4 The event was filmed and later aired on PBS in May 1992 as part of the Millennium Series, *A poor man shames us all.*
5 This is a reference to a myth in which a crocodile carries a horse across a body of water.
6 I draw here very broadly on Mary Steedly's term (1993: 199) although I mean something more specific and sociolinguistic by it.
7 According to Max Weber (Bendix 1960), the evolving empowerment of the autonomous reasoning individual within the framework of a legal bureaucratic state was the hallmark of modern citizenship. While Roman and Greek citizenship was guaranteed partly by cult participation and kinship ties, it eventually became, with the rise of burghers in the European cities, an individual contract with the state. Christianity also helped to weaken the bonds of the family by creating a confessional community of individuals rather than an association of kinship-based cults. The religious idiom later became an important source of imagining community in the organization of the modern nation (Anderson 1991). What guided this process of evolution for Weber was the inevitable progress of rationalization and secular "disenchantment" as it ramified through areas of commerce, religion, and law.
   Critics contend that Weber was ethnocentric in his conception of "reason," and in his teleological view that secular Western-type social values were the inevitable endpoint of such historical development. As Jean Comaroff (1994) has pointed out, many Asian systems of authority have "defied disenchantment" and have maintained a central role for religion and ritual in their modern polities even as they have redefined them.
8 Waitz (1933: 57) concludes his *memoire* with a Calvinist manifesto: "The Soembanese wants to be ruled with an iron hand. Be strong, but fair. Weakness will be punished . . . much patience and tact is required of the administrator. Stay cheerful."

9 *Langsung*, "Direct" *Umum*, "General, Public," *Bebas*, "Free" *Rahasia*, "Secret."

10 "*Pemilu ini, tidak usah lagi. Buat apa kita bikin susah diri dengan pemilu? Bagaimana? Kalau saya jadi calon presiden, akan saya dipilih? Sama sekali tidak mungkin. Apa yang akan terjadi, akan terjadi. Lebih baik, yawao, pulang sudah.*"

5. Ideologies of personal naming and language shift

1 Hoskins (1993) has pointed out – and Geertz himself seemed presciently aware of this (1973: 409) – that when the Geertzes were conducting fieldwork in the late 1950s prior to the bloody anti-communist reprisals of 1965 and 1966, "time may have *appeared* immobilized, but after many thousand Balinese were killed in the wake of an alleged coup no one could deny the force of national history and its ability to disrupt even the most carefully calibrated ceremonialism" (1993: 71).

2 I was told that some clans have their own *ngara katto* ("hard names") for the standard names. For instance, for *Lende*, the Mangu Tana clan uses *Gado*, while the Baliloko clan may use *Ngedo*, while the Lewata uses the standard *Rua*.

3 Onvlee says this also occurs with verb roots (1930: 241). I did not find this to be a common occurrence in Weyewa.

4 Some people have a *ngara kambaila*, a "secret name," that they acquire through dreams, miraculous encounters in the forest, or from ancestors. Such secret spiritual counterparts are known as *zora*, "spiritual counterpart." One rich man, who was widely accused of being stingy and greedy, was said to have a secret name that derived from his occasional encounters with a civet cat in the jungle, whom he consulted for magical powers. He shared the name with the civet cat after meeting it in the forest, and the two were *tamo* ("namesakes"), but he would not tell anyone else the name.

5 Refers to the water buffalo's ability to *doda* ("flatten out, conquer") the grasses in the rice field during pre-planting preparation of soil.

6 Refers to the dog's habit of accompanying its owner on trading expeditions.

7 Refers to the great length of the spear.

8 Girls' identities, to some extent, are differentiated for them by the institution of marriage, in which a girl is spatially and emotionally separated from her parents when she moves in with her husband.

9 Enjoyment of physical consumption is only a part of the service yielded by goods; the other is the enjoyment of sharing names. Mary Douglas and Baron Isherwood (1979: 75).

10 The dog was said to be named after a raid on a village in Lombo in which many people were killed.

11 Very large water buffalo are useful for preparing the soil of rice fields, and one with great strength who can "crush the earth" is particularly valuable.

12 Figure 9 only includes numbers from the Protestant Church for West Sumba because figures for the Catholic Church do not date back as far. In the past twenty years, however, the Catholic church has experienced similarly explo-

sive growth, and the number of Christians overall in West Sumba is over 70 percent (Kantor Statistik Sumba Barat 1992).

13 It is still possible to address someone as *tamo* ("namesake") on the basis of a shared last name.

14 Since these family names often derive from the older system of "hard" and "soft" names, this Western-derived patronymic system could – ironically – become a vehicle for the survival of this native system.

15 Common Indonesian names for bemos derive from the (rather sentimental) themes of pan-Indonesian Chinese urban culture: "fruits of love" (*buah cinta*), "golden diamond" (*intan mas*), "ocean" (*samudra*), "ray of hope" (*sinar harapan*).

16 The bemo names in Weyewa are occasionally lines from a couplet: one bemo was named *manda elu* ("beautiful view") which everyone knows is paired with *pada eweta* ("fertile meadow").

17 Land and buildings are sometimes also given couplet names, but these items are not seen as standing for or exchangeable for the owner so much as the referent.

6. From miracles to classrooms: changing forms of erasure in the learning of ritual speech

1 Another objection the Sumbanese raised was that the children would have to cut their hair:

> They feel that an animist should not do this. Christians cut their hair, and this is a way one can often tell whether someone is christian or heathen. When I gave permission for them to have long hair, there was some relief. But I insist they be hygienic and well washed! The custodial issues over the children also posed nagging problems: They seem to assume that the children would be my personal possession . . . After a [few weeks at school, the parents would say] "when the child finally becomes grown up and intelligent, take them off to Java or Holland." On an island where children are units of alliance and exchange between families, this is implies serious economic, political and social obligations on the part of the missionary.

2 The Dutch were suggesting that responsibility for educational performance transcended age categories; in a way, they were asking the Sumbanese to trade in age hierarchies for a more class-based system. As the Sumbanese came to see it, selected elite Sumbanese Indonesians, both young and old, had a responsibility to accommodate to the upper-class Dutch norm. If they did so, rich rewards could be theirs, which could be passed down through generations. Instead of seeing hierarchy in terms of age, they were being urged to see it more in terms of class.

3 "[By training native leaders], the mistakes that are made will not be blamed so much on us but rather on their own compatriots." They could save money by "replacing European officials wherever possible with Native officials [who] will be paid at a lower salary based on the low standard of living of the people" (Cohen-Stuart in Penders 1968: 111).

4 That is, since the rise of colonialism in Indonesia.

5 *mai yemmi ne* ("come heres you") is ungrammatical Weyewa. As is common

in Indonesia, this teacher is from another language group, and her knowledge of the local language is poor.

6 As I was preparing to leave for the US during my last visit, I stayed in a new (three years old in 1994) hotel in Waikabubak. In the hotel were about half a dozen tourists, mostly from western Europe. Germany, the Netherlands, Britain, and Japan are among the more important sources of tourists in West Sumba. One night after returning to my hotel room, I walked through the tiled lobby and was approached by a young man wearing a traditional headcloth and waistcloth, and perfectly faded Levi's jean jacket.

"You like guide?" he asked me in English. I was fascinated, because while such cultural brokerage and guiding was commonplace in Bali, this was the first time I had ever been approached on the street, so to speak, by someone marketing his skills as a guide to Sumbanese culture. I asked him what kind of services he offered. He listed for me a number of rituals he could escort me to: (1) a stone-dragging ceremony in Wanukaka to take place in two days; (2) a house-building ceremony in Weyewa in a week; (3) a feast in Laboya. I asked him how he knew about all these events. He said all these events were with the "families of rajas," with which he had a "close connection." What was his connection? He was a relative of an East Sumbanese raja who had worked in a Waikabubak Chinese shop for many years, thus bringing him into contact with Sumbanese elites from many parts of the island who had come to trade in the town. He became familiar with them, and began to trade on his acquaintances for economic benefit, not always to the satisfaction of the "rajas" he claimed to know so well.

He mentioned that there was a guide book sold in the art shop established near the market in downtown Waikabubak that could provide detailed English-language explanations of local culture; I went and picked up a copy (about US$10 for thirty-five photocopied and bound pages) and was surprised to discover many quotes and illustrations from my own earlier book (Kuipers 1990) staring me in the face.

APPENDIX

Ritual-speech survey of twelve-year-olds students 1979–1994

The multiple-choice tests were administered in classrooms in Kalimbundaramane to sixty-three sixth graders (twelve-year-olds) in 1980 and seventy-one in 1994. Although the number of students who claimed to be "Christian" in 1994 was much higher, non-Christians did not do significantly better on the tests; nor did the religion of their parents affect the score. Boys did somewhat better than girls.

I. Data-data pribadi: tulis jawaban yang tepat.
[personal information: write the appropriate answer]

Nama: [name]
Umur [age]
tempat tinggal [residence]
kelamin P L [sex: F M]
dibaptis: sudah belum [baptized: yes or no]
agama orang tua: prot kat marapu islam [religion of parents: prot cath marapu islam]

*II. Arti-arti daripada beberapa baitan: melinkari jawaban yang tepat [the meanings of some couplets: circle the right answer. Note: asterisk * indicates the correct answer]*

1. a ndita we'e   [who fills the water cisterns]
   a powi api   [who keeps the fires burning]
   a) orang yang menyanyi [person who sings]
   b) orang yang rasa dingin [a person who feels cold]
   c) orang yang mendiami rumah adat [a person who lives in an ancestral house]*
   d) binatang yang mengisi tempat air dengan guna2 [animal that fills cisterns with magic]
2. mate moro longge [die with blue-black hair]
   zeda kaka ngundu [die with white teeth]
   a) pemuda [a young man]
   b) meninggal karena sakit [die of an illness]
   c) orang yang meninggal masih mudah [person who dies young]*
3. mata we'e pawali [water source of origin]

162

pola punge darra [base of the tree]
a) pihak om [mother's brother's side of the family]*
b) mata air [spring]
c) pohon yang besar [a large tree]

4. karere rawi wola [flowering tendrils of the cucumber]
karobo rawi uwa [blossoming vines of the gourd]
a) keturunan dari seorang leluhur [descendants of an ancestor]*
b) tanaman-tanaman [cultivated plants]
c) hasil dari sesuatu kegiatan [fruits of an activity]

5. maliti a pambewa [a shady banyan tree]
kadokke a panganggo [a sheltering banyan tree]
a) pohon ayng besar [a large tree]
b) orang yang berkuasa [a powerful person]*
c) tempat yang sejuk [a shady, cool place]

6. kapingge ndappa rutto [water spider without blood]
kaballa ndappa ate [grasshopper without a liver]
a) hama-hama yang makan padi [rice pests]
b) orang yang bodoh [a stupid person]
c) orang yang belum pengalaman [a person with little experience]*

7. ndara ndende kiku [horse with a standing tail]
bongga mette lomma [dog with a black tongue]
a) orang pembicara yang hebat [a great ritual spokesman]*
b) orang yang diiringi oleh kuda dan anjing [a person accompanied by a dog and horse]
c) tempat pesta besar [place of a large feast]

8. kadu ndappa toda [horn that cannot be pollarded]
ulle ndappa roro [tusk that cannot be trimmed]
a) pesta yang tidak bisa ditundu [feast that cannot be postponed]
b) orang yang tidak bisa dikalahkan [person who cannot be dominated]*
c) hewan yang belum bisa dipotong [livestock not ready for slaughter]

9. ndappa zuma ngara [name that cannot be mentioned]
ndappa tekki tamo [title that cannot be uttered]
a) orang yang dihormati [person who is respected]
b) leluhur [ancestors]
c) Tuhan Yang Mahaesa [the Supreme Being]*

10. wengowe kuru [chest rash]
rarangge mata [blushing face]
a) orang yang mengadakan urrata [a person performing divination]*
b) orang yang sakit [a sick person]
c) orang yang marah [an angry person]

11. nguru-nguru mawo wengga [rumbling in the shadow of Wengga]
nyangi-nyangi loko toza [tinkling of the Toza brook]
a) bunyi-bunyi dari orang menyanyi [the sounds of someone singing]
b) gong zaizo [the gongs of the placation rite]*
c) bunyi-bunyi dari daerah Laboya [sounds from the Laboya region]

12. a pazangera parawi inna [who stand next to ancestral heirlooms]
a pazadidi parawi ama [who accompany the ancient works]

    a) a zaizo [the singer in placation rites]*
    b) leluhur [ancestors]
    c) orang yang tua [an old person]

13. a kalete towona [who rides the brow]
    a kazonga balena [who travels on the shoulders]
    a) kawan dalam perjalanan [a fellow traveler]
    b) jin-jin jahat [evil spirits]
    c) dewa yang melindungi [protector spirits that protect]*

14. a rukutana wazu [who splinters the wood]
    a lekatana umma [who demolishes the house]
    a) orang jahat [a evil person]
    b) angin hebat [a strong windstorm]
    c) dewa yang jahat [an evil spirit]*

15. lambe a mbeleka [wide rat disk]
    parii a kalada [tall house pillar]
    a) umah yang besar [a large house]
    b) jiwa leluhur [ancestral spirit]*
    c) orang yang kaya [a rich person]

Cocokkan [matching – respondents were asked to draw]

1. bongga ole urra [dog soulmate]   mbatu rutta [pull the weeds] [3]
2. a nonga powi [who blows the flute]   a bale dungga [who plays in response] [2]
3. ndari tana [work the land]   ndara ole ndewa [horse of common spirit] [1]
4. manu a mawenna [the right chicken]   rawi rato [feast of princes] [5]
5. wolo pondi [gathering of nobles]   tangana kandauke [match the words] [8]
6. mattu mata [faces are complete]   nduru api [tend the fire] [7]
7. mbeika teppe [lie on the mat]   tanga wiwi [the lips are paired] [6]
8. nggobbana panewe [pair the words]   wawi a manoto [the exact pig] [4]
9. nyura lele mayango [curling ivory]   we'e paboba yarra [bubbling water] [9]

REFERENCES

Abu-Lughod, Lila 1986 *Veiled sentiments: honor and poetry in a Bedouin society.* Berkeley: University of California.

Adriani, N. 1932 Indonesische Priestertaal. In *Verzamelde Geschriften*, vol. III, pp. 1–21. Haarlem: De Erven F. Bohn.

Agnew, Jean-Christophe 1986 *Worlds apart: the market and the theatre in Anglo-American thought 1550–1750.* Cambridge: Cambridge University Press.

Alisjahbana, Sutan Takdir 1976 *Language planning for modernization: the case of Indonesian and Malaysian.* The Hague: Mouton.

1986 The relation of Language, Thought and Culture as Reflected in the Development of the Indonesian Language. *International Journal of the Sociology of Language* 62: 25–49.

Allerton, D. J. 1987 The linguistic and sociolinguistic status of proper names. *Journal of Pragmatics* 11: 61–92.

Anderson, Benedict O'G. 1990 *Language and power: exploring Indonesia's political cultures.* Ithaca, NY: Cornell University Press.

1991 *Imagined communities: reflections on the origin and spread of nationalism,* revised edn. London: Verso.

1996 Colonial language policies in Indonesia and the Philippines: a contrast in intended aims and unintended outcomes. In Laura Garcia-Moreno and Peter Pfeiffer, eds., *Text and nation: cross-disciplinary essays on cultural and national identities.* Columbia, SC: Camden House.

Anonymous 1922 Paarden en buffelfokkerij in de onderafdeeling West Soemba. *Nederlandsch-Indische Balden Voor Dieren Geneeskunde en Dierenteelt* 36: 220–228.

Anttila, Raimo 1980 Totality, relation and the autonomous phoneme. *Cahiers de L'institut de linguistique de Louvain* 6.(3–4): 49–64.

Babcock, Barbara, ed. 1977 *Reversible worlds.* Ithaca, NY: Cornell University Press.

Bakhtin, Mikhail 1979 *Rabelais and his world* .Cambridge, MA: MIT Press.

1986 *Speech genres and other late essays,* trans. Vern McGee, Michael Holquist and Caryl Emerson. Austin, TX: University of Texas Press.

Barraud, Cecile and Jos Platenkamp, eds. 1992 Rituals and sociocosmic order in Eastern Indonesian societies (2 vols). *Bijdragen tot de Taal, Land, en Volkenkunde* 145/6.

Bauman, Richard and Charles Briggs 1990 Poetics and performance as critical perspectives on language and social life. *Annual Review of Anthropology* 19: 59–88.

Bean, Susan S. 1980 Ethnology and the study of proper names. *Anthropological Linguistics* 22: 305–16.

Bendix, Reinhard 1960 *Max Weber: an intellectual portrait.* Garden City, NY: Doubleday.

Berg, C. C. 1951 *De Problematiek an het Bahasa Indonesia Experiment.* Jakarta: Wolters.

Bernstein, Basil 1974 *Class, codes and control: theoretical studies towards a sociology of language*, revised edn. New York: Schocken Books.

Bickerton, Derek 1983 Creole languages. *Scientific American.* 249 (July): 116–122.

Biro Statistik 1984 *Sumba Barat Dalam Angka.* Waikabubak: Biro Statistik.

Bowen, John 1986 On the political construction of tradition: gotong royong in Indonesia. *The Journal of Asian Studies* 45: 545–61.

　1991 *Sumatran politics and poetics: Gayo history 1900–1989.* New Haven, CT: Yale University Press.

　1993 *Muslims through their discourse.* Princeton, NJ: Princeton University Press.

Brenneis, Donald 1997 Comment on "Against constructionism: an historical ethnography of emotion" by William Reddy. *Current Anthropology* 38.(3): 340–1.

Cambier van Nooten, W. H. J. 1928 *Vervolg Memorie Van Overgave van de Afdeeling Soemba, Augustus 1928.* [Zug, Switzerland: Interdocumentation].

Campbell, Lyle and Martha Muntzel 1989 The structural consequences of language death. In Nancy Dorian, ed., *Investigating obsolescence: studies in language contraction and death*, pp. 181–96. Cambridge: Cambridge University Press.

Chambers, J. K. and Peter Trudgill 1980 *Dialectology.* Cambridge: Cambridge University Press.

Clifford, James and George Marcus, eds. 1986 *Writing culture: the poetics and politics of ethnography.* Berkeley: University of California.

Comaroff, Jean 1994 Defying disenchantment. In Charles F. Keyes, Laurel Kendall, and Helen Hardacre, eds., *Asian visions of authority: religion and the modern states of East and Southeast Asia* Honolulu: University of Hawaii Press.

Couvreur, A. J. L. 1914 *Memorie van Overgave.* Afdeeling Soemba [Memoires]. Unpublished archival material. Zug, Switzerland: Interdocumentation.

　1917 Aard en Wezen der inlandsch zelfbesturen op het eiland Soemba. *Tijdschrift van het Binnenlandsch Bestuur* 52: 206–19.

Cunningham, Clark E. 1964 Order in the Atoni House. *Bijdragen tot de Taal- Land- en Volkenkunde* 120: 34–69=8.

Curtius, Edward 1953 *Literature and the European Middle Ages.* Princeton, NJ: Princeton University Press.

Dapawole, L. 1965 *Sumba Membuka Tabir* [Sumba opens the curtain]. Waika- bubak: Dewan Raja-raja.

Dijkstra, H. [1920] 1987 De Plaats van het onderwijs in de zendingsarbeid. In Th. Van Den End, ed., *Gereformeerde Zending Op Sumba 1859–1972* <Nether- lands>: Uitgave van de Raad voor de Zending der Ned. Herv. Kerk, de Zending der Gereformeerde Kerken in Nederland en de Gereformeerde Zendingsbond in Ned. Herv. Kerk.

Direktorat Jenderal Pertanian, 1973 *Monografi Daerah Sumba Barat, Propinsi Nusa Tenggara Timur.* Jakarta: Direktorat Jenderal Pertanian.

Dorian, Nancy ed. 1982 Defining the speech community in terms of its working margins. In Suzanne Romain, ed., *Sociolinguistic variation in speech commu- nities*, pp. 25–33. London: Edwards.

1989a Introduction. In Nancy Dorian, ed., *Investigating obsolescence: studies in language contraction and death*, pp. 1–10. Cambridge: Cambridge University Press.

1989b *Investigating obsolescence: studies in language contraction and death.* Cambridge: Cambridge University Press.

Douglas, Mary and Baron Isherwood 1979 *The world of goods.* New York: Basic Books.

Duranti, Alessandro 1984 Ethnography of speaking: towards a linguistics of the praxis. In Frederick Newmeyer, ed., *Linguistics: the Cambridge Survey. Vol. IV: Language: socio-cultural context*, pp. 210–28. Cambridge: Cambridge University Press.

Ecklund, Judith 1977 Marriage, seaworms and song: ritualized responses to cultural change in Sasak life. PhD dissertation, Department of Anthropology, Cornell University, Ithaca, NY.

Eco, Umberto 1997 *The search for the perfect language.* Oxford: Blackwell.

Ellen, Roy F. 1976 The development of anthropology and colonial policy in the Netherlands: 1800–1960. *Journal of the History of the Behavioral Sciences* 12: 303–324.

Emeneau, Murray 1980 *Language and linguistic area.* Stanford, CA: Stanford University Press.

Errington, J. Joseph 1985a *Language and social change in Java: linguistic reflexes of modernization in a traditional royal polity.* Athens: Ohio University Monographs in International Studies. Southeast Asia Series, No. 65.

1985b On the nature of the sociolinguistic sign: describing the Javanese speech levels. In Elizabeth Mertz and Richard Parmentier, eds., *Semiotic mediation: sociocultural and psychological perspectives*, pp. 287–310. New York: Academic Press.

1986 Continuity and change in Indonesian language development. *Journal of Asian Studies* 45.(2): 329–353.

1992 State speech for peripheral publics in Java. 11-page unpublished manuscript.

Fischer, D. Th. 1934 *Priestertaalan: Een Ethnologiese Studie.* s'Gravenhage: Martinus Nijhoff.

Fishman, Joshua 1978 The Indonesian language planning experience: what does it teach us? In S. Udin, ed., *Spectrum: essays presented to Sutan Takdir Alisjahbana on his seventieth birthday*, pp. 333–339. Jakarta: Dian Rakyat.

Florey, Margaret 1993 The reinterpretation of knowledge and its role in the process of language obsolescence. *Oceanic Linguistics* 32.(2): 295–309.

Forth, Christine 1982 An analysis of traditional narrative in Eastern Sumba PhD dissertation, Department of Anthropology, Oxford University.

Forth, Gregory L. 1981 *Rindi: an ethnographic study of a traditional domain in eastern Sumba.* The Hague: Martinus Nijhoff. Verhandelingen van het Koninklijk Instituut voor Taal-, Land- en Volkenkunde no. 93.

1983 Blood milk and coconuts: a study of intracultural variation. *Man* 18.(4): 654–668.

1988 Fashioned speech, full communication. In James J. Fox, ed., *To speak in pairs: essays on the ritual languages of eastern Indonesia.* Cambridge: Cambridge University Press.

Fox, James J. 1980 *The flow of life: essays on eastern Indonesia.* Cambridge, MA: Harvard University Press.

1988 *To speak in pairs: essays on the ritual languages of eastern Indonesia.* Cambridge: Cambridge University Press.

Fox, James J. and Clifford Salter, eds., 1996 *Origins, ancestry and alliance: explorations in Austronesian ethnography.* Canberra: Department of Anthropology, Australian National University.

Freud, Sigmund 1961 *Civilization and its discontents* translation of *Das Unbehagen in der Kultur.* New York: W. W. Norton.

Gal, Susan 1995 Language and the "arts of resistance." *Cultural Anthropology* 10.(3): 407–424.

Gal, Susan and Judith Irvine 1995 The boundaries of language and disciplines: how ideologies construct differences. *Social Research* 62.(4): 967–1001.

Geertz, Clifford 1968 *Islam observed.* Chicago: University of Chicago Press.

1973 *Interpretation of culture.* New York: Free Press.

1980 *Negara: the theatre state in nineteenth century Bali.* Princeton, NJ: Princeton University Press.

1983 *Local knowledge: further essays in interpretive anthropology.* New York: Basic Books.

1994 Life on the edge [book review of] *In the realm of the diamond queen* by Anna Lowenhaupt Tsing. *New York Review of Books* 41.(7): 3–4.

Gellner, Ernest 1983 *Nations and nationalism.* Ithaca, NY: Cornell University Press.

Germani, Gino 1980 *Marginality.* New Brunswick, NJ: Transaction Books.

Goody, Esther, ed., 1978 *Questions and politeness.* Cambridge: Cambridge University Press.

Goossens, Jan 1977 Wat is dialectologie? In Bernard T. Tervoort, ed., *Wetenscap & taal,* pp. 173–189. Muiderberg: Coutinho.

Gorkom, Karel Wessel van 1896 *Gids Voor de controleurs bij het Binnenlands Bestuur.* Batavia: Kolff.

Gouda, Frances 1995 *Dutch culture overseas: colonial practice in the Netherlands Indies, 1900–1942.* Amsterdam: Amsterdam University Press.

Grimes, Charles E. and Kenneth Maryott 1994 Named speech registers in Austronesian languages. In *Language contact and change in the Austronesian world.* Tom Dutton and Darrell T. Tryon, eds., pp. 275–319. New York: Mouton de Gruyter.

Groeneboer, Kees 1992 *Weg tot het Westen: het Nederlands voor Indie, 1600–1950: een taal politieke geschiedenis.* Leiden: KITLV Uitgeverij (Verhandeling van Koninklijk Instituut voor Taal- Land- en Volkenkunde no. 158).

Groeneveld, F. J. 1931 *Memorie van Overgave van de gezaghebber van West Soemba, loopende over het tijdperk van 23 November to 2 Oktober 1931.* Zug, Switzerland: Interdocumentation.

Gronovius, D. J. van den Dungers 1855 Beschrijving van het eiland Soemba van Sandelhout. *Tijdschrift voor Nederlandsch Indie* 17: 277–312.

Hall, Robert Anderson 1955 *Hands off pidgin English!* Sydney: Pacific Publication Pty Languages.

Hamka 1987 *Tenggelamnya Kapal Van Der Wijck.* Kuala Lumpur: Pustaka Antara.

Hangelbroek, H. 1910 *Soemba: land en volk.* Assen: G. F. Hummelen.

Hanks, William 1987 Discourse genres in a theory of practice. *American Ethnologist* 14.(4): 668–692.

Hansen, David O. et al. 1989 Determinants of access to higher education in Indonesia. *Comparative Education Review* 33.(3): 17–33.

Hansen, Miriam 1995 *Babel and Babylon: spectatorship in American silent film.* Cambridge, MA: Harvard University Press.

Haripranata 1984 *Sejarah Gereja di Sumba dan Sumbawa* [History of the church in Sumba and Sumbawa]. Ende: Arnoldus.

Haugen, Einar 1972 *The ecology of language*, ed. Anwar Dil. Stanford, CA: Stanford University Press.

Heath, Shirley Brice 1984 Linguistics and education. *Annual Review of Anthropology* 13: 251–274.

Heine-Geldern, Robert 1942 Conceptions of state and kingship in Southeast Asia. *Far Eastern Quarterly* 2: 15–39.

Heryanto, Ariel 1989 Berjangkitnya bahasa-bangsa di Indonesia [The spread of language and ethnicity in Indonesia]. *Prisma* 18.(1): 3–16.

Hill, Jane 1993 Structure and practice in language shift. In Kenneth Hyltenstam and Viberg Ake, eds., *Progression and regression in language: sociocultural, neuropsychological, and linguistic perspectives*, pp. 69–93. Cambridge: Cambridge University Press.

Hirsch, Eric Donald 1987 *Cultural literacy: what every American needs to know.* New York: Vintage Books.

Hoekstra, Peter 1948 *Paardenteelt op het eiland Soemba.* Batavia: John Kappee.

Hoffman, J. 1979 A foreign investment: Indies Malay to 1901. *Indonesia* 27: 65–92.

Hollan, Douglas and Jane C. Wellenkamp 1994 *Contentment and suffering: culture and experience in Toraja.* New York: Columbia University Press.

hooks, bell 1990 *Yearnings: race, gender and cultural politics.* Boston: South End Press.

Hoskins, Janet 1985 "So my name shall live: stone dragging and grave-building in Kodi, West Sumba. *Bijdragen tot de Taal, Land- en Volkenkunde* 132: 31–51.

1993 *The play of time: Kodi perspectives on calendars, history and exchange.* Berkeley: University of California Press.

ed. 1996 *Headhunting and the sacred imagination in Southeast Asia.* Stanford, CA: Stanford University Press.

Hoven, W. 1930.*Verslag van den ambtenaar bij de afdeeling Bestuurszaken der Buitengewesten van het Department van Binnenlandsch Bestuur, Residentie Timor en Onderhoorigheden, in maanden October en November 1930.* Unpublished archival material.

Hunt, Lynn Avery 1992 *The family romance of the French Revolution.* Berkeley: University of California Press.

Hymes, Dell 1974 *Foundations in sociolinguistics.* Philadelphia: University of Pennsylvania Press.

Irvine, Judith T. 1982 Language and affect: some cross-cultural issues. In H. Byrnes, ed. ,*Contemporary perceptions of language: interdisciplinary dimensions*, pp. 31–47. Washington DC: Georgetown University Roundtable in Language and Linguistics.

1990 Registering affect: heteroglossia in the linguistic expression of emotion. In Catherine A. Lutz and Lila Abu-Lughod, eds., *Language and the politics of emotion*, pp. 126–161. Cambridge: Cambridge University Press. Studies in Emotion and Social Interaction.

Irvine, Judith and Susan Gal 1998 Language ideology and linguistic differentiation. In Bambi B. Schieffelin, Kathryn A. Woolard, and Paul Kroskrity, eds., *Language Ideologies: practice and theory.* New York: Oxford University Press.

Jay, Martin 1984 *Marxism and totality: the adventures of a concept from Lukacs to Habermas.* Berkeley: University of California Press.

Johnson, James H. 1995 *Listening in Paris: a cultural history*. Berkeley: University of California Press.

Jonker, Johann 1885 *Een Oud Javaansch Wetboek vergeleken met Indisch Rechtsbronnen*. Leiden: E.J. Brill.

Kantor Statistik Sumba Barat 1984 *Sumba Barat Dalam Angka*. Waikabubak: Kantor Statistik Sumba Barat.

1989 *Sumba Barat Dalam Angka*. Waikabubak: Kantor Statistik Sumba Barat.

1992 *Sumba Barat Dalam Angka*. Waikabubak: Kantor Statistik Sumba Barat.

Kapita, Umbu Hina 1976 *Masyarakat Sumba dan Adat Istiadatnya* [Sumbanese society and its customs]. Waingapu: Gereja Keristen Sumba.

Kay, Paul 1977 Language evolution and speech style. In Ben G. Blount and Mary Sanches, eds., *Sociocultural dimensions of language change*, pp. 21–33. New York: Academic Press.

Keane, Webb 1997a Knowing one's place: national language and the idea of the local in eastern Indonesia. *Cultural Anthropology* 12.(1): 37–63.

1997b *Signs of recognition*. Berkeley: University of California Press.

Kern, H. 1913 Woordverwisseling in het Galelareesch. In *Verspreide Geschriften*. 's-Gravenhage: Martinus Nijhoff.

Keyes, Charles, eds. 1991 *Reshaping local worlds: formal education and cultural change in rural Southeast Asia*. Monograph 36. Yale Southeast Asia Studies. New Haven, CT: Yale Center for International and Area Studies.

Kloosterhuis, G. 1936 Afschrift: De dienst der Volksgezondheid in West Soemba. Unpublished archival material.

Koentjaraningrat, ed. 1993 *Masyarakat Terasing*. Jakarta: Gramedia.

Kridalaksana, Harimurti 1979 Lexicography in Indonesia. *RELC Journal: A Journal of Language Teaching and Research in Southeast Asia* 10.(2): 57–66.

1993 The future of regional languages in Indonesia. In Andre Crocheteria, et al., eds., *Actes du XVe Congres International des Linguistes*, pp. 161–164. Saintes-Foy: PU Laval.

Krijger, L. P. [1948] 1987 Feestelijkheden bij zelfstandigwording der gemeenten. In Van Den End, Th. ed. *Gereformeerde Zending Op Sumba 1859–1972*, pp. 512–514. <Netherlands>: Uitgave van de Raad voor de Zending der Ned. Herv. Kerk, de Zending der Gereformeerde Kerken in Nederland en de Gereformeerde Zendingsbond in Ned. Herv. Kerk.

Kripke, Saul F. 1972 Naming and necessity. In D. Davidson and G. Harman, eds., *Semantics of natural language*, pp. 253–355. Dordrecht: Reidel.

Kroskrity, Paul, ed., 1992 *Language ideologies: practice and theory* Special Issue of *Pragmatics* 2.(3): 235–453.

Kuipers, Joel 1986 Talking about trouble: gender differences in Weyewa speech use. *American Ethnologist* 13.(3): 448–462.

1990 *Power in performance: the creation of textual authority in Weyewa ritual speech*. Philadelphia: University of Pennsylvania Press.

1993 Obligations to the word: ritual speech, performance and responsibility in Weyewa, eastern Indonesia. In Jane Hill and Judith Irvine, eds., *Responsibility and evidence in oral discourse*, pp. 123–146. Cambridge: Cambridge University Press.

Kulick, Don 1992a Anger, gender, language shift and the politics of revelation in a Papua New Guinean village. In Paul Kroskrity, ed., *Language ideologies: practice and theory* Special Issue of *Pragmatics* 2.(3). (1992), pp. 282–296.

1992b *Language shift and cultural reproduction: socialization, self and syncretism in a Papua New Guinean village*. New York: Cambridge University Press.

Kuter, L. 1989 Breton vs. French: language and the opposition of political, economic, social and cultural values. In Nancy Dorian, ed., *Investigating obsolescence: studies in language contraction and death*, pp. 75–89. Cambridge: Cambridge University Press.

Lambooy, P. J. [1932] 1987 Zending en volksgewoonten op Soemba. In Rh. Van Den End, ed., *Gereformeerde Zending Op Sumba 1859–1972*, pp. 340–342. <Netherlands>: Uitgave van de Raad voor de Zending der Ned. Herv. Kerk, de Zending der Gereformeerde Kerken in Nederland en de Gereformeerde Zendingsbond in Ned. Herv. Kerk.

Lanz, C. E. 1919 *Memorie van Overgave Afdeling Soemba*. Memorie Soemba. Augustus 1919. Unpublished archive materials 64.

Leonteva, N. N. 1974 On the semantic incompleteness of texts. In V. Rozencvejg, ed., *Machine translation and applied linguistics, vols. I and II*, vol. II, pp. 119–145. Frankfurt am Main: Athenaion.

Lévi-Strauss, Claude 1962 *The savage mind*. Chicago: University of Chicago Press.

Levy, Robert 1984 Emotion, knowing and culture. In Richard Schweder and Robert LeVine, eds., *Cultural theory*. Cambridge: Cambridge University Press.

Lewis, Martin W. 1992 *Wagering the land: ritual, capital and environmental degradation in the Cordillera of northern Luzon 1900–1986*, Berkeley: University of California Press.

Liddle, R. William 1970 *Political participation in Indonesia*. New Haven, CT: Yale University, Southeast Asian Studies.

Lockard, Craig 1996 Popular musics and politics in modern Southeast Asia: a comparative analysis. *Asian Music* 27.(2): 149–199.

Maier, Henk M. J. 1993 From heteroglossia to polyglossia: the creation of Malay and Dutch in the Indies. *Indonesia* 56: 37–61.

Mannheim, Bruce 1991 *The language of the Inka since the European invasion*. Austin: University of Texas Press.

May, Herman Josef 1979 *Die Insel Sumba: Machte und Mythen der Steinzeit im 20. Jahrhundert*. Bonn: Hofbauer Verlag.

Mehan, Hugh 1979 *Learning lessons*. Cambridge, MA: Harvard University Press.

Merton, Robert 1949 *Social theory and social structure*. Glencoe, IL: The Free Press.

Mertz, Elizabeth 1983 A Cape Breton system of personal names: pragmatic and semantic change. *Semiotica* 44:(1/2): 55–74.

Metzner, Joachim 1977 Pemeliharaan Ternak di Daerah Agraria di Pulan Sumba Dan Masalah Paceklik Musiman. Kupang, Timor, Indonesia: Biro Penelitian, Universitas Nusa Cendana.

Mitchell, David 1982 Endemic gonorrhea in Sumba. Unpublished paper prepared for the Asian Studies Association of Australia, Monash University, 10–14 May 1982.

Mithun, Marianne 1980 Principles of naming in Mohawk. In Elizabeth Tooker, ed., *Naming systems*. Proceedings of the 1980 American Ethnological Society, pp. 40–54. Washington DC: American Ethnological Society.

Mougeon, Raymond and Edouard Beniak 1989 Language contraction and linguistic change: the case of Welland French. In Nancy Dorian, ed., *Investigating obsolescence: studies in language contraction and death*, pp. 287–312. Cambridge: Cambridge University Press.

Myers-Scotton, Carol 1992 Code-switching as a mechanism of deep borrowing, language shift, and language death. In Matthias Brenzinger, ed., *Language death: factual and theoretical explorations with special reference to East Africa*, pp. 31–58. Berlin: Mouton de Gruyter.

Needham, Rodney 1980 Principles and variations in the structure of Sumbanese society. In James J. Fox, ed., *The flow of life: essays on eastern Indonesia*, pp. 21–47. Cambridge, MA: Harvard University Press.

1983 Sumba and the Slave Trade. Melbourne: Center for Southeast Asian Studies, Monash University. Working Paper number 31.

Ochs, Elinor 1983 Making it last: repetition in children's discourse. In Elinor Ochs and Bambi Schieffelin, *Acquiring conversational competence*. London: Routlege & Kegan Paul.

1986 From feelings to grammar: a Samoan case study. In Bambi Schieffelin and Elinor Ochs, eds., *Language socialization across cultures*, pp. 251–272. Cambridge: Cambridge University Press.

1988 *Culture and language development: language acquisition and language socialization in a Samoan village*. Cambridge: Cambridge University Press.

Onvlee, Louis 1930 *Palatalisatie in eenige Soembaneesche dialecten. Feestbundel tegenover het 150–jarig bestaan van het Bataviaasch Genootschap*, Deel II, pp. 234–245. Batavia: Bataviaasch Genootschap.

1951 Letter to the India Committee of Netherlands Bible Society, 31 May 1951. In Th. Van Den End, ed., *Gereformeerde Zending Op Sumba 1859–1972*, pp. 539–531. Zeist: Zendingzentrum.

1973 *Cultuur als Antwoord*. Leiden: Verhandeling van het Koninklijk Instituut voor Taal-Land- en Volkenkunde.

1977 The construction of the Mangili dam. In P. E. de Josselin de Jong, ed.. *Structural anthropology in the Netherlands*, pp. 151–163. The Hague: Martinus Nijhoff.

1980 The significance of livestock on Sumba. In James J. Fox, *The flow of life: essays on eastern Indonesia*, pp. 195–207. Cambridge, MA: Harvard University Press.

n.d. *A Laiko Lara. Spelboekje in de taal van Waijewa, West Soemba*. Djakarta: Nederlands Bijbelgenootschaap.

Onvlee, Louis, Umbu Hina Kapita and P. J. Luijendijk 1984 *Kamberaas (Oost Soembaas): Nederlands Woordenbooek met Nederlands Kamberaas register*. Leiden: Koninklijk Instituut voor Taal- Land- en Volkenkunde.

Oort, W. B. 1906 Het gevecht op Prai Meditta (Soemba). *Indisch Militair Tijdschrift* 2: 749–753.

Osborne, John 1957 *Look back in anger*. London: Faber & Faber.

Pateman, Carole 1988 *The sexual contract*. Stanford, CA: Stanford University Press.

Pemberton, John 1994 *On the subject of "Java"*. Ithaca, NY: Cornell University Press.

Penders, Christiaan L. M. 1968 "Colonial education policy and practice in Indonesia, 1900–1942". Canberra: Australian National University. PhD Thesis.

Philips, Susan Urmston 1983 *The invisible culture: communication in classroom and community on the Warm Springs Indian Reservation*. Prospect Heights, IL: Waveland Press.

Pratt, Mary Louise 1987 Linguistic utopias. In N. Fabb, ed., *The linguistics of writing*, pp. 48–66. Manchester: Manchester University Press.

Prins, A. H. O. 1916 *Memorie Van Overgave betreffende het bestuur der afdeeling Soemba, ultimo juni 1916*. Zug, Switzerland: Interdocumentation.

Rafael, Vincent 1990 Patronage and pornography: ideology and spectatorship in the early Marcos years. *Comparative Studies in Society and History* 13.(2): 282–304.

Reddy, M. 1979 The conduit metaphor – a case of frame conflict in our language about language. In A. Ortony, ed., *Metaphor and Thought*. Cambridge: Cambridge University Press.

Reid, Anthony 1988 *Southeast Asia in the age of commerce. Vol I: Lands below the winds*. New Haven, CT: Yale University Press.

Riekerk, G. H. M. 1936 *Bestuurs Memorie van den Controleur van West Soemba*. Zug, Switzerland: Interdocumentation.

Rodenwalt, Ernst 1923 De biologische toestand van de bevolking van het eiland Soemba. *Geneeskundig Tijdschrift voor Nederlandsch-Indie* 63: 448–464.

Rodgers, Susan 1979 Advice to the Newlyweds. In Edward Bruner and Judith Becker, eds., *Art, ritual and society in Indonesia*. Athens, OH: Ohio University, Center for International Studies.

Roo van Alderwerelt, J. de 1906 Historisch Aantekeningen over Soemba. *Tijdschrift voor de Taal- Land- en Volkenkunde* 48: 185–316.

Ronkel, Philippus Samuel van 1929 *Adat Radja-radja Melajoe naard drie Londensche handschriften, met steun van de adat rechtstichting*. Leiden: E.J. Brill.

Roos, Samuel 1872 Bijdrage tot de kennis van taal, land, en volk van het eiland Soemba. *Verhandelingen van het Bataviaasch Genootschap van Kunsten en Wetenschappen* 36: 1–125.

Rosaldo, Michelle Z. 1980 *Knowledge and Passion: Ilongot notions of self and social life*. Cambridge: Cambridge University Press.

1982 The things we do with words: Ilongot speech acts and speech act theory in philosophy. *Language in Society* 11(2): 203–237.

1983 The shame of the headhunters and the autonomy of self. *Ethos* 11: 135–151.

Rumsey, Alan 1990 Wording, meaning, and linguistic ideology. *American Anthropologist* 92.(2): 346–361.

Sapir, Edward 1921 *Language, an introduction to the study of speech*. New York: Harcourt, Brace and Company.

1930 Totality. *Language Monographs* 6. Baltimore: Linguistic Society of America.

1949 *Culture, language and personality: selected essays edited by David Mandelbaum*. Berkeley: University of California.

Sastrodihardjo, R. Soekardjo 1958 *Beberapa Tjatatan tentang daerah Sumba* [Some notes on Sumba]. Jakarta: Pusat Djawatan Petanian Rakjat Bagian Publikasi & Dokumentasi.

Schmidt, Anna 1985 *Young people's Dyirbal: an example of language death from Australia*. Cambridge: Cambridge University Press.

Schwartz, Adam 1994 *A Nation in waiting* Boulder, CO: Westview Press.

Scott, James C. 1990 *Domination and the arts of resistance*. New Haven, CT: Yale University Press.

Searle, John 1958 Proper names. *Mind* 67: 166–173.

Siegel, James T. 1986 *Solo in the new order: language and hierarchy in an Indonesian city*. Princeton, NJ: Princeton University Press.

1997 *Fetish, recognition, revolution*. Princeton,NJ: Princeton University Press.

Silverstein, Michael 1979 Language structure and language ideology. In Paul Clyne et al. eds., *The elements: parasession on linguistic units and levels*, pp. 193–247. Chicago: Chicago Linguistic Society

1981 The Limits of Awareness. Sociolinguistic Working Paper 84. Austin, Texas: Southwest Educational Development Laboratory.

1985 Language and the culture of gender: at the intersection of structure, usage and ideology. In Elizabeth Mertz and Richard Parmentier, eds., *Semiotic mediation: sociocultural and psychological perspectives.* New York: Academic Press.

Stallybrass, Peter and Allon White 1986 *The politics and poetics of trangression.* London: Methuen.

Steedly, Mary 1993 *Hanging without a rope.* Princeton, NJ: Princeton University Press.

Sweeney, Amin 1987 *A full hearing: orality and literacy in Malay literature.* Berkeley: University of California Press.

Tambiah, Stanley Jeyaraya [1977] 1985 The Galactic Polity in Southeast Asia. In *Culture, thought and action: an anthropological perspective,* pp. 252–286. Cambridge, MA: Harvard University Press.

Taylor, Allan 1989 Problems in obsolescence research: the Gros Ventres of Montana. In Nancy Dorian, ed., *Investigating obsolescence: studies in language contraction and death,* pp. 167–179. Cambridge: Cambridge University Press.

Taylor, Paul Michael, ed., 1994 *Fragile traditions: Indonesian art in jeopardy.* Washington, DC: Smithsonian Institution Press.

Teeuw, Andries 1994 *Van Der Tuuk as lexicographer.* Denpasar: Panitia Simposium Internasional Kajian Budaya Austronesia.

Ten Kate, Herman 1894 Verslag eener reis in de Timor en Polynesie. *Tijdschrift van het Koninklijk Aardrijkskundig Genootschap* 11: 541–638.

Traube, Elizabeth 1986 *Cosmology and social life: ritual exchange among the Mambai of East Timor.* Chicago: University of Chicago Press.

Tsing, Anna Lowenhaupt 1990 Gender and performance in Meratus dispute settlement. In Jane Atkinson and Shelly Errington, eds., *Power and difference: gender in island Southeast Asia.* Stanford, CA: Stanford University Press.

1993 *In the realm of the diamond queen: marginality in an out-of-the-way place.* Princeton, NJ: Princeton University Press.

Tsitsipis, Lukas 1988 Language shift and narrative performance: the structure and function of Arvanitika narratives. *Language in Society* 17.(1): 61–86.

1989 Skewed performance and full performance in language obsolescence: the case of an Albanian variety. In Nancy Dorian ed., *Investigating obsolescence: studies in language contraction and death,* pp. 117–137. Cambridge: Cambridge University Press.

Tuan, Yi-Fu 1991 Language and the making of place: a narrative-descriptive approach. *Annals of the Association of American Geographers* 81.(4): 684–696.

Turner, Victor 1974 *Dramas, fields metaphors: symbolic action in human society.* Ithaca, NY: Cornell University Press.

Van Den End, Th., ed., 1987 *Gereformeerde Zending Op Sumba 1859–1972.* Zeist: Zendingszentrum.

Van Dijk, T. [1925] 1987 Tegen ongeloof Nederlandstalig onderwijs. In Th. Van Den End, ed., *Gereformeerde Zending Op Sumba 1859–1972,* pp. 245–246. Baarn: Zendingszentrum.

[1914] 1987 Verslag over het volksonderwijs in 1914. In Th. Van Den End, ed., *Gereformeerde Zending Op Sumba 1859–1972,* pp. 182–186. <Netherlands>: Uitgave van de Raad voor de Zending der Ned. Herv. Kerk, de Zending der Gereformeerde Kerken in Nederland en de Gereformeerde Zendingsbond in Ned. Herv. Kerk.

Van Vollenhoven, Cornelius 1934 *Verspreide Geschriften*, Vol. I. Haarlem: H. D. Tjenk Willinck.

Ventresca, Marc 1995 *When states count*. Phd dissertation, Department of Sociology, Stanford University.

Versluys, J. D. N. 1941 Aantekeningen omtrent geld- en goederenverkeer in West-Soemba. *Koloniale Studien* 25: 433–483.

Waitz, E. W. F. J. 1933 *Bestuursmemorie van den gezaghebber van West Soemba, 19 Oktober 1931 t/m 10 April 1933*. Zug, Switzerland: Interdocumentation.

Watson, Seosamh 1989 Scottish and Irish Gaelic: The giant's bedfellows. In Nancy Dorian ed., *Investigating obsolescence: studies in language contraction and death*, pp. 41–59. Cambridge: Cambridge University Press.

Webb, Paul 1986 *Palms and the cross: socio-economic development in Nusatenggara 1930–1975*. Townsville, Australia: Centre for Southeast Asian Studies, James Cook University of North Queensland.

Weinreich, Uriel 1966 *Languages in contact: findings and problems*. The Hague: Mouton.

Wielenga, Douwe Klaas [1904] 1987 Prediking in de landstaal. In Th. Van Den End, ed., *Gereformeerde Zending Op Sumba 1859–1972*, pp. 136–137. <Netherlands>: Uitgave van de Raad voor de Zending der Ned. Herv. Kerk, de Zending der Gereformeerde Kerken in Nederland en de Gereformeerde Zendingsbond in Ned. Herv. Kerk.

1912 Reizen op Soemba. *Macedonier* 15: 328–334.

1916 I. Historie 1873–1874: Controleur Roskott. *De Macedonier* 21: 3–11.

1928 *Oemboe Dongga, het kampong hoofd van Soemba*. Kampen: Kok.

Wilken, G.A. 1892 *Handleiding voor de vergelijkende volkenkunde van Nederlandsch-Indie*. Leiden: Brill.

Winichakul, Thonchai 1994 *Siam mapped: a history of the geobody of a nation*. Honolulu: University of Hawaii Press.

Wolff, Hans 1959 Language intelligibility and interethnic attitudes. *Anthropological Linguistics* 1: 34–41.

Woolard, Kathryn and Bambi Schieffelin 1994 Language ideologies. *Annual Review of Anthropology* 23: 55–82.

Wouters, Cas 1987 Development of behavioural codes between the sexes: the formalization of informalization in the Netherlands 1930–85. *Theory, Culture and Society* 4: 405–427.

Wurm, Stephen O. and Shiro Hattori, eds., 1983 *Language atlas of the Pacific area*. Pacific Linguistics, Series C. No. 66. Canberra: Australian Academy of the Humanities in Collaboration with the Japan Academy.

Yampolsky, Philip 1989 *Hati Yang Luka*, an Indonesian hit. *Indonesia* 1–17.

Zentgraaff, H.C. 1912 *Pacificators in Midden Soemba*. Soerabaia: Nijland.

INDEX

Abu-Lughod 15, 42
adat
  performances 123
  secular meanings of 4
  Van Vollenhoven 9, 11
address forms
  Christian names 117
agriculture
  rhetoric of, in politics 67
  see dispersal 34
  work group performance 92
Alisjahbana 68, 136, 137, 149
Allerton, J. 96
Anderson 10, 68, 149
anger
  and "angry men" 43
  and change 63, 64
  and expressive styles 14
  and gender 48
  as ideology 5
  as *kasar* "crude" behavior 63
  as status 43, 100, 107, 109
  Christianity and 4, 43
  comparative perspectives on 42, 48, 49
  cultural organization of 42, 43, 47
  definition of 48
  Dutch views of 14, 43, 44, 79, 133, 148, 151
  in laments 60, 62
  in learning practices 107, 125, 134, 143
  Japanese 81
  leadership 45, 73
  modern life 4
  performance features 49, 73
  versus humility 51
angry man 55, 152
  as anachronism 63
  as exemplary citizen of traditional polity 92
  colonial discovery of 44, 46

naming 98, 101, 108
  social status of 97, 48, 49
  verbal competence of 48, 49, 68
animal names 97, 106, 112, 120, 121, 122
  name 98
applause
  see audiencing practices 76
areal linguistics
  see place, linguistic study of 22
audience 94
  and laments 54, 82
  and learning 130, 134
  and names 110
  and the theatre state 69, 70
  as citizenship 20, 67, 68, 88, 90, 91
  changing structure of 8, 5, 20, 79, 146, 150, 152
  comparative perspectives on 79
  completeness 6, 12, 36, 68, 69, 70, 74, 83, 90
  convening of 73, 122
  Dutch as 60, 69, 70, 76, 71, 78, 150, 151
  for laments 36
  imagery of 52
  Lende Mbatu as convenor of 70, 71, 73
  practices 67, 75, 76, 79, 92
  practices as learning practices 125
  response 49
  see citizenship 67
  see spectatorship 67
  work group as 67, 88, 91
audiences
  changing structure of 68
  convening of 67
authority xi
  and orphans 61
  angry man and 20, 29, 48, 70, 151
  centers of 8, 9, 29, 34, 150
  changing system of 2, 34, 35, 37, 38, 78, 79, 90, 120, 141, 143, 147, 151, 152

STUDIES IN THE SOCIAL AND CULTURAL FOUNDATIONS
OF LANGUAGE

14. Don Kulick
    Language shift and cultural reproduction; socialization, self and syncretism in a Papua New Guinea village

15. Jane H. Hill and Judith T. Irvine (eds.)
    Responsibility and evidence in oral discourse

16. Niko Besnier
    Literacy, emotion, and authority: reading and writing on a Polynesian atoll

17. John J. Gumperz and Stephen C. Levinson (eds.)
    Rethinking linguistic relativity

18. Joel C. Kuipers
    Language, identity, and marginality in Indonesia: the changing nature of ritual speech on the island of Sumba